Travel Planning on the Internet

By Drs. Ron and Caryl Krannich

TRAVEL AND INTERNATIONAL BOOKS

International Jobs Directory
Jobs For People Who Love to Travel
Mayors and Managers in Thailand
Politics of Family Planning Policy in Thailand
Shopping and Traveling in Exotic Asia
Shopping in Exotic Places
Shopping the Exotic South Pacific
Travel Planning on the Internet
Treasures and Pleasures of Australia
Treasures and Pleasures of China
Treasures and Pleasures of Egypt
Treasures and Pleasures of Hong Kong
Treasures and Pleasures of India
Treasures and Pleasures of Indonesia
Treasures and Pleasures of Israel and Jordan
Treasures and Pleasures of Italy
Treasures and Pleasures of Paris and the French Riviera
Treasures and Pleasures of the Philippines
Treasures and Pleasures of Rio and São Paulo
Treasures and Pleasures of Singapore and Bali
Treasures and Pleasures of Singapore and Malaysia
Treasures and Pleasures of Thailand

BUSINESS AND CAREER BOOKS AND SOFTWARE

101 Dynamite Answers to Interview Questions
101 Secrets of Highly Effective Speakers
201 Dynamite Job Search Letters
Best Jobs For the 21st Century
Change Your Job, Change Your Life
The Complete Guide to International Jobs and Careers
The Complete Guide to Public Employment
The Directory of Federal Jobs and Employers
Discover the Best Jobs For You!
Dynamite Cover Letters
Dynamite Networking For Dynamite Jobs
Dynamite Resumes
Dynamite Salary Negotiations
Dynamite Tele-Search
The Educator's Guide to Alternative Jobs and Careers
Find a Federal Job Fast!
From Air Force Blue to Corporate Gray
From Army Green to Corporate Gray
From Navy Blue to Corporate Gray
Get a Raise in 7 Days
High Impact Resumes and Letters
Interview For Success
Job-Power Source CD-ROM
Jobs and Careers With Nonprofit Organizations
Military Resumes and Cover Letters
Moving Out of Education
Moving Out of Government
Re-Careering in Turbulent Times
Resumes & Job Search Letters For Transitioning Military Personnel
Savvy Interviewing
Savvy Networker
Savvy Resume Writer
Ultimate Job Source CD-ROM

TRAVEL PLANNING ON THE INTERNET

The Click and Easy™ Guide

Ronald L. Krannich, Ph.D.
Caryl Rae Krannich, Ph.D.

IMPACT PUBLICATIONS
Manassas Park, VA

Library of Congress Cataloguing-in-Publication Data

Krannich, Ronald L.
   Travel planning on the internet: the click and easy guide / Ronald L.
Krannich, Caryl Rae Krannich
      p. cm.
   Includes bibliographical references and index.
   ISBN 1-57023-142-7
   1. Travel – Computer network resources. 2. Internet. 3. World Wide Web.
I. Krannich, Caryl Rae. II. Title

G155.A1 K693 2000
025.06'91 – dc21   00-046125

Publisher: For information on Impact Publications, including current and forthcoming publications, authors, press kits, online bookstores, and submission requirements, visit Impact's main website: *www.impactpublications.com*.

Publicity/Rights: For information on publicity, author interviews, and subsidiary rights, contact the Media Relations Department: Tel. 703-361-7300, Fax 703-361-7300, or email: *travelmedia@impactpublications.com*.

Sales/Distribution: All bookstore sales are handled through Impact's trade distributor: National Book Network, 15200 NBN Way, Blue Ridge Summit, PA 17214, Tel. 1-800-462-6420. All other sales and distribution inquiries should be directed to the publisher: Sales Department, IMPACT PUBLICATIONS, 9104 Manassas Drive, Suite N, Manassas Park, VA 20111-5211, Tel. 703-361-7300, Fax 703-335-9486, or email: *sales@impactpublications.com*.

Contents

Travel Planning on the Internet

worldroom.com
We Make Business Trips Work

500 Miles

Lufthansa

中文版

City Guides
Select a Region
- [Select a City] -

News Center
Travel News
Executive Briefing
Dow Jones News
Markets & Finance

Channels
Career Manager
Women'sWorld
Travel Health
Trip Tech
Off the Shelves
TravelTalk

Travel Monitor
Flights
Hotels

About Us
I-Quest Corporation
Advertising
Worldroom Hotels
Press Center
Career Opportunities
Contact Us
Privacy Policy

Headlines

Travel News
Updated Sep 13 0613 GMT
- Sydney Fumes Fell Passengers
- Computer Glitch Hits Continental
- Emirates: Free First-Class for Life
- ThatWeb Adds Mobile Functions
- Typhoon Batters Japan
- More Travel News

Executive Briefing
A Pall Cast on Malaysian Tourism
Kidnappings raise fears about the future of the booming industry.
September 13, 2000   read

BP Amoco Dealt Blow in Russia
Big bank's debt restructuring deal hurts troubled Russian oil business.
September 13, 2000   read

Bimantara Shines in Indonesian Gloom
Stock remains attractive in the long term because of a raft of quality assets.
September 13, 2000   read

Dow Jones News
- UN, Norway To Help Finance Future Elections In Pakistan
- Both Sides Discuss Plea Bargain For Wen Ho Lee
- Death Toll From Car Bomb At Jakarta Bourse Rises To 10
- J.P. Morgan/Chase Open -3: Deutsche Bank Cuts Q1 View
- J.P. Morgan/Chase Open -2: Dilution Concerns Weigh In
- More News

by DOW JONES

City Guide Spotlight
More Than a Restaurant

A very up-market Beijing restaurant successfully combines a touch of east and west in its menu and ambiance, and boasts not only of a great chef, but also of avant-garde Chinese artists. full text

- Worldroom Guide to Beijing
- Beijing Dining & Leisure

Worldroom Guides-to-Go
Restaurant reviews. Recommended bars. Useful numbers. Now available on your handheld -- enough information to get there, get around and get the job done. Download guides for Asian cities.

Worldroom Wireless
Get key data and information even if you're stuck in traffic, waiting in line, or the batteries on your laptop have run out. Access Worldroom's guides for Asian cities through your WAP-enabled mobile phone. full text

Channels

Women'sWorld
What Do Working Women Want in the 21st Century? new!
Compliments and high performance ratings no longer cut it. "Show me the promotion" is what women are saying. full text

Career Manager
Getting Your Message Across new!
The savings from getting your corporate communications right the first time are enormous. Your audience gets your message the way you want -- with maximum creativity, clarity and impact. full text

Travel Health
Advice from Dr. Deb: Golden Rules of Healthy Travel
Even if you do nothing else, following these simple rules will help you avoid many potential health hassles on the road. full text

Off the Shelves
Guide to Choosing, Serving & Enjoying Wine new!
Who says wine has to be intimidating? Here's a sparkling guide to wine basics that provides practical advice on tasting and ordering with confidence, even when you're dining with an important business associate. full text

Trip Tech   sponsored by COMPAQ
Quick Fixes for More Efficient Computing new!
Application error? Loss of disk space? Problems downloading from the Net? When you're on the road, you can't always turn to tech support for help. Learn a few tricks yourself. full text

1

The Savvy Internet Traveler

WHERE IN THE WORLD WOULD YOU LIKE TO GO for your next trip? What types of things would you like to do? Where would you like to stay? What will it cost? Where are the best places to dine? How much cash should you take? Where can you find an ATM? What's the local custom on tipping? What groups share your travel interests? How do you access your email in China? Are Iran and Cuba good places to visit these days? What health precautions should you take in Egypt? Is it safe to fly Aeroflot? Where's the best place to go trekking in Nepal? Is it better to honeymoon in Jamaica or Bali – at the Four Seasons, Ritz-Carlton, or the Aman Resorts? Who offers a two-week culinary tour of Northern Italy? Do you know of any great last minute deals for Paris this weekend? Is a Crystal Harmony cruise as fabulous as they say?

Whatever your questions, however general or esoteric, you'll find answers on the Internet – if you know where to look, whom to contact, and how to sort the good, the bad, and the ugly.

From Dependence to Independence

Today's sophisticated traveler has lots of interests and questions as well as limited time and patience. Seeking greater independence and control over travel decisions, an increasing number of travelers also have access to a 24-hour a day information hotline, travel advisor, and potential problem-solver – the Internet. Unlike many travelers who are dependent on "travel professionals" for most destination information and services, today's Internet savvy traveler is his own travel professional. He has quick access to a bewildering array of information that can, if managed properly, help him make intelligent travel decisions both prior to and during his travels. He may still use a travel professional, but he first does Internet research so he can better communicate his interests and needs to the professional. A busy and "wired" new world traveler who often plans his travels on-the-go, he may use the Internet at 30,000 feet or call his technology butler to check his in-room Internet connection.

Your Best Travel Friend

Whether booking airline tickets, making hotel reservations, reviewing local news, reconfirming flights, checking arrival and departure times, accessing email, joining tour groups, selecting top restaurants, deciding on evening entertainment, identifying great shopping opportunities, or learning a few useful phrases in the local language, the Internet is increasingly becoming a traveler's best friend. It's even becoming a trusted friend as the quality of Internet information and services improves. And like a good friend, the 24-hour a day Internet is always there when you need it. Travelers aware of the Internet's tremendous information and service potential use the Internet to enhance their travel experiences both before and during their travels. For them, the Internet is an essential tool that saves time and money and results in a much more rewarding travel adventure.

Freeing travelers from dependence on others, the Internet promotes a more independent and intelligent style of travel. It's increasingly becoming a traveler's best friend – always there when you need it.

It's All About Empowerment

But the Internet is much more than a convenient resource for information and services. Freeing individuals from dependence on travel agents, tour groups, guides, advertisements, hotel concierges, and outdated guidebooks, the Internet also promotes a more independent and intelligent style of travel. It empowers travelers by offering them choices which were unheard of only a few years ago or which were largely controlled by other individuals and groups.

The Internet also has led to the proliferation of new travel questions and issues that have further enriched the field of travel. As such, there is an Internet-style of travel that opens up a whole new world of travel possibilities for individuals who value greater freedom and predictability in their travels.

Planning as the Process

If you have lots of travel interests, questions, and decisions to make, you should find this book especially useful for pre-trip planning as well as for traveling on the road. Road warriors on assignment in distant places may find this book to be an important travel lifeline. Indeed, you may quickly find the title to this book to be somewhat of a misnomer. For no longer is the Internet used just for pre-trip travel planning. Within the past year or two it has become an intricate part of the travel process for many travelers – both business and leisure – who have learned to frequently use the Internet while traveling. In fact, many travelers are too busy to engage in lengthy pre-trip planning; knowing where they want to go, they plan the details on the go – with the help of a good guidebook and the Internet. For example, travelers staying in many of the major hotels in Hong Kong, Manila, Singapore, and Bangkok can now instantly access one of the most useful websites for travelers – *www.worldroom.com* – to stay in touch with everything from local news, entertainment, restaurants, and attractions to their email account back home. Flying into Bangkok next week from Hong Kong? Why not make a reservation at one of the hottest new restaurants in Bangkok you've just learned about from the new restaurant report that appeared on your Worldroom connection in Hong Kong? Other types of Internet connections, from cybercafes to wireless Internet access via cell phones, enable travelers to more and more integrate travel information and services on the Internet with their ongoing travels. As a result, many travelers are experiencing a whole new world of travel linked to the Internet – they have literally become "wired travelers". Unfortunately, only part of the world is sufficiently wired to enable them to fully use the power of the Internet for travel. Within the next few years this will all dramatically change with the increasing prevalence of wireless Internet connections in the air and on the ground.

In fact, this is not a book about pre-trip planning on the Internet. It's a book about using the Internet for enhancing your travel experiences, from beginning to end. It's a book about the whole new world of travel in which the Internet plays an important role at all phases of the travel process. In this sense, planning and the travel process go hand in hand.

The Way Things Were

Not long ago most business and leisure travelers relied on time-honored methods for acquiring travel information and purchasing travel services – newspapers, magazines, newsletters, guidebooks, brochures, catalogs, videos, word-of-mouth, and travel agencies. They often limited the nature of their questions to the likely answers they would get from such information sources. If you were interested in the hottest destinations, you might survey recent glossy magazine articles or contact a travel agent. If you needed information on visa requirements and the best places to stay, you might examine a travel guidebook or contact a travel agent. If you were interested in the cheapest airfares to Paris, you might consult ads in the Sunday travel section of a major newspaper, contact a travel agent, or call a consolidator. In many respects, travel planning was relatively simple because of the role of the travel agent, travel publications, and the telephone. A trusted travel magazine, guidebook, and agent could provide you with a wealth of travel information and services. Better still, the services of travel agencies were ostensibly free to the consumer. So why not use them?

But travel planning as we've known it is no longer solely focused on the print media and travel agents nor is it as free for the asking. With the explosive growth of the travel industry has also come increased complexity and options centered around the role of the Internet in travel planning. Today, you have a bewildering array of options, mainly focused on the Internet, that both adds increased complexity and options to your overall travel planning.

Embrace the Chaos

If you are even a casual Internet user, one thing you quickly learn is that the Internet is a place of great chaos despite all the keyword search engines and indexes that attempt to make the process more coherent. It's also a very seductive medium that can suck up more time than you ever imagined. Our task in this book is to bring some degree of useful order to the chaos, based upon our understanding of the travel planning process, so that you can better plan and implement various aspects of your travels without incurring the high costs of sucking up time with bad Internet choices. Our goal is to save you time and minimize the frustrations and headaches inherent in trying to untangle the chaos of the Internet.

If you've not yet embraced the Internet, chances are you will at least embrace the travel portion of the Internet by the time you finish this book – or definitely understand why more and more people have become seduced by this medium. As you will quickly discover, the Internet displays some of its greatest capabilities to make life more convenient, economical, and fun when it comes to the business of travel. It adds value and dispenses many personal benefits that are very difficult to acquire through other means. And if travel is one of your passions, you may also develop a passion for travel on the Internet – an electronic form of wanderlust that may further complicate your life! It's truly seductive.

> *The Internet displays some of its greatest capabilities to make life more convenient, economical, and fun when it comes to the business of travel. It adds unique value and dispenses many personal benefits.*

A New Game For an Old Business

Travel planning on the Internet is a relatively new phenomenon which coincides with major new developments in the travel industry during the past five years. These new developments have been nothing short of revolutionary.

By the mid-1990s, the Internet began making major inroads into the travel industry which would inevitably revolutionize it like few other industries. In many respects, much of this industry was ideally suited for the Internet – an information and transaction rich industry that relied heavily on a variety of commissioned middlemen to supply such basic travel services as airline tickets, hotel reservations, and car rentals. Indeed, the 10-15 percent agency commission on selling travel services was the financial glue that kept this industry of travel suppliers, wholesalers, and retailers happily humming for many years. Once major revenue streams of travel agencies, these agency-centered services recently have been severely eroded by a combination of new Internet-based travel services and travel suppliers, especially airlines, who have restructured the whole commission relationship in favor of the suppliers. Only cruises and packaged tours now remain the major domains of travel agents.

The advent of new and aggressive online booking services, such as Sabre's Travelocity and affiliate auction site Priceline.com and Micro-soft Network's Expedia, substantially impacted on the way traditional bricks and mortar travel agencies did business. As a result, many traditional travel agencies closed their doors in the face of a new and challenging business environment.

By the year 2000 more than 10,000 Internet sites had sprung up to provide travel information and services and thousands more will launch within the next year or two. The Internet had quickly become crowded with a variety of sites, from pure e-commerce sites to websites of traditional travel suppliers. While billions of dollars in transactions take place over the Internet each day – most in the form of airline, hotel, and car rental bookings – few pure e-commerce sites were actually profit-able. With the impending launch of the new airline-operated Orbitz booking system and its affiliate Hotwire auction site in Spring 2001, to challenge the dominance of Travelocity and Expedia, the Internet travel gold rush is anything but over.

Meet Your Technology Butler

But the really good news for travelers is that more and more major hotels, especially those geared toward business travelers, recognize the increasingly important role the Internet plays in travel. Many hotels are rapidly converting their business centers into Internet centers as well as rewiring rooms so guests can have instant Internet access. In many older properties, certain blocks of rooms may be set aside for computers and Internet access as the hotel undergoes technological renovation. Many new hotels are fully in-room Internet compliant with special Internet modem lines, Web TV, and/or in-room computers connected to the Internet.

The good news for Internet savvy travelers is that they no longer need to use the hotel's business center or prowl the streets for a cramped backpacker's Internet café to use the Internet. The Internet is simply a "must have service" in many hotels. It's no surprise hotel chains such as the Ritz-Carlton recently created the position of "technology butler" for all its properties. If a guest has a problem connecting to the Internet or difficulty with his hard drive or programs, like the hotel doctor, the Ritz's technology butler is on call to assist the troubled guest. Other hotels will do the same as they recognize how important the Internet is to their guests – just as important as the in-room television, mini-bar, and fax machine. Hotels with a competitive edge are those that are wired to the Internet.

Stay Connected at 30,000 Feet

The Internet revolution for travelers goes far beyond Internet cafés and Internet compliant hotel rooms and business centers. Within the next year several airlines will be offering wireless Internet connections in the sky. While flying at 30,000 feet you'll be able to check your email, make restaurant reservations, shop online, and surf your favorite sites. Initially offered by InflightOnline (*www.inflightonline.com*), this wireless Internet technology for airlines will probably become a standard service within the next five years. As a result, more and more travelers will be efficiently using their flying downtime by doing travel planning in the sky while on their way to their next destination!

The Consumer as King

Internet travel business has become big business. Indeed, travel businesses that failed to embrace the Internet seem destined to be out of business within the very near future as more and more business and leisure travelers turn to the Internet for travel information and services.

The major benefactor of the numerous travel sites that have evolved over the past few years is you, the consumer. However confused, never before in the history of the travel industry has the consumer become such a king. Websites live and die on the number of visitors they attract and keep as loyal users. Many venture capital (VC) sites, such as *travelocity.com, priceline.com, biztravel.com, away.com, iexplore.com,* and *novica.com*, are willing to burn through millions of dollars on advertising and giveaways and remain unprofitable in order to get your attention. In so doing, they give away trips, deep discount airfares and hotels, provide money-back guarantees on trips, offer free newsletters and travel updates, and attempt to build brand loyalty through all types of financial incentives. The war for your computer mouse, eyeballs, and wallet has never been so intense as on the Internet today. You are the travel king.

But as you may have learned long ago, nothing is really free nor private, even for kings. By definition, anyone using the Internet is swimming in a huge fish bowl of sharks – advertisers, marketers, and list managers. Like most other commercial sites, travel websites track the behavior of users for sales and marketing purposes. The travel sites you visit will most likely result in a profile of your "travel behavior" which will then be marketed to travel firms that offer services related to your interests. If, for example, your primary interest is in cruising and you tend to visit the numerous cruise sites outlined in Chapter 10, chances are you will be targeted by enterprising companies with ads, emails, mailings, and phone calls relating to cruise services, because they know from your behavioral profile that you may be cruise-anxious.

Put It in Perspective

When approaching travel planning on the Internet, it's important to cut through a great deal of Internet and travel hype that can mislead you. Indeed, there are a lot of myths about travel planning on the Internet that often accompany over-exuberance for new technology. For example, many people believe it's cheaper to purchase an airline ticket and make a hotel reservation online than to do so through a traditional travel agent or by contacting the supplier directly. Studies continue to show that the evidence is at best mixed; many popular online reservation systems actually are more costly than using a seasoned travel professional. In fact, you often get the best hotel rates by calling a hotel front desk and asking for their best rate rather than by using an Internet hotel reservation system. Individuals who rely solely on the Internet for making travel purchases often pay a premium for such so-call electronic convenience. Consequently, you are well advised to shop around, both online and offline, for the best travel deals. Better still, and as we discuss in Chapter 11, go directly to the producer's or service provider's website where you may be offered special "cyberbuyer" discounts!

When using the Internet for travel purposes, please keep in mind the importance of using both online and offline resources. Learn to link the two types of resources rather than rely solely on one or the other. Here are a few tips that should prove useful:

1. **Don't neglect savvy travel agents:** We love the Internet as well
   as our travel agent who also is Internet savvy – and a professional.
   Just because many travel agencies have gone out of business does
   not mean they are a dying breed nor have they lost their usefulness. Not surprising, there's a new breed of travel agents operating today – the survivors – who offer new and improved services
   to both business and leisure travelers. The great Darwinian
   principle of the survival of the fittest has recently claimed many
   agents who failed to adapt to the new environment of the Internet
   and declining commissions. As more and more consolidation
   takes place in this business, more and more travel agencies have
   become more highly specialized in meeting the needs of their
   clients. They use the Internet to assist their customers. A good
   trusted travel agent can still save you a great deal of time and
   money. After all, they are travel professionals who know the "ins"
   and "outs" of their business which are considerable. Regardless
   of how proficient you become on the Internet, you're still an
   amateur at the travel game. Learn how to best use a travel agent
   in reference to your own work on the Internet. For example, don't
   assume you are getting the best airline ticket deal on the Internet
   because a site tells you it's so. Because of their own commission
   structures, which often involve another layer of middlemen who
   operate "affiliate programs", Internet booking sites are notorious
   for misrepresenting the full picture of discounts which agents
   know very well. At the same time, don't assume all travel services
   are equally represented on the Internet. Cruises and packaged
   tours are still best arranged through travel agents. In fact, cruise
   lines and tour groups have very close relationships with wholesalers and retail travel agents wholesale their products. Their relationships are as strong as ever and will most likely continue in the
   foreseeable future; they are not currently threatened by the Internet. Indeed, the Internet is likely to further strengthen agency
   relationships with cruise lines and tour groups as more and more
   agencies market their specialty cruises and tours through their
   own websites. If you are the type of travel planner who would
   love to join a cruise or tour group, don't waste a great deal of time
   on the Internet trying to find the right cruise or tour for you. Call
   your travel agent and have him do the work for you. When you
   call a travel agent, you have a person to talk to – real customer
   service – who can give you instant information and advice that is
   largely absent on most Internet travel sites.

2. **Be critical of travel services offered over the Internet – they may not be great deals.** Welcome to cut-throat capitalism on the Internet! Make no assumption that the best deals are always found on the Internet. The best Internet deals are often found during the first year when a start-up Internet business – backed by venture capital and using a high cash-burn approach – decides to literally "give away the store" by offering at cost or below cost services in order to attract brand loyalty. In bricks and mortar businesses, this is called the "lost leader phenomenon" – a business offers products and services at or below cost in order to bring you into their store where you will hopefully purchase other full retail items. Amazon.com is a classic example of how to engage in such traditional business practices on the Internet and thus wipe out the competition (in this case, independent bookstores with already low profit margins). If you know what you are doing, you can get some good deals in such give-away environments. But more often than not, an established Internet site that has moved into a profit-making mode may not offer many price advantages. Using leading airline booking sites, you will sometimes pay 10 to 20 percent more for an airline ticket than if you used a traditional consolidator or travel agent who has access to better discounted tickets. Whatever you do, make sure you always compare prices both online and offline. The day you forget to do this is the day you will likely pay more for the so-called convenience of using the Internet to do your own travel planning. You may be surprised to discover your favorite online travel site, however user-friendly and entertaining, is no longer such a great financial deal nor your best friend!

3. **Use the Internet if you love to plan and control everything yourself . . . and have lots of Internet-time on your hands.** Many people love to plan and control all aspects of their travels and seem to have lots of Internet time in their lives. Indeed, they often have more fun at the planning stage than in actually doing the trip which may involve lots of uncontrollable hassles. If you love to plan and control, you'll love using the Internet for travel planning. However, if planning and control is not your thing, don't spend a great deal of time on the Internet. It may frustrate you. You may spend hours and hours trying to plan small details or to save $10 on an airfare or hotel when picking up the phone

and using a toll-free number can achieve the same or better result in one-tenth the time. As many intermittent Internet users quickly discover, they have much better things to do with their time than "surfing the net" for information that can be readily gotten through more efficient means, such as a travel agent or toll-free number.

4. **Approach the Internet as a place where you can enhance your travel experience through research and networking.** The Internet can be a powerful travel planning and implementation tool if used intelligently. Embrace it but don't become totally seduced by it. The quality of information and services it yields is only as good as the quality of your questions and searches. Learn to ask the right questions and locate the right sites.

5. **Discover the joys of serendipity both before and during your travels.** One of the great joys of travel is found in the planning process which is often serendipitous. It's where ideas take shape, dreams become crystalized, and new anticipations arise. If used serendipitously, the Internet will help shape your dreams and anticipations in many exciting ways – you'll encounter rewarding chance occurrences that arise when looking for one thing but discovering another. You'll discover new places, identify new things to do, make new friends, and raise new questions. At the same time, the Internet should play an important role during your travels. You should be able to access important information about your location, from restaurants, shops, and sightseeing to local news, entertainment, and special events. The Internet should become an important travel companion wherever in the world you travel. We're convinced the sooner you get wired with travel on the Internet, the more exciting and enriching will be your travel adventures.

6. **Plan your trip around quick and easy Internet access.** One of the real joys of traveling is the ability to use the Internet on the road for work and play. As you plan your trip, identify hotels that have Internet access as well as survey centers for using the Internet. For example, Netcafe (*www.netcafe.com*) provides a directory of over 2,000 cybercafes in 113 countries. If you're staying in a budget hotel which lacks Internet access, you may want to visit this site to locate a cybercafe near your hotel. In fact,

one important criterion you may want to include in selecting a hotel is whether or not it has in-room Internet access. While you may pay a little more for such a service, you also may find it more than pays for itself in the long run as your Internet friend joins you in enriching your travel adventure.

A New World of Possibilities

The Internet opens up a whole new world of travel possibilities. It enables users to do many things they might normally do by other means or avoid altogether – from acquiring information and purchasing products and services to arranging the details of travel and solving problems. Specific things you can currently do on the Internet include the following:

- book airline tickets
- make hotel and car rental reservations
- explore cruise options
- contact tour operators
- identify and book specialty tours
- obtain train and bus passes
- review subway routes and stops
- make restaurant reservations
- reserve tickets for special events
- view video clips
- check on passport and visa requirements
- complete visa applications
- review travel articles and guidebooks
- read newspapers around the world
- download travel guides
- check email and send messages
- acquire health and safety information
- contact tourist offices
- access maps and directions
- review hotel and resort facilities
- locate quaint bed and breakfast inns
- take virtual tours of destinations
- join travel groups and clubs
- participate in online chats and discussion groups
- compare travel costs

- bargain for travel products
- identify special interest travel groups
- become an air courier
- review travel radio and television programs
- read travel magazines and newsletters
- check airline schedules
- reconfirm airline tickets
- review airline safety records
- monitor frequent flier miles
- preview layouts of airports, aircraft, and cruise ships
- ask questions of travel experts and fellow travelers
- contact embassies and consulates
- check on customs regulations
- arrange shipping
- locate cybercafes and ATMs
- translate foreign language phrases
- learn a foreign language
- calculate currency rates
- shop for travel gear
- explore specific destinations
- acquire travel tips and advice
- win a trip
- take a travel quiz
- assess your travel interests
- calculate distance
- check on world times
- review the weather
- develop a personalized 3-day weather forecast
- consult a Feng Shui master
- contact hotel concierges
- access email, voice mail, and faxes
- make free long-distance phone calls
- create a personalized travel planner/scheduler
- acquire travel insurance
- complain about destinations and services

The list of things you can do over the Internet goes on and on. While once a relatively passive information resource for travelers, today's rapidly changing Internet has become much more interactive with increasing emphasis on customizing key communication functions appropriate for travelers. The interactivity now goes far beyond chat rooms and discussion groups. One of the best examples of where the Internet is going for travelers is the innovative Worldroom.com:

www.worldroom.com

While designed primarily for business travelers, the site also is very useful for any type of traveler who seeks essential travel information and services. The site now allows users to download travel guides and maps on PDAs; customize three-day weather forecasts; create a communication tool box for instantly accessing email, voice mail, and faxes; and consult a Feng Shui master, just in case the furniture in your hotel room needs to be rearranged! We expect many more interactive and customized travel features to come out of this unique site.

What You Can Do Well on the Internet

In many respects, we are still at a first generation stage of Internet development for travel. Right now the Internet is especially popular for booking airline, hotel, and auto reservations – the bread and butter revenue streams that keep many websites alive – and dispensing peripheral free information and advice in the form of travel "tool kits" and semi-interactive chat rooms and discussion groups. But this situation will not remain static for long. Within the space of a year or two, or perhaps even a few months, we expect sites using new and innovative software will push travel to a whole new stage of development. Indeed, over the next couple of years we expect these sites to be much more interactive as they become designed to enhance the overall travel experience through the use of multi-media. More and more travelers will be able to "travel" to their locations and acquire information and advice even before leaving home. They will "try out" locations to see if there is a good "fit" before visiting the destination. Or they may just enjoy virtual travel rather than leave their homes. The whole communication function will change as travelers become wired to the Internet 24-hours a day. They will truly become global travelers with the resources for instantly accessing travel information and advice on the go.

Enrich Your Travel Experience

The remainder of this book examines several major Internet travel sites which you should find useful in planning and implementing your travels.

Given the nature of the Internet phenomenon, this is by no means an exhaustive directory to such sites. Indeed, many sites come and go at an alarming rate. Some are very comprehensive, busy, complex, and well financed and staffed sites; they are constantly undergoing changes in order to improve their information and services as well as attract and keep users. Others are small under-financed and under-staffed sites that offer useful information but which may best be termed "cobwebs" because of their infrequent changes. For example, how often do you need to change a site that reviews the history and culture of a destination or lists the addresses and phone numbers of embassies, tips on packing, and translation of foreign language phrases? A lot less than sites that provide information on weather, currency, safety warnings, and airline schedules.

The websites reviewed here represent some of the most useful sites we have found for both planning and implementing a travel adventure. We've used many of them for pre-trip planning and while traveling around the globe. As you will quickly discover, some are more useful than others. Except for a few all-encompassing travel sites, each deals with a particular aspect of travel. Many are redundant in that they provide similar information. And much of the redundancy is a function of the nature of many Internet travel sites – many are plugged into larger affiliate programs which use the same databases but under a different name. Taken together, our featured sites constitute a powerful collection of websites for travel planning and implementation.

Whatever you do, make sure you incorporate the Internet into your travels. Not only will you find it to be a rich resource for planning your travels, we're confident you'll find it will enrich your overall travel experience. In the end, that's what useful travel resources should be all about!

Advanced Search - Language, Display, & Filtering Options

[Google Search] [I'm Feeling Lucky]

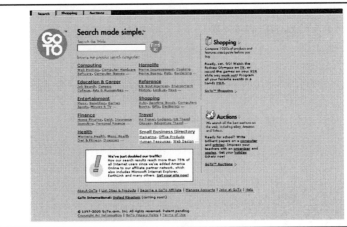

2

Getting Started in the Right Direction

ETTING STARTED ON THE INTERNET IS RELATIVELY easy as long as you have the proper communication equipment, a willingness to learn, some basic organizational skills, and time to explore the Internet. In the end, time may be your worst enemy, especially if you become addicted to the Internet – a common affliction of Internet users. Regardless of your level of technical expertise, the Internet is very easy to learn with most people requiring only a few minutes of basic orientation. Really savvy Internet users invest a great deal of time in learning relatively sophisticated organizational and communication techniques.

Basic Guidance

If you are an Internet novice, you may want to pick up a basic book, written in plain English, on how to use the Internet. You don't need anything complex, cute, or expensive. Get a book that goes over Internet basics, such as setting your home page, bookmarking sites, saving and copying Web pages, downloading files, using search engines, customizing Web browsers, and using the Usenet, mailing lists, and e-mail. Two good books that demystify the Web with great brevity and clarity include:

> *Teach Yourself the Internet*, David Crowder and Rhonda
> Crowder (Foster City, CA: IDG Books)

The Rough Guide to the Internet, Angus J. Kennedy (New York: The Rough Guides)

Both books complement each other. The first book is a large text that is best reviewed before you leave home. The second book by Kennedy is ideal for travel since it is designed as a small pocket-sized reference guide. For your convenience, both books are available through Impact Publications (see page 259). You also can access the Kennedy book online and use it free of charge, including hotlinks to hundreds of recommended sites, by going to this section of the publisher's website:

www.roughguides.com/internet/directory/index.html#tools

A Library and an Orchestra

There are two organizational/disorganizational dimensions to the Internet worth noting as you prepare to use the Internet: specific locations (URLs) and communities of interests (Usenet newsgroups, mailing lists, bulletin boards/forums). People go to the Internet to both find things (seek out specific locations by URL) and participate in discussions (join communities).

> *The Internet is like an orchestra of amateur players without a director who are trying to play a coherent tune or compose a composition without knowing what their fellow players are up to.*

Imagine a library where millions of books are just thrown helter-skelter in one huge room. Or imagine an orchestra of amateur players without a director – where most participants are of questionable talent and are at times both in the orchestra and in the audience – trying to play a coherent tune or compose a composition. In this chapter we'll examine the case of the library in need of classification, labeling, and location codes. In Chapter 3 we'll look at the case of the orchestra of amateurs without a director (virtual travel communities).

In the case of the library, nothing is labeled nor classified – even the covers are missing! While you may wander through the mess and serendipitously find an interesting resource, chances are you will be lost, confused, and frustrated about where to start and what you can expect to find along the way. You may just give up and decide this type of library is not for you. Without some form of organization and classi-fication system these millions of resources may be meaningless to you.

The Internet is like a huge library where few things have been classified and put on the shelves. It's rich with information but chaotic in terms of organization. While this book classifies travel sites and identifies specific resources by name and location (URL), the Internet also includes a variety of organizational elements – variously called search engines, search agents, and directories – that enable users to access resources in a relatively coherent manner. Not one, but hundreds of search engines, agents, and directories are available for exploring the Internet. Indeed, one site, *www.gogettem.com*, alone identifies over 2,500 search engines and directories! Creating a high level of redun-dancy, this multiplicity of search elements is extremely functional for anyone interested in accessing useful information on the Internet. The redundancy is often created by the fact that many search engines use the same databases (several use the Inktomi database system) and are powered by affiliate programs or parent companies which operate other search engines. Not surprisingly, a search conducted on one search engine may produce nearly identical results as the same search conducted using an ostensibly different search engine.

While most of the sites identified in this discussion are often subsumed under the general category of "Search Engines," we've broken them into three categories of search elements:

- Search engines
- Search agents
- Directories

These are important distinctions because they can lead to different approaches to using the Internet and thus yield different qualities of information. In the end, your searches are only as good as the quality of your questions. The sooner you improve the quality of your questions, the sooner you will generate quality information on the Internet.

Once you begin using these various search elements, you'll begin seeing some major differences in how you query various sites and how databases are organized and information presented. **Search engines**, for example, use software with "spiders" to literally crawl the Internet for keywords, phrases, addresses, and page titles that you specify should be part of your search. On the other hand, **search agents** appear to be search engines but with one major difference – they explore various search engines simultaneously so that you get the benefit of multiple searches. **Directories** consist of compilations of websites, usually done by individuals, which are classified under a variety of subject headings; directories typically identify the most popular sites relevant to a particular subject.

When you use a search engine or search agent, you are basically asking a question, in the form of keywords and phases, for which you desire an answer. When you use a directory, you are presented with a list of sites, by subject category, with little relevance to any particular questions; directories merely expose you to lots of popular sites which may, in turn, raise questions in your mind. If you have lots of questions for which you seek answers, by all means perfect your keywords and phrases and use search engines and search agents. But if you're not sure what questions to ask, you may want to start with directories that expose you to many different related sites. After examining several sites in the directory, you should have a better idea of the types of questions you would like to ask of the search engines and search agents.

Please note that many search engines also incorporate elements of search agents and directories, and vice versa. In these cases, you should be aware that the search element functions very differently from the directory element.

Search Engines

An essential starting point for Internet users are the various search engines that enable them to literally search millions of Web pages for information relevant to their particular interests and queries. Entering keywords and phrases into a search engine's query form, the search engine quickly returns a list of "hits" based upon your defining criteria. If, for example, you're interested in finding the best places to go bungy jumping in New Zealand, you might enter "bungy jumping New Zealand" in your favorite search engine in the hopes that you will get lots of good "hits" that will help you determine the best places to take that big leap.

However, not all search engines are equal. Some have larger databases than others. Some use more sophisticated software than others. Some are much faster than others. And some are simply more intelligent and user-friendly than others. You may find, for example, that one search engine will only yield two references to bungy jumping in New Zealand whereas another search engine will give you over 20 such references. Since the quality and depth of various search engines differ, you are well advised to use more than one search engine when looking for resources on the Internet. Indeed, we regularly switch back and forth with five of our favorite search engines with often dramatically different results. Our current favorite is no-nonsense Google which has proved very reliable and yields some of the best travel sites:

www.google.com

A few of our other favorite search engines include iWon, GoTo, Northern Light, and HotBot:

iWon:	*www.iwon.com*
GoTo:	*www.goto.com*
Northern Light:	*www.northernlight.com*
HotBot:	*www.hotbot.com*

In our example of "bungy jumping New Zealand," our five favorite search engines recently yielded this number of "hits":

www.google.com	24
www.iwon.com	3,437
www.goto.com	240
www.northernlight.com	10
www.hotbot.com	7

You'll discover numerous other search engines for exploring the Internet. Going beyond our favorite five, these search engines also should prove useful for conducting Internet travel searches:

AltaVista:	*www.altavista.com*
AOL Search:	*http://search.aol.com*
C4.com:	*www.c4.com*
CEO Express:	*www.ceoexpress.com*
Debriefing:	*www.debriefing.com*
EuroSeek:	*www.euroseek.com*
Excite:	*www.excite.com*
FAST Search:	*www.alltheweb.com*
Go/InfoSeek:	*www.go.com*

inFind:	*www.infind.com*
Looksmart:	*www.looksmart.com*
Lycos:	*www.lycos.com*
Magellan:	*www.mckinley.com*
Microsoft Network:	*www.msn.com*
Netscape:	*www.netscape.com*
Raging Search:	*www.raging.com*
Searchbeat:	*www.searchbeat.com*
Snap:	*www.snap.com*
Thunderstone:	*www.thunderstone.com*
Webcrawler:	*www.webcrawler.com*
Yahoo:	*www.yahoo.com*

However, after sampling numerous alternatives, you may conclude our top five, and especially Google and iWon, are the "best of the best" search engines.

Search Agents

Also known as searchbots, search agents basically search a few key search engines and directories simultaneously in response to search queries. These search agents are not equal since each conducts simultaneous searches using a different set of search engines and directories. For example, MetaGopher simultaneously searches eight major search engines: Yahoo, Google, Spinks, Goto.com, HotBot, Go Network, WebCrawler, and AltaVista. MetaCrawler simultaneously searches Yahoo, InfoSeek, Lycos, Excite, and AltaVista. Matilda simultaneously searches 13 international and Australian search engines. One of the stand-out sites, which requires downloading special software, is **Copernic**. Some of the most popular and useful search agents include:

Ask Jeeves:	*www.ask.com*
Copernic:	*www.copernic.com*
DogPile:	*www.dogpile.com*
EuroFerret:	*www.euroferret.com*
Go2Net:	*www.go2net.com*
Matilda:	*www.aaa.com.au*
MetaCrawler:	*www.metacrawler.com*
MetaGopher:	*www.metagopher.com*
ProFusion:	*www.profusion.com*

Directories

Several sites that primarily function as search engines also include a directory section. This section includes a unique set of sites under specific subject headings, such as autos, cities, games, money, parenting, real estate, shopping, and travel. Some of these sites tend to subsume "Travel" under the general category of "Recreation." The real star directory is **About.com** which has a reputation for compiling one of the most comprehensive listings of sites by subject matter. Previously known as **Miningco.com**, this site is now part of the About.com site:

About.com:	*www.about.com*
Ask Jeeves:	*www.ask.com*
Britannica:	*www.britannica.com*
DogPile:	*www.dogpile.com*
Excite:	*www.excite.com*
Go:	*www.go.com*
iWon:	*www.iwon.com*
Looksmart:	*www.looksmart.com*
Lycos:	*www.lycos.com*
Magellan:	*www.mckinley.com*
Microsoft Network:	*www.msn.com*
Netscape:	*www.netscape.com*
Open Directory:	*http://dmoz.org*
WebTop:	*www.webtop.com*
Yahoo:	*www.yahoo.com*

Most Popular Search Engines

But there are a lot more search engines, agents, and directories than the ones we've discussed above. In August 2000, for example, the following search engines were identified by Top9.com (*www.top9.com/top99s/ top99_search_engines.html*) as the most frequently used. Representing a combination of search engines, agents, and directories, many of these sites also represented the most popular sites on the Web with millions of visitors using them each week to search for information and solve problems:

List Rank	Overall Web Rank	Search Engine	Unique Visitors (x000)
1	1	www.yahoo.com	52,212
2	3	www.msn.com	41,153
3	8	www.lycos.com	20,718
4	9	www.altavista.com	20,718
5	13	www.excite.com	17,472
6	14	www.netscape.com	17,293
7	17	www.iwon.com	14,511
8	19	www.about.com	13,522
9	23	www.looksmart.com	11,523
10	24	www.goto.com	11,517
11	26	www.go.com	11,482
12	36	www.snap.com	9,511
13	63	www.google.com	6,604
14	113	www.go2net.com	4,899
15	125	www.4anything.com	4,518
16	129	www.dogpile.com	4,427
17	161	www.directhit.com	3,761
18	213	www.mamma.com	3,105
19	226	www.gohip.com	3,011
20	248	www.webcrawler.com	2,734
21	264	www.clickheretofind.com	2,600
22	267	www.hotbot.com	2,584
23	310	www.rocketlinks.com	2,332
24	370	www.metacrawler.com	1,984
25	393	www.myway.com	1,929
26	432	www.search.com	1,766
27	511	www.gotoworld.com	1,511
28	526	www.ignifuge.com	1,474
29	542	www.northernlight.com	1,428
30	563	www.efind.com	1,391
31	831	www.ditto.com	986
32	842	www.boomerank.com	974
33	900	www.findwhat.com	932
34	904	www.37.com	929
35	978	www.searchalot.com	870
36	998	www.sprinks.com	852
37	1,099	www.megaspider.com	784

38	1,197	*www.planetclick.com*	738
39	1,261	*www.suite101.com*	704
40	1,271	*www.ah-ha.com*	699
41	1,426	*www.homepageware.com*	635
42	1,459	*www.bomis.com*	623
43	1,624	*www.alltheweb.com*	572
44	1,634	*www.searchcactus.com*	565
45	1,657	*www.yahoo.com.au*	560
46	1,704	*www.411web.com*	542
47	1,861	*www.yahoo.ca*	499
48	1,916	*www.blomp.com*	485
50	1,954	*www.yep.com*	476
51	2,079	*www.webhideout.com*	448
52	2,211	*www.find.com*	422
53	2,214	*www.pointcom.com*	421
54	2,961	*www.top9.com*	320
55	2,977	*www.msn.co.uk*	319
56	3,085	*www.supercybersearch.com*	308
57	3,219	*www.resoftlinks.com*	296
58	3,259	*www.oingo.com*	293
59	3,367	*www.powerclick.com*	283
60	3,517	*www.100hot.com*	270
61	3,603	*www.searcharrow.com*	263
62	3,648	*www.searchhawk.com*	260
63	3,760	*www.secondpower.com*	252
64	3,892	*www.startingpage.com*	244
65	4,301	*www.quacko.com*	221
66	4,449	*www.why.com*	215
67	4,549	*www.stpt.com*	211
68	4,958	*www.hotlinks.com*	193
69	4,994	*www.allonesearch.com*	192
70	5,068	*www.wordplanet.com*	189
71	5,129	*www.locate.com*	186
72	5,195	*www.jumpforce.com*	184
73	5,208	*www.savvy.com*	183
74	5,485	*www.pageseeker.com*	175
75	5,586	*www.annotate.net*	171
76	5,658	*www.swoopit.com*	169
77	5,691	*www.seekon.com*	168
78	5,721	*www.firstbookmark.com*	167
79	5,760	*www.7search.com*	166
80	6,114	*www.langenberg.com*	156

81	6,275	www.raging.com	152
82	6,284	www.clickheretofind.net	152
83	6,682	www.surfy.com	142
84	6,693	www.hotsheet.com	142
85	6,832	www.c4.com	138
86	6,965	www.canada.com	136
87	7,091	www.megago.com	134
88	7,288	www.verica.com	130
89	7,296	www.earthcommerce.com	130
90	7,506	www.virtualfish.com	126
91	7,830	www.pokok.com	121
92	8,012	www.hotindex.com	118
93	8,129	www.einet.net	116
94	8,437	www.globesearch.com	112
95	8,439	www.hotrate.com	112
96	8,765	www.lycos.co.uk	108
97	9,085	www.onecenter.com	104
98	9,163	www.sycast.com	103
99	9,374	www.buildingonline.com	101

In addition to the key search engines, agents, and directories we identified in previous sections, you may want to explore the travel capabilities of the many additional search engines identified in this list of 99 top
search engines.

For information on even more search engines, as well as tips on
how to best use them, we recommend visiting Search Engine Watch:

www.searchenginewatch.com

This site also includes a comprehensive listing of search engines for
identifying search engines, such as *www.directoryguide.com*, *www.
searchiq.com*, *www.allsearchengines.com*, and *www.goget tem.com*.

Travel Site Comparisons and Ratings

While most Web directories identify the most popular sites by category,
other sites actually rank sites by popularity. If you're interested in the
most popular travel sites, visit these three sites which provide rankings
of various travel sites:

Scorecard	Ratings
www.scorecard.com	

This site rates consumer experiences with various industries, companies, and websites. In the case of travel, it identifies consumer ratings of the top travel websites and travel services relating to airlines, car rentals, cruises, hotels, and travel agents. It also includes reviews and consumer comments (lots of unhappy consumers vent about certain dependably late airlines). If you're interested in what others are saying about travel on and off the Web, be sure to check out this site.

Top9	Ratings
www.top9.com/travel_transport	

If you're interested in identifying the most popular travel websites based on the number of visitors, as well as seeing how each site ranks in comparison to all websites, be sure to bookmark this site. It ranks the top 9 websites for 13 different travel categories:

- Online agents
- Airlines
- Resources/Reviews
- Hotels/Resorts
- Destinations
- Hotel Booking
- Transport
- Rental Cars
- Vacations and Tours
- Adventure Travel
- Timeshares
- Bed and Breakfast
- Cruise Lines

In addition, it identifies nine up-and-coming hot websites as well as related sites for each category.

100Hot   **Ratings**
www.100hot.com/directory/lifestyles/travel.html

This site ranks the top 100 travel sites on a weekly basis based
on the number of "hits" each receives. For the week of August
18, 2000, for example, the top 10 sites included:

1. Intellicast
2. MapQuest
3. Yahoo Travel!
4. Lonely Planet Online
5. Spanair
6. Travelocity
7. American Express
8. TravelNow Online Travel Reservations
9. Delta SkyLinks
10. Canada.com

If you're interested in learning where everyone is hanging out
online for travel information and services, be sure to periodically visit this site.

Saving Time and Effort

Getting started with travel planning on the Internet can be a very
laborious and disorienting process if you primarily rely on search
engines, search agents, and directories for identifying useful travel sites.
While such organizational helpers are unquestionably useful, they also
can be very time consuming and the results are often disappointing
because of the hit and miss nature of such sites. At best these devices
will identify the most popular sites in terms of the number of "hits" they
receive on a monthly basis. Such popularity may reflect more on the size
of a site's advertising budget, publicity efforts, and marketing prowess
– by seeding their site with keywords and META tags – than on the
actual quality and usefulness of the site's content. For example, the
popular AOL Search (*http://search.aol.com*) is nearly useless for many
users who find the first few hundred sites identified under "Travel" to
be all individual book titles for the Lonely Planet travel series –
supposedly AOL's most popular travel sites! While Yahoo.com is the

most popular search engine (ranks #1 in terms of "hits"), we find Google.com, which ranks thirteenth in search engines, to be much more useful.

In the pages that follow, we identify specific travel sites that we have found especially useful for travel planning. Many of these sites are of exceptional quality. Some may seldom appear, or they appear very low, on the standard search engines. You may want to sample these sites before venturing in the world of search engines, search agents, and directories. Indeed, you can save a great deal of time and effort by going directly to several of the gateway travel sites we identify in the next chapter. Once you locate quality sites, be sure to bookmark them and return to them often. In so doing, you may discover your time is better spent going directly to the special travel sites identified in subsequent chapters than in using the search engines, search agents, and directories identified in this chapter. Whatever your choices, you will at least be heading in the right direction for planning your travels on the Internet.

3

Virtual Travel Communities

T HE INTERNET IS MUCH MORE THAN A COLLECTION of websites from which to access travel information and services. It's first of all a *community of individuals and organizations* that come together because of common interests and goals. You use the search engines in Chapter 2, for example, because you are looking for something very specific or because you wish to expose yourself to new information and experiences that can lead to a more rewarding travel adventure. In so doing, you may encounter individuals and organizations that can assist you. Hopefully you will make many new friends along the way.

Information Communities

While most of this book focuses on the organizational players on the Internet – locations that have URLs, staffs, commercial operations, and perhaps venture capital subsidizing their efforts – the Internet also is made up of thousands of individuals who have formed specialized communities that are focused on information rather than commerce. Most such communities are very loosely structured for exchanging information and advice. They are virtual networks designed for information, advice, and referrals. Some are linked to commercial websites whereas others are independent nonprofit community websites or they reside elsewhere (Usenet) on the Internet. Individuals can easily join and leave such groups. Held together virtually by the Usenet and email, these communities are a mixed bag for travelers. Some are very useful whereas others are dreadful wastes of time. Some stay together for many months whereas others may only last a few weeks, depending on the quality of their participants and the benefits they dispense to their "members". Few such communities will last more than a couple of years.

You should be aware of your community options before you explore specific travel sites on the Internet. You will normally find three types of communities in three different places on the Internet:

- Usenet newsgroups
- Mailing lists
- Message boards of websites

While each of these communities has limitations, all potentially offer some very important travel information and advice. If you participate in these communities, you'll most likely come away with some very timely information that cannot be found from other sources on the Internet. The information comes directly from individual travelers and laymen rather than from travel businesses and professionals.

> *These virtual communities are a mixed bag for travelers. Some are very useful whereas others are dreadful wastes of time.*

Usenet Newsgroups

If you are used to communicating with others by email, you know the importance and timeliness of such communication. Indeed, many people now have a hard time living without their email. At the same time, many people have discovered the communication advantages of newsgroups which for many travelers is better than email. Some become addicted to them.

Newsgroups are one of the most interactive aspects of the Internet. Also known as Usenet, this is the virtual community aspect of the Internet – the largest electronic public discussion forum in the world. In fact, nearly 40,000 newsgroups currently function on the Internet. These are loose communities of shared interests where members or participants ask questions, share experiences, post alerts, review subjects, introduce new activities, spread gossip, and sometimes create mischief. Depending on the nature of the subject and the particular mix of participants, many of these groups are fun, educational, and exciting to join; others lack energy and are often boring, stressful, and useless. Newsgroups tend to live and die based upon the quality of the participants, on-going communication dynamics, and benefits offered to the group. While all the so-called "news" of these groups is not fit to print, much of it is useful. For travelers, travel newsgroups can be very educational and timely, especially if you encounter quality travelers who share their experiences and offer useful tips.

Similar to the many discussion and chat groups found on the major travel sites, newsgroups function like public bulletin boards. Someone posts a message which can be read by everyone who accesses the newsgroup. Viewers, in turn, post replies within the community for all to read or privately send an email to the individual who originally posted the message.

The UseNet is one section of the Internet, separate from the World Wide Web, which has its own networks, servers, and routers for handling newsgroups. In order to participate in newsgroups, you must have special software, called a newsreader, installed on your browser. Netscape Navigator and Microsoft Internet Explorer browsers come with this software pre-installed.

Newsgroups are an especially rich resource for travelers who know how to best use them for travel planning. Indeed, some travelers may spend 80 percent of their Internet time using various travel newsgroups. Seeking timely information, they ask about best restaurants, hotels, and things to do as well as seek answers to hundreds of travel questions, such as when is the best time to visit the Grand Canyon, do you need to take shots to visit South Africa, or does anyone know where to buy good quality rubies in Myanmar? However, you should also be cautious about the information acquired through such "open" forums. Since newsgroups are not moderated, they are highly susceptible to spam, disinformation, and irritating participants, such as individuals trying to market their products or constantly asking inane questions. The quality of information is often questionable since you really never know who is providing the information – a nine-year old, a sociopath, inexperienced travelers, self-appointed travel experts, or a real travel expert? Many of the travel newsgroups tend to attract a disproportionate number of young, inexperienced, and excitable budget travelers who view themselves as instant travel experts after a three-week trip backpacking through Europe. They also attract a few wackos who have personal political agendas, such as boycott certain countries because of its politically incorrect government or its cruel treatment of animals, or the disgruntled airline passenger who wants you to boycott an airline because the toilet wasn't working properly on his last flight. Take, for example, a recent discussion in one newsgroup on the best travel guidebook on Hong Kong. One person recommended the Lonely Planet City Guide but thought it was too expensive to buy new ($14.95) so they recommended trying to get a used copy online through eBay. You may be able to live without such insightful advice! Indeed, if you are a different age, class, and disposition of traveler, you may find their discussions at best naive and at worst weird and useless for your own interests; they can be great time wasters as you "hang out" with people who seem to have a lot of idle time on their hands. In other words, newsgroups are often gateways to a virtual world of questionable information and advice. You often meet troubled travelers in these groups. Use them but don't rely on them for quality travel information and advice.

For information on how to best use newsgroups, as well as tips on which newsgroups might best meet your needs, visit these useful sites:

DejaNews:	*www.dejanews.com*
Liszt:	*www.liszt.com/news*
Usenet Info Center:	*http://metalab.unc.edu/usenet-i/ home.html*
Questions:	*www.xs4all.nl/~wijnands/nnq/ grouplists.html*

You'll find several newsgroups on the Internet. However, you'll need a specialized search engine to find newsgroups related to your particular travel interests. The largest and most popular such search engine is Deja News (*www.dejanews.com*).

Deja News   **Newsgroups**
www.dejanews.com

This is the granddaddy directory of newsgroups. It includes useful search engines for finding discussion groups by subject and name. For example, if you search for "Travel", you'll find the following discussion forums:

rec.travel.cruises
rec.travel.air
rec.travel.asia
rec.travel.europe

At the same time, you'll find discussions of specific countries
and U.S. states under its "Regional" heading. For example,
you'll find separate discussion forums organized around
Australia, France, Hong Kong, Israel, Japan, Poland, Russia,
Spain, and the Ukraine. However, most of the regional discussion focus on non-travel topics. Some questions receive no
response whereas others may generate hundreds of responses
(airline delays) and new discussion "threads" that lead into
separate travel topics. This newsgroup also provides product
reviews. For example, if you search for a particular country,
you'll find how visitors rate various cities in that country. In
the case of Thailand, both Mae Hong Son and Chiang Mai
received the highest ratings of travelers in Thailand.

Liszt	**Newsgroups**
www.liszt.com	

This powerful site, which is also part of Deja, provides a
directory to over 30,000 Usenet newsgroups as well as a
directory to more than 90,000 mailing lists, and 25,000 IRC
chat channels. Like Deja News, its search engine allows you to
type in your interests and then it lists all relevant mailing lists.

Mailing Lists

Mailing lists are another useful way to access travel information on the
Internet. Unlike spontaneous newsgroups that require you to take
initiative in posting your own messages and/or checking on other
publicly posted messages, mailing lists are more structured and are often
moderated by the individual who initially created the list. While most
are open to the public, many also are private – only certain individuals
who meet membership criteria can join. At the same time, mailing lists
have the potential of automatically driving tons of email to your
address. Indeed, with mailing lists you become a "member" or "sub-

scriber" to the list by giving the group your email address. When messages are posted to the group, you automatically receive copies of the messages. Subscribe to a few active mailing lists and you may see a dramatic increase in your daily email volume. You'll no longer feel lonely with only receiving two or three messages a day – you could easily end up with 100 messages a day. After awhile, you may think your membership is an exercise in self-directed spam!

The purpose of most mailing lists is to disseminate information and/or encourage the exchange of ideas amongst members who have a common interest in the same subject. Some lists are excellent forums for acquiring useful news and information whereas others wander off on the deep end as they generate lots of useless email from individuals who need to get a life. The long-term viability of mailing lists depends on the quality of the information. Members tend to come and go ("subscribe" and "unsubscribe") by completing online subscription forms that officially put their email into the mailing list. Many mailing lists become defunct because of the lack of time and interest on the part of the creator.

If you are interested in participating in mailing lists, a good starting point is the following site which serves as a useful directory to more than 7,500 mailing lists:

http://paml.net

You can search the directory by keyword or go directly to an alphabetical index of mailing lists by names and subjects. For example, if you are interested in China, you can subscribe to several different mailing lists such as *www.egroups.com/list/ china-info* and *www.chinakontor.de/list CH.htm*. If you are interested in particular travel subjects, look under "Travel" and you'll find a variety of interesting specialized travel lists:

Costa Rica:	*www.egroups.com/list/Costa_Rica*
Gems in Israel:	*www.gemsinisrael.com/subscribe.html*
Irish Cottage:	*www.onelist.com/community/irishcottage*
Wedding News:	*www.egroups.com/group/weddingnews*
West Africa:	*www.topica.com/lists/westafrica*

One of the largest directories to "mailing lists" is operated by Liszt:

www.liszt.com

It includes over 90,000 mailing lists in its database as well as maintains a directory of Usenet newsgroups. By using the search engine or clicking onto a relevant topic ("Travel" is subsumed under "Recreation" and includes 67 mailing lists), you can survey available mailing lists.

If you are interested in creating your own mailing list – maybe your travel passion is diving for World War II shipwrecks and you would like to bring together a community of individuals with similar interests – check out these sites:

eGroups:	*www.egroups.com*
Topica:	*www.topica.com*
Liszt:	*www.liszt.com*
Listbot:	*www.listbot.com*
Coollist:	*www.coollist.com*

These sites provide information on how you can create your own free mailing list.

Because mailing lists have the potential of creating such high volumes of email, you may want to consider unsubscribing if you are traveling for a lengthy period of time. If not, you may be overwhelmed trying to sort through your email when you return from your trip. And you probably don't want to access such email while you are traveling since it can be very time consuming.

Message Boards of Websites

Message boards are similar to newsgroups but with one major exception – they are found on websites. Numerous travel websites include a community section which is variously called "community", "forum", "message board", "discussion group", or "chat group". Most are free flowing forums (anyone asks and answers questions) whereas others may be periodically hosted by travel experts. These sections enable visitors to ask questions in anticipation of receiving responses from other site users or hosts. Most such message boards are relatively static – you must revisit the message board to look for replies. However, a few sites such as iAgora (*www.iagora.com*) provide automatic email responses from message boards. In other words, if you leave a message, all responses will autonomically appear on the message board as well as be routed to your email.

Some of the best, and most active, message boards are found on such travel websites as *www.fodors.com, www.frommers.com,* and *www.lonelyplanet.com.* We tend to prefer the message boards of such websites, especially Fodor's site which generates some of the best quality questions and answers (fewer questions from budget and inexperienced travelers), to the more general newsgroups and mailing lists. For more information on these sites, see our discussion of travel guidebook publishers in Chapter 8.

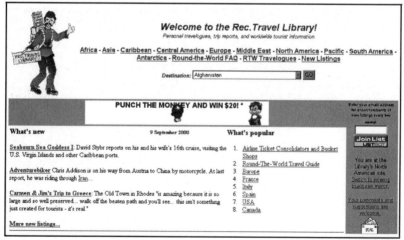

4

Gateway Travel Sites

O NE OF THE QUICKEST WAYS TO GET STARTED ON
the Internet is to go directly to several key gateway travel
sites. Focusing only on travel, these sites function as search
engines, directories, or indexes. By using these sites, you'll
be able to identify over 70 percent of all travel sites on the Internet. If
used in conjunction with the search engines, search agents, and
directories identified in Chapter 2, you should be able to cover over 90
percent of all Internet travel sites.

Global Directories and Linkages

We strongly recommend exploring several of the following websites.
These key sites provide linkages to a rich variety of travel Websites.

Kasbah	Directory
www.kasbah.com	

Wow! This site will save you lots of search time and enrich
your online travel experience. If you have time to visit only one
travel site, make sure it's Kasbah. This is our favorite travel
search engine. It claims to include over 150,000 handpicked
travel sites from 230 countries. You can casily search by single
keywords (accommodations, business, dining, fishing, gay,

museum, shopping, transport), towns, cities, countries, and regions. The site also includes a reservation center (airline, hotel, car rental, last minute, cruise, budget, bed and breakfast), specialty travel (golf, adventure, scuba diving, eco-travel), travel tools (maps, currency converter, weather, ATM locators), international news, and numerous travel resources (publications, shopping, food and drink, arts and entertainments, sports, fun and trivia, and additional search engines). If, for example, you're interested in reviewing travel publications, go to the section called "Travel Magazines" and you'll be instantly linked to more than 200 publications, from *Condé Nast Traveler* and *Travel and Leisure* to *Cruising World Magazine* and *Discovery Online*. Best of all, if you can't find what you're looking for using Kasbah's search engine, directories, and indexes, it gives you 20 additional search engines on this site from which to conduct additional searches, some (WebTop and EuroFerret) of which can be done in several foreign languages:

FAST Search:	*www.alltheweb.com*
C4.com:	*www.c4.com*
Google:	*www.google.com*
inFind:	*www.infind.com*
Debriefing:	*www.debriefing.com*
HotBot:	*www.hotbot.com*
Thunderstone:	*www.thunderstone.com*
Northern Light:	*www.northernlight.com*
EuroFerret:	*www.euroferret.com*
SavvySearch:	*www.savvysearch.com*
WebTop:	*www.webtop.com*
Husky Search:	*www.huskysearch.cs. washington.ed*
ProFusion:	*www.profusion.com*
EuroSeek:	*www.euroseek.com*
Snap:	*www.snap.com*
Meta Gopher:	*www.metagopher.com*
Matilda:	*www.aaa.com.au*
Netcraft:	*www.netcraft.com*
SearchKing:	*www.searchking.com*
Looksmart:	*www.looksmart.com*

The site also includes special travel sections on Canada, United Kingdom, Australia, and New Zealand.

Travel Library	Directory
www.travel-library.com	

This site provides thousands of links to travel sites. Its destination search engine identifies numerous websites relevant to particular destinations. For example, if you're interested in Morocco, just type in Morocco and the search engine identifies many general tourism sites as well as tour operators, travel agents, and travel articles on Morocco. They also include a special section on transportation (air, bicycle, cruise, motorcycle, train) and lots of informative sites and travel tips (packing, health, tourism offices, safety, scams, working, clubs). Its simple front page is somewhat deceptive; start clicking and you'll uncover a wealth of travel information under each of its subject headings.

VirtualTourist	Directory
www.virtualtourist.com	

This is an unusual gateway site. It consists of a community of more than 80,000 members who share travel information, experiences, and insights. Rich in discussions and online chats, the site is especially useful for anyone interested in getting first-hand information and advice from seasoned travelers. The stories and insights tend to be very personal and appeal to individuals who appreciate up-to-date travel reports. The site also rates the top members, provides a friend finder, offers online postcard, and includes a currency converter, time zones, and a travel store. A useful search engine enables users to search the site by location, member, and keywords. For example, if you are interested in Thailand, you'll find the site includes 66 members who live there, 1,280 members who have visited there, and 103 members who plan to visit soon. If you tap into this network of travelers, you'll be able to access a tremendous amount of information on destinations.

Community Directories

The following sites function as community directories – focus on major cities. Some are very city-specific whereas others serve as search engines for several destinations. Most include a comprehensive set of travel planning tools, from booking systems to news, message boards, and newsletters, that can be used for planning a trip.

Citysearch.com	**Directory**
www.citysearch.com	

This site functions as a search engine for exploring where to go, what to do, and how to get things done in nearly 100 U.S., Canadian, and Australian cities (90 percent are U.S. cities). Each site includes a wealth of information on everything from restaurants, bars, movies, arts, sports, and shopping to yellow pages, news, and careers. The site consists of a combination of Citysearch and partnership sites. For example, Chicago, Cincinnati, and Sydney are Citysearch sites whereas Washington, DC is a partnership site linked to WashingtonPost.com. Citysearch is also part of Ticketmaster Online (*www.ticket master.com*) and Matchmaker (*www.match.com*). This is a well financed site which can be found on the Nasdaq: TMCS. A very rich site for exploring major cities.

Exes	**Directory**
www.exes.com	

Primarily functioning as a travel search engine, this site also includes several useful travel resources: hotel directories, airlines, airports, embassies, traffic conditions, news groups, weather, maps, car rentals, immigration, and links to several official destination sites, such as Australia, Egypt, Mexico, Cannes, and New York. Its TravelActive channel includes links to numerous sites that have exciting travel content.

Travelnotes   Directory
www.travelnotes.org

This site provides a wealth of travel information from detailed country backgrounds to reviews of websites and travel articles. It includes a travel forum, tips, quiz, and mailing list. The site also includes an affiliate airline, car rental, and hotel booking system. But the best part of this site is its rich destination section which links to most countries around the world. If you need quick information on a particular country or city, just go to the destination section and you'll most likely find much more information than you anticipated.

My Travel Guide   Directory
www.mytravelguide.com

This comprehensive travel site includes a wealth of information and services: city travel guides, travel news, message boards, U.S. parks guide, reservation center, travel newsletter, online chat, and travel tools.

Trip Finders and Assessments

Several websites focus on assisting travelers with all aspects of their travels. The following sites reveal numerous travel services as well as shared observations from travelers:

Opinionated Traveler   Directory
www.opinionatedtraveler.com

Operated by a group of eight professional travel journalists and broadcasters, this site offers lots of first-hand observations and analyses of travel around the globe. Includes destination reviews as well as numerous travel links through its "Opinionated Travel Network" section. Also offers a travel store based on affiliate relationships.

Travel-Finder   **Directory**
www.travel-finder.com

This travel search engine covers more than 8,000 travel-related sites operated by over 4,000 hosts. Its "spider" allows you to search by activity, category, type of traveler, state, province (U.S. and Canada), country, region, and continent. Using this site, you should be able to narrow your travel interests considerably. Except for its irritating interactive "Punch the Monkey and Win $20" ad, this is a useful site, although it is not as comprehensive as you might expect.

TravelPage   **Directory**
www.travelpage.com

This is not your typical redundant travel website. This award-winning gateway travel and adventure site provides a great deal of practical travel information, from news, weather, maps, currency, money, safety, health, and passport/visa requirements to chats, news, and features focused on specific destinations, hotels and resorts, cruise travel, and air travel. It also includes a reservation center for airlines, hotels, car rentals, and vacation packages. If, for example, you are interested in cruises, just click onto its "Cruise Travel" section and you'll discover a wealth of information and linkages including reviews of over 11,000 cruises, a cruise club, cruise specials, profiles of favorite cruises and cruise lines, reviews of ports, live camera views of ports, and U.S. government ship inspection scores.

Travel-Guide   **Directory**
www.travel-guide.com

It's not clear what this site is all about until you start clicking onto its various sections. Affiliated with Columbus Publishing in London, this site includes lots of travel book content produced by Columbus Publishing. Its destination sections, for example, are linked to World Travel Guide (*www.wtgonline. com*) and include overview travel information provided by Columbus Publishing in London. Its airport section is linked to World Airport Guide (*www.worldairportguide.com*). And its ski guide section goes directly into World Ski Guide (*www. worldskiguide.com*). Various sections of the site can also be accessed in German and Spanish. The site also offers a limited product line of two travel CD-ROMs, three books, and a map.

Bookings and Linkages

The following sites provide booking services as well as a comprehensive listing of related services:

AOL	**Directory**
http://www.aol.com/webcenters/travel/home.adp	

Nothing original here but the site does aggregate a wealth of travel information, services, and feedback. In addition to the standard booking departments for airline tickets, car rentals, accommodations, cruises, packages, and hot deals, the site includes several useful travel tools such as weather, international phone numbers, safety information, and travel tips. Its lifestyle section focuses on tips for gay and lesbian travelers. An interesting quiz sections allows users to assess whether or not a particular type of trip (cruise, national parks, Hawaiian Islands, Caribbean Islands) is right for them. The site also includes a useful search engine for searching AOL, news, and the web. Its city guide section is linked to AOL's popular DigitalCity. Not surprising, given AOL's extensive affiliation relations, this site's booking section is operated by Sabre's Travelocity (*www.travelocity. com*). Destination information is provided with affiliate relations with Frommer's, Lonely Planet, and Rough Guides as well as TravelFile.

Web-Street-Secrets   **Directory**
www.web-street-secrets.com

This site emphasizes two elements – booking travel online and linking to other travel sites. The booking section is more educational than commercial; it teaches you how to best book travel online by presenting four guides to online booking: Booking Travel Online, Booking Engines, Finding Insider Travel Information, and Using Essential Travel Resources. The travel links section is what makes this an important gateway travel site. User-friendly, it provides a very comprehensive listing of linkages to airlines, booking engines, car rentals, cruise lines, discount travel, general travel resources, hotels, hotel discounters, newsgroups, search engines, travel magazines and newsletters.

Gateway Commerce

Travel.com   **Directory**
www.travel.com

This is a one-stop-shop designed for purchasing every conceivable type of travel product and service. It's also the ultimate patchwork affiliate site. Built with numerous affiliate relationships (hundreds of vendors link into this site to provide seamless e-commerce), its online mall includes airfares, business meetings, cruises, currencies, events/tickets, golf vacations, insurance, lodging, publications, rail passes, rental cars, skiing vacations, sporting goods, travel packages, and travel products. The site also includes useful free travel information such as travel advisories, airports, ATM locator, driving directions, embassies, flight information, and weather. A search engine operated by the leading adventure travel Website, Gorp, allows users to specify their travel interests for finding appropriate travel adventures.

5

Travel Communities

NUMEROUS INTERNET SITES ARE ORGANIZED FOR communities of shared travel interests. If you're a budget traveler, female, traveler with kids, Jewish, or a senior, you'll find websites specially designed to respond to your particular needs. You'll be able to reference sites which focus on your particular travel interests and affiliations.

In this chapter we identify some of the major specialty groups. If you identify with any of these groups, you may want to check out the accompanying websites. If you belong to another group not featured here, use the major search engines or check out the Usenet newsgroups and mailing lists in Chapter 4 to locate your particular community. Chances are you'll find relevant groups of like-minded travelers. If, for example, you are an African-American, student, disabled, gay, female, Jewish, or a senior, you may discover special tours designed especially for you and others who share similar group interests and affiliations. You'll find articles, chat groups, and innovative tours focused on your special travel issues. Best of all, you may make many new travel friends in the process of visiting these sites.

African-Americans

African-Americans are increasingly interested in traveling to places that are rich in African-American history, culture, and entertainment. Many also are interested in patronizing African-American travel businesses,

from tours and resorts to restaurants and entertainment establishments. One of the best sites for Afrocentric travel is Soul of America:

SoulOfAmerica	African-Americans
www.soulofamerica.com	

This site is dedicated to publishing travel information relevant to Afrocentric culture and entertainment in major U.S. cities and the Caribbean islands. It includes useful sections on black cities, towns, resorts, colleges, and history. It also includes a hotel reservation system, a travel store, and information on festivals, sports, and linkages to other sites. You can subscribe to their e-Newsletter which includes informative articles on travel relevant to African-Americans. One of the most focused and informative African-American travel sites.

GlobalMecca, Inc.	African-Americans
www.globalmecca.com	

Travel is one of 13 channels on this website designed for promoting the personal and economic empowerment of African-Americans. Founded in February 1999, the site aims at being the leading content provider for this community. The travel channel includes many standard features which are provided through an affiliate relationship with Expedia (airline, hotel, car rental reservations, travel forums, travel tools). Includes some unique content such as a recent feature on The Black Panther Legacy Tour.

Pathfinders Travel	African-Americans
www.pathfinderstravel.com	

This is the online version of a glossy quarterly travel magazine designed for people of color. Includes many feature articles on exotic U.S. and international destinations, such as recent pieces on "A Sharecroppers Daughter Goes to Paris" and "Sleeping Inn at Black Bed and Breakfasts." New sections focus on restaurants ("Chef's Table") and travel group specials.

Budget and Student Travelers

Budget travelers constitute one of the largest and most ubiquitous groups of independent travelers in the world. They also make up a particular subculture of travelers who have their own attitudes and approaches to travel and who support an important segment of local economies. Preoccupied with finding cheap airline tickets, accommodations, restaurants, tours, and local transportation, they support the budget end of the travel industry that is dependent upon servicing a high volume of budget travelers. Indeed, without budget travelers, a whole segment of the travel industry would collapse, especially in Third World countries. While many budget travelers are young single students who have limited financial resources and love to travel with their Lonely Planet, Let's Go, Moon, and Rough Guide travel guides and stay connected to Internet cafés, many others are older and enjoy the independent budget travel style which often involves backpacking, staying in hostels, dining in inexpensive establish-

> *Budget travelers make up a particular subculture of travelers who have their own attitudes and approaches to travel and who support an important segment of local economies.*

ments, and hanging out at cheap bars where they feel they get to really meet the people and learn about the local culture. And other less adventuresome budget travelers join budget tours that may involve using hostels, one- and two-star hotels, and public transportation. While many travel websites are designed for independent budget travelers – especially booking sites for inexpensive airline tickets and accommodations (see Chapter 11) – the following websites represent the major budget sites:

BudgetTravel	Budget/Students
www.budgettravel.com	

Wow! This is the *kasbah.com* for budget travelers. If you are looking for a fantastic collection of linkages relating to travel in general and budget travel in particular, it doesn't get any better than this site. Indeed, you can easily spend hours getting lost in this site as you go from one linkage to another. This is a very rich gateway site to various dimensions of budget travel worldwide. It includes numerous linkages to individual countries, from embassies, tourist offices, and visas to travel agents, maps, weather, accommodations, recreation, and health. Includes many special features, such as a monthly special, message board, travelogs, featured destinations of the month, adventure travel, travel agents, hostels, and shopping worldwide.

Frommer's	Budget
www.frommers.com	

One of the largest and most popular budget travel websites designed to promote budget travel and offer travel savings to users. Operated by budget travel guru Arthur Frommer who continues to dispense useful budget travel tips and advice through his daily online newsletter and the popular "Arthur Frommer Budget Travel Magazine" and Frommer travel guides which provide the major content for this site. A very busy site, it enables users to book airline tickets, hotels, cruises, car rentals, and tours as well as purchase travel books and subscribe to the magazine. Offers a useful destination search engine as well as message boards, an "Ask Arthur" section, travel specials, vacation ideas, and recommended hot spots. A rich site for exploring the world of budget travel. Offers a free issue of the offline magazine.

Hostels	Budget/Students
www.hostels.com	

Students and budget travelers who prefer staying in hostels will find this site very useful. Surveying the world of hostels, the site includes useful travel articles, message boards, tips on hostelling, and a comprehensive listing of hostels. The site also includes online travel stores (rail passes, travel gear, flights, car rentals, books, and maps), travel tools, travelers tales, news, deals, and a free newsletter.

Backpacker.net	Budget/Students
www.backpacker.net	

If you're planning to travel on the cheap, be sure to check out this site. Focusing on inexpensive hostels and bargain flights, the site also includes message boards, linkages to other budget travel sites, planning tips, a hostel index, tip of the day, Q&A, and announcements. Since many such travelers often seem to attract trouble – get robbed or cheated – the tips and travel tales sections provide useful warnings and advice for those who may be first-time, naive travelers. Since many budget travelers also look for cheap highs in cheap places, the site includes an interesting but rather juvenile "Beer Index" – a comparative chart for identifying the cheapest places in the world to get drunk! Now that's one way to get into trouble, especially when you can't find your hostel at night or you end up stretched out on the beach and get robbed in the process. Offers a free mailing list.

Crazy Dog Travel	Budget/Students
www.crazydogtravel.com	

This well organized site includes lots of useful linkages for budget travelers as well as other types of travelers. Includes special sections on travel planning, packing, money, documents, guides, airlines, accommodations, health, safety, scams, getting around, food, water, communications, photography, maps, female travelers, student travelers, travel bookstore, news, and articles.

ThriftyTraveler	Budget/Students
www.thriftytraveler.com	

Focused on marketing editor Mary VanMeer's *Thrifty Traveler.com* newsletter (both online and offline versions) and *Thrifty Traveling* book, this site is dedicated to teaching visitors the secrets of finding cheap air fares, accommodations, cruise deals, car rentals, attractions, and tours. In addition to informative articles, the site includes travel specials, over-50 news, net-surfing tips, hotel discounts, news, and travel tips and strategies.

Other useful budget sites, many of which are operated by the major budget travel guide publishers, include:

Lonely Planet:	*www.lonelyplanet.com*
Let's Go:	*www.letsgo.com*
Moon Handbooks:	*www.moon.com*
Rick Steves:	*www.ricksteves.com*
Rough Guide:	*www.roughguides.com*
Art of Travel:	*www.artoftravel.com*
Travelog:	*www.travelog.net/links/budget.htm*
Shoestring Travel:	*www.stratpub.com/linktrav.html*
Izon's Backpacker:	*www.izon.com*
BootsnAll:	*www.bootsnall.com*
International Student Travel Confederation:	*www.istc.org*
Council on International Educational Exchange:	*www.ciee.org*
STA Travel:	*www.statravel.com*
Budget Travel:	*www.tenting-hostls.com/Budget-Travel-Links/*
Trippinout:	*www.trippinout.com*
Air Courier:	*www.aircourier.org*
Hostelling International:	*www.hiayh.org*
Hostels of Europe:	*www.hostelseurope.com*

Business Travelers

Business travelers make up a very special and lucrative segment of the travel industry. Like budget travelers, business travelers constitute a very special travel culture. But unlike budget travelers, they spend a lot of money on travel and their attitudes toward travel are very different from students and backpackers who are often in search of a cultural experience. Some business travelers follow Winston Churchill's famous comment: *"My needs are very simple – I simply want the best of everything."* While many business people fly coach and stay in four-star or first-class hotels, others occupy those business and first-class airline seats and stay at five-star or deluxe hotels such as the Ritz-Carlton and Four Seasons – in business you are where you sit and stay! This is the quality end of the travel business. From travel agencies to airlines to hotels to car rentals to restaurants, business travel is the bread and butter of the travel industry. Indeed, many travel agencies primarily specialize in the more lucrative and predictable business travel market rather than the more unpredictable leisure travel market. Since business travelers tend to travel frequently and have special information and service needs, numerous websites have been developed to handle those needs. These sites address the special concerns of business travelers:

> *From travel agencies to airlines to hotels to restaurants, business travel is the bread and butter of the travel industry.*

- Booking flights, hotels, and car rentals.

- Checking on flight delays, frequent flier miles, directions, traffic conditions, and road closures.

- Reviewing city-specific information on weather conditions, restaurants, culture, entertainment, banking, health, safety, jobs, and local news.

- Using the Internet for accessing email, faxes, and voice mail on the road; scheduling appointments; transferring files with the home office; and conducting video conferences.

- Acquiring tips on everything from using a laptop, PDA, and cell phone to overcoming jet lag, shopping for gifts, using local transportation, and handling the local tipping, and hospitality cultures.

- Accessing information on global markets and international news.

- Catching up with the rest of their life rather than making more money (these are busy, decisive, career-oriented people who tend to work hard and play hard).

While many business websites are basically booking engines, such as Biztravel, others, such as Worldroom, are comprehensive sites to assist business travelers with many of their information needs. Examine a few of these sites and you'll be up and running for acquiring some very special information and services relevant to business travelers:

Worldroom   **Business Travel**
www.worldroom.com

This is our idea of a terrific business and travel website designed to make business travel more convenient than ever. Indeed, its slogan is very much on target – "We Make Business Trips Work." Since we travel a great deal in Asia, this has become one of our favorite business travel sites. Based in Hong Kong and Manila, this is one of the most useful sites for travelers – whether business or leisure – a model for many other websites. Operated by I-Quest Corporation, it is closely linked to many five-star business hotels which also offer Worldrooms. These are special rooms which include computers and printers directly connected to the Worldroom site. Other rooms are part of Worldroom Connect which provide a direct modem link to this gateway business site. The site is extremely rich with business tools and information. Its Business Center enables users to directly access their email, faxes, and voice mail online through the Worldroom site. Other sections include city guides to many Asian as well as European cities which include information on everything from hotels and restaurants to entertainment and news. It also includes a travel monitor, travel tools, health, women's, career, tech, and talk sections. Worldroom wireless enables users to download the free city guides onto their PDAs. If you travel to Asia – whether on business or pleasure – you'll want to put this site at the very top of your "best of the best" site lists. Indeed, use it to plan your trip to Asia. Since Worldroom is rapidly moving into Europe, you may want to include it in your European travel plans.

Biztravel   Business Travel
www.biztravel.com

Backed by venture capital and an affiliate of the huge bricks and mortar travel operator Rosenbluth International, here's the popular business booking site that received a great deal of media buzz in 2000 for offering a money-back guarantee on a variety of possible flight delays. If, for example, a flight booked through Biztravel is delayed for more than one hour, purchasers receive a refund of $100. This novel offer in an industry notorious for its flight delays supposedly resulted in an initial 40% increase in Biztravel bookings. It also resulted in a higher than anticipated level of refunds – more than $40,000 a month! How long this offer will last is anyone's guess. Nonetheless, this site also offers several special features for business travelers, such as city information (both U.S. and international), travel tool kit (wireless services, maps, directions, weather, flight tracker, country alerts, currency converter, tips, and links), travel news, and travel columns (views). The site's Brancatelli File (Joe Brancatelli), MileMaster (Randy Petersen), Travel Technologist (Christopher Elliott), Tactical Traveler (Joe Brancatelli), and Road to Good Health (Dr. Eliot Heher) columns are especially popular with business travelers.

Trip   Business Travel
www.trip.com

This online travel information and reservation company is very popular with business travelers. Focused on both small business owners and large corporations that have too many "schedule-weary 'road warriors' who travel too frequently," their typical site visitor has an average annual household income of $77,000 and works with a company with 10 to 500 employees. The site's Trip Planner section enables users to book flights (also find lowest airfares and airport codes) and reserve cars and hotels. Its Tools for Travel section includes destination guides (from Reed Travel), flight tracker, maps, airport guides, currency converter, world clock, federal per diems, international holidays, and wireless technology tips. Its NewStand section allows users to access useful travel articles, ask questions, and participate in an online community of travel experts. Marketplace is a shopping center that features numerous merchants (linked to Infospace). Vacations offers leisure travel options, from resorts to adventure travel. And the flightTRACKER section keeps you up-to-date on the status and arrival times of all fights in the U.S. Overall, this is a very information- and service-rich site for business travelers.

| **Business Travel**
www.businesstravel.com | **Business Travel** |

At first glance this site does not seem to have a lot of content. However, click on a few buttons at the bottom of your screen and you'll find there is more here than what initially meets the eye. This site is devoted to providing quality information for business travelers. While much of the information is general, and comes from affiliate relationships with About.com and the Wall Street Journal (*www.travel.wsj.com*), much of it constitutes a set of useful linkages for business travelers: finance, investment, stock quotes, food, entertainment, weather, computers, shipping, employment, and media. Its travel section consists of numerous linkages to airlines, hotels, destination guides, state travel offices, travel advisories, and travel aids (currency converter, subway navigator, travel expense calculator, foreign languages, airport guide). The site also includes booking engines for making airline, hotel, and car rental reservations.

| **Wall Street Journal**
www.travel.wsj.com | **Business Travel** |

As you might expect from the Wall Street Journal, this site is very focused on providing travel information and services relevant to business people. In addition to the obligatory booking engines for reserving airline tickets, hotels, and cars, the site includes travel news, mileage updates, city guides, weather forecasts, a currency converter, and airport maps. It also provides subscription information for acquiring the paper versions of two of the Dow Jones & Company publications, *The Wall Street Journal* and *Barron's*.

Skyguide	Business Travel
www.sky-guide.com	

Operated by American Express Publishing, Skyguide is a subscription-based site ($69 for 12 monthly issues) that dispenses travel information and services to business travelers. It claims to have 360,000 subscribers. However, it's unclear what additional value one gets from this site compared to similar information and services available through Worldroom, Trip, and Biztravel. The free sections on this site are similar to the same section on other travel sites. The sections include weather, airport tips, airlines, ground transportation, safety, travel tips, and a business traveler's library. A rich collection of articles and linkages for the business traveler.

About.com	Business Travel
www.businesstravel.about.com	

This well organized business travel site is literally "in your face" with everything you need, or want to know, about travel. In addition to providing airline ticket, car rental, and hotel reservation services, the site includes airline seat maps, advisories, frequent flyer programs, airports, banking, currency, jet charter, city guides, travel services, customs and etiquette, hotel directories, passport and visa information, restaurant linkages, travel insurance, travel technology, travel tips, weather, and advice for women travelers. Includes numerous linkages to related sites as well as many informative travel articles.

For other websites relevant to business travelers, including online business magazines, visit these sites:

Cities:	*www.citynet.com*
	www.digitalcity.com
City/country guides:	*www.fodors.com*
Etiquette:	*www.traveletiquette.com*
Events:	*www.whatsgoingon.com*
Jazz clubs:	*www.jazz-clubs-worldwide.com*
Language:	*www.travlang.com*
Leading hotels:	*www.lhw.com*
Luxury:	*www.entreenews.com*
	www.luxury4less.com
Magazines:	*www.concierge.com*
	www.economist.com
	www.fortune.com
	www.forbes.com
	www.businessweek.com
News:	*www.newsdirectory.com*
	www.cnn.com
	www.usatoday.com
	www.btnonline.com
Restaurants:	*www.zagat.com*
	www.restaurantrow.com
Small luxury hotels:	*www.slk.com*
Shopping:	*www.ishoparoundtheworld.com*
	www.luxuryfinders.com
Spas:	*www.spafinders.com*
Sports:	*www.golfnow.com*
Technology:	*www.avantgo.com*
	www.omnisky.com
	www.onthegosoftware.com
Trade show/conferences:	*www.expoguide.com*
Women:	*www.womenbusinesstravelers.com*
	(see others on pages 75-76)

Disabled and Special Needs

Nearly 43 million Americans have disabilities that can make travel even more challenging than usual. Responding to the growing number of disabled travelers, the travel industry has increasingly recognized the special travel needs of the disabled by offering special tours, travel tips, and encouragement. At the same time, special needs travelers have formed their own websites to share information and advice on how to engage in trouble-free travel. These sites cover a wide range of disabilities. Some of the best such sites include:

Access-Able   **Disabled/Special Needs**
www.access-able.com

This is the premier online resource for accessible travel information. Operated by pioneers Bill and Carol Randall, it has developed into a global network of individuals who are knowledgeable about accessibility in their communities. Includes a frequently asked question (FAQ) section; information on cruise lines with accessible ships; relay and voice phone numbers for airlines, hotels, and car rentals; travel agents that have tours or plan trips for special needs; and forums and bulletin boards. A very rich site that addresses the full range of disability issues including traveling with oxygen, finding a hotel room, airlines, cruise ships, service animals, blind and low vision, and finding transportation.

Global Access   **Disabled/Special Needs**
www.geocities.com/Paris/1502

This network for disabled travel includes a wealth of information and resources. The site includes numerous articles on disabled travel – from camping in Europe to traveling with a wheelchair in Northern India – tips, resources, linkages, and readers' comments. The linkage section includes many useful accessibility sites in destinations such as the United Kingdom, Ireland, Germany, Denmark, Norway, Italy, Spain, Greece, France, Portugal, and the U.S.

Actcom   **Disabled/Special Needs**
www.actcom.co.il/~swfm/

Includes advice on how to rent a car with hand controls – something most local travel agents and reservation offices of international rental companies will or cannot do. The site also includes a list of related linkages for the disabled traveler.

World on Wheels   **Disabled/Special Needs**
www.geocities.com/Heartland/6295/

This site focuses on travel in a wheelchair. It includes numerous first-person accounts about the accessibility of particular locations.

Emerging Horizons   **Disabled/Special Needs**
www.emerginghorizons.com

This online newsletter, published by Candy and Charles Harrington, focuses on accessibility travel news. The site includes frequently asked questions (FAQ) and a listing of useful travel resources, including a section on destinations. For example, if you're traveling to Japan, you'll find a site devoted to accessible hotels, transportation, museums, parks, and shopping in Japan.

Dialysis Finder   **Disabled/Special Needs**
www.dialysisfinder.com

Use this site's database to locate dialysis clinics around the world. Includes numerous resources relating to dialysis, medical advice, and accessible travel.

Several other related websites also are relevant to travelers with disabilities:

Disabilities:	*www.disabilityworld.com*
	www.disabilitytravel.com
	www.dis-abilities.com
Food and Chemical	
Sensitivities:	*www.livingwithout.com*
Global Dialysis:	*www.globaldialysis.com*
Human Rights:	*www.escape.ca/~dpi/*

Mobility:	*www.miusa.org/index.html*
Resources:	*www.eskimo.com/~jlubin/disabled*
Society:	*www.sath.org*
Travel With Oxygen:	*www.breathineasy.com*
Wheelchairs:	*www.wheelchair-getaways.com*

Gays and Lesbians

For many gays, lesbians, bisexuals, and transgender individuals, travel is a very liberating experience centered around the notion of "community." Constituting a distinct subculture within the travel business, gays and lesbians can travel to places where they enjoy their lifestyles in relative anonymity and in the company of others who share their interests. The number of gay and lesbian travelers is difficult to estimate, although some publications report that nearly 20 percent of all leisure travelers are gays and lesbians. Whatever their numbers, they constitute a very vocal, well organized, and active group of travelers who often travel to destinations that are gay and lesbian-friendly. They increasingly patronize cruises, tours, hotels, restaurants, clubs, and entertainment establishments that welcome gays and lesbians. Since gays and lesbians also represent one of the more affluent groups of travelers, much of the travel industry either caters to or is especially sensitive to the travel needs of this group. Indeed, many gay and lesbian professionals are regular clients of luxury hotels, resorts, tours, and cruises. While discrimination still takes place, the economic and organizational clout of gays and lesbians has helped establish this group as an important one for the travel industry. Gays and lesbians have their own travel websites that focus on their particular community interests, from featuring gay and lesbian vacations, organizing calendars, and providing tips on traveling with a pet to sharing traveler's tales and operating message boards. Some of the best such sites include:

PlanetOut	**Gays/Lesbians**
www.planetout.com	

This is the premier worldwide community website for gays, lesbians, and bisexuals. It includes a travel channel with information on gay and lesbian vacations, a directory to gay-friendly travel agents, destination guides, features on gay urban areas, message boards, travel columnists, traveler's tales, travel tips, a reservation section, and more.

Rainbow Query	Gays/Lesbians
www.rainbowquery.com	

This is one of the largest search engines for the gay community. Includes a huge community directory with travel as a separate subject. Incorporates informative travel articles and gay guides to cities, outdoors, accommodations, travel providers, and travel guides.

Out & About Online	Gays/Lesbians
www.outandabout.com	

This is a rich sight for locating all types of information relating to gay and lesbian travel. It includes back issues of the "Out & About Newsletter," a reference library (gay travel calendar, health tips, ratings), travel stories, links to gay tour operators, travel agents, and travel sites.

Home Suite Hom	Gays/Lesbians
www.gaytrip.com	

Previously known as Gayscene, this is an international travel club with informative travel articles and recommendations relevant to gays, lesbians, bisexuals, and the transgender community. Lists gay bars, clubs, shops, and restaurants in North America, Australia, Europe, and Southeast Asia.

Other websites with travel content and linkages of special interest to gays and lesbians include:

Cruises:	*www.gaycruisevacations.com*
Gay Travel:	*www.gay-travel.com*
Gay Yellow Pages:	*www.gayellowpages.com*
Gay Guide:	*www.gayguide.net*
Gay Wired:	*www.gaywired.com*

Gay Mag:	*www.guidemag.com*
Now Voyager:	*www.nowvoyager.com*
Our World Mag:	*www.ourworldmag.com*
PrideNet:	*www.pridenet.com*
Q-Net:	*www.q-net.com*
Travelook:	*www.travelook.com*
Venture Out:	*www.venture-out.com*
ViajarTravel:	*www.viajartravel.com*

Family and Kids

Traveling with kids involves a lot more than just heading for Disney-land. Families with children are increasingly traveling the globe and finding such family adventures extremely rewarding – if done right. In recognition of the growth in family travel, more and more travel groups are providing special services to families. Some travel agencies, such as Grand Travel (*www.grantvl.com*), specialize in vacation travel programs for grandparents and grandchildren who wish to travel together. The following sites are especially useful for families that travel with kids:

Family.com   **Familes/Kids**
www.family.go.com/Categories/Travel

This is a comprehensive family website with many different channels relevant to families and kids – from babies to pets. Its travel channel includes useful travel checklists, such as things to take into a theme park, tip of the day, a guide to Disney resorts worldwide, family-friendly travel guides, travel tips, informative articles, special travel deals, and an online reservation system operated by Vacation Together. This is a good place to learn about the many issues relating to family travel.

About.com   **Families/Kids**
www.travelwithkids.about.com

Like so much of the About.com family of sites, this one is jam-packed with useful information relevant to family travel. It includes numerous articles relevant to traveling with kids and family travel deals. It also includes special sections on family resorts, travel games, travel with babies, vacation deals, vacations with teens, and traveling with kids in Canada, the Caribbean, Europe, California, Florida, Hawaii, and several other U.S. states. Provides extensive linkages to related About.com sites such as Parenting, Toddlers, and Theme Parks.

Family Travel Files	Families/Kids
www.familytravelfiles.com	

This site is dedicated to providing useful information on travel with kids. It includes sections on family travel news, vacation ideas, special family vacation packages, family-friendly events, and linkages to other sites. Sign up for the free Ezine for practical advice, product reviews, and travel features.

Gorp.com	Families/Kids
www.gorp.com/gorp/eclectic/family.htm	

If your family loves the outdoors, you'll find this site has lots of useful advice for enhancing an outdoor family adventure. This is the community section of the popular Gorp.com adventure travel site which focuses on providing tips on how families can best enjoy the outdoors together. Provides parenting tips, expert advice, a family discussion forum, and vacation recommendations. Recent articles identified the 10 best rivers for kids; how to help kids identify and avoid poison ivy; tricks for getting kids into the outdoors; family activities in Nepal and Southern Thailand; and taking bathroom breaks with kids outdoors. Well done and informative.

Travel & Leisure Family	Families/Kids
www.tlfamily.com	
www.pathfinder.com/travel/TL/family	

There's not a lot to this site but it does include family travel articles from the magazine "Travel & Leisure Family." It also includes family sections in the bulletin boards and chat.

Family Travel Guides   Families/Kids
www.familytravelguides.com

Operated by Pamela Lanier, this site dispenses information and advice on family travel. Sections on accommodations, food, outdoors, travel packages, travel tips, and deals and specials are the most useful for families.

Other family-related sites worth visiting include:

Adoption Travel: *www.adoptiontravel.com*
Family Go: *www.family.go.com*
Family Fun: *www.familyfunvacations.com*
Family Haven: *www.familyhaven.com*
Family Travel Forum: *www.familytravelforum.com*
Family Travel Times: *www.familytraveltimes.com*
Grandparents: *www.grandtrvl.com*
Roadside: *www.roadsideamerica.com*
Travel With Kids: *www.travelwithkids.com*
Vacation: *www.vacation.com/family*

Pet Lovers

Can't travel without taking your loving pet with you? Here's help for those who want to travel with Fido but feel discriminated against by travel providers who prefer that you leave your animal at home. The sites are rich with essential travel planning tips, lists of pet-friendly travel providers, and rules and regulations governing the importation and transportation of pets. If you love to camp, sightsee, lie on the beach, or go shopping, cruising, or dining with your pet, you'll find several of these sites extremely informative.

Pets Welcome   Pet Lovers
www.petswelcome.com

This site claims to be the Internet's largest pet/travel resource. Use this site for identifying over 25,000 hotels, B&Bs, ski resorts, campgrounds, and beaches that are known for being pet-friendly. Includes a listing of pet-friendly airlines, tips on traveling with your pet, and an Info Xchange section for travel-pet stories. Includes a reservation system for accommodations at pet-friendly places and travel club. Join the mailing list and you automatically enter a contest to win a travel food bowl!

Dog Friendly   **Pet Lovers**
www.dogfriendly.com

Dog lovers who can't part with their pooch when traveling, sightseeing, shopping, or working will like this site (a recent message posted on this site said it all – *"Take your pet to work is better than stock options!"*). It includes a travel guide to dog-friendly hotels, stores, and employers; numerous dog articles and tips; and linkages to other dog sites, such as cruising with canines. Travel tips focus on travel dog etiquette; preparing your dog for a flight, cruise, or road trip; and emergency pet services.

Traveling With Your Pet   **Pet Lovers**
www.avma.org/care4pets/safetrav.htm

Sponsored by the American Veterinary Medical Association, this site provides many practical safety tips for traveling with your pet. Includes warnings on traveling to places with heartworm disease, such as Alaska; avoiding sedating or tranquilizing your pet when traveling; planning and preparation; interstate travel regulations; travel by air, car, bus, or train; camping with pets; post-trip examinations; pet stores; advice on buying a pet; and even travel tips for kids.

USDA   **Pet Lovers**
www.aphis.usda.gov:80/vs/sregs/
www.aphis.usda.gov/travel/pets.html

Operated by the U.S. Department of Agriculture's Animal and Plant Health Inspection Service, these two sites provide a wealth of information on rules and regulations governing the importation of pet birds, traveling with your pet, state regulations relating to animals; and linkages to the U.S. Customs Service and the Centers for Disease Control and Prevention.

Religious Groups

Each year thousands of churches and religious groups organize specialty tours to a variety of religious sites. The largest group of religious travelers are the Muslims. Indeed, millions of Muslims travel to the holy city of Mecca each year to fulfill their religious obligation or hadj. Travel agencies throughout the Muslim world specialize in these hadj trips which usually involve chartering numerous planes to Mecca in Saudi Arabia.

But the Muslims are not alone. Each year millions of Christians make pilgrimages to some of Christianity's most holy and popular sites – the Vatican in Rome and Jerusalem. Hundreds of thousands of Jews also travel to Israel. While most of these travel groups are organized through Christian churches and Jewish community centers, two websites also specialize in travel for Christians and Jews:

| **Christian Travellers**   **Religious Groups** |
| *www.christiantraveller.org* |

Obviously designed for Christian travelers, this site includes travel information and travel linkages of interest to Christians. Somewhat difficult to navigate and often unclear what the site is all about, although the webmaster confesses he or she doesn't have enough time to do everything, especially creating country links! Represents a patchwork of travel linkages.

| **Jewish Travel**   **Religious Groups** |
| *www.jewishtravel.com* |

The Christians could learn a lot from the Jews when it comes to doing travel websites for assisting their community. Indeed, the Jews know how to develop a useful website for their community of travelers. This site is rich in travel articles, travel discounts, and travel links. It addresses one important issue facing Jewish travelers – the challenge of traveling kosher. The site includes an interesting community section with a House Exchange, Bulletin Board, and Travel Tips from Readers. The Jewish TraveLinks section includes databases for local kosher restaurants, reliable kosher symbols, Synagogues and Chabad houses around the world, candlelighting times and times for prayer, and a guide to Israel travel (hotels, attractions, news, weather). Recent articles on Jewish travel revealed that kosher food could indeed be found in Austin (don't pack that tuna!) and Rule One for bundling your teenager off to Israel was "never let 'em see you cry."

Seniors

For the most part, seniors are not budget travelers who enjoy carrying backpacks, staying in hostels, and looking for cheap eats. Travel for them is often a quality of life issue – they would like to travel in style where they can enjoy the good life, from nice hotels to fine restaurants.

Indeed, the largest percentage of travel expenditures is made by travelers 50 years and older. Within the over-50 group, the fastest growing group of travelers are ages 65 and older – primarily retirees who see travel as one of the major benefits of retirement and who have been putting off major travel for years. Not surprisingly, they travel often and for two to four-week periods at a time. While they frequently join tours and cruises, many seniors also love to travel independently. Having financial clout in the travel industry, seniors are a much

Having financial clout, seniors are a much sought-after group of travelers by travel agents and suppliers.

sought-after group of travelers by travel agents, tour operators, airlines, car rental companies, hotels, and resorts. Many of these groups, such as United Airline's Silver Wings Plus program, offer special senior travel discounts and special tours and travel programs, such as learning vacations, that respond to the travel interests of seniors. Many also develop what might be best termed "soft adventure" tours for seniors – safaris, ecotourism, and river cruising – who love adventure travel but not the extreme physical demands that are often required of more youth-oriented adventure travel. Adventure travel often comes in the form of educational adventures, such as those offered by Elderhotel, Travel Learn, and Learning. Nonetheless, groups like Skiers Over 50 (*www.skiersover50.com*) focus on an active lifestyle. Many of the sites we discussed earlier for disabled and special needs travelers (pages 59-62) also are relevant to many seniors. Overall, since seniors have more income and time to travel, they also prefer higher quality travel than younger travelers who have less money and time.

Elderhostel.org	Seniors
www.elderhostel.org	

Focusing on adults 55 years and older, this not-for-profit organization has been organizing educational adventures for more than 25 years. Most are short-term programs that are very affordable. Indeed, many of the hundreds of programs sponsored by Elderhostel might rightly fall into the category of budget travel for seniors. On the other hand, many of the programs also can be expensive (a 13-day history and culture tour of Bhutan goes for nearly $4,700 per person). This site permits users to search three online catalogs (U.S. and Canada, International, Adventures Afloat) to identify an appropriate program. If you're interested in travel ideas and specific destinations, this is great site for exploring numerous travel options. Each program includes detailed itineraries and costs.

Seniors Search	Seniors
www.seniorssearch.com	
(www.seniorssearch.com/cgi-bin/page.asp?cn+15)	

This is a search engine and web directory for seniors. Its travel directory includes 25 travel categories, such as budget travel, cruises, disabilities, ecotourism, home exchange, resorts, tour operators, restaurants, train travel, travel agents, travel insurance, and travel tips and tools. While limited in content at present, it's potentially a rich resource for locating senior-centered travel information and services.

Travel Learn   **Seniors**
www.travelearn.com

This site is operated by one of the major learning tour companies that specializes in education tours and travel. Working with more than 300 universities and colleges in the U.S., their international learning vacations are for adults ages 30-80, with a disproportionate number of clients being seniors. The site offers an online newsletter (e-zine), the "TravLearn Cybertravel Newsletter," which includes website recommendations, book and video selections, recipes, travelers' quotes, trivia, and a geography quiz related to a single destination featured in each issue. The site also archives previous issues of the newsletter.

Learning   **Seniors**
www.learn.unh.edu

Operated by the University of New Hamphire (Continuing Education), this site features Interhostel/Familyhostel educational travel programs. The Interhostel program is designed for those over 50 who want to travel and learn about different cultures. It includes such programs as "Christmas Around the World" (11 different tours). The Familyhostel learning vacations are designed for three generations of travelers – grandparents, parents, and children.

AARP   **Seniors**
www.aarp.org/travel

Boasting a membership of over 40 million, the American Association of Retired Persons has millions of members who love to travel. Accordingly, its travel section includes numerous travel articles, an interactive bulletin board, and discounts on hotels, airlines, car rentals, cruises, sightseeing, and vacation packages.

Seniors Site   **Seniors**
http://senior-site.com/travel/index.html

Claiming to be the ultimate resources guide for all senior subjects, this site includes linkages to several major travel sites. Includes a handy list 37 search engines for exploring the web.

Senior Women   **Seniors**
http://seniorwomen.com/travel.htm

This informative site includes travel articles written by and for women. Incorporates linkages to many travel websites relevant to senior women.

Other travel sites relevant to seniors include:

Adventure Women:	*www.adventurewomen.com*
Access-Able:	*www.access-able.com* (see page 60)
Elder Treks:	*www.eldertreks.com*
Friendship Force:	*www.friendship-force.org*
Grantvl:	*www.grantvl.com*
Poshnosh:	*www.poshnosh.com*
Seniors Home Exchange:	*www.seniorshomeexchange.com*
Senior Travel Tips:	*www.seniortraveltips.com*
Senior Net:	*www.seniornet.org*
Skiers Over 50:	*www.skiersover50.com*
Silver Wings Plus:	*www.silverwingsplus.com*
Yahoo:	*http://dir.yahoo.com/Recreation/ Travel/Seniors/*

Weekend and Last-Minute Trippers

Are you too busy to take a week or two off but still want to travel? Why not join the growing number of "quick trippers" who have learned the joys of taking three-day weekend trips? They've also learned that some of the best travel deals can be found on the Internet for last-minute travel planners. Indeed, the following sites are ideal for such travelers.

Weekends   **Quick Trippers**
www.weekends.com

If you live in or near New York City, San Francisco, Boston, Los Angeles, and Washington, DC and have the itch to get away for the weekend, this may be the perfect site for you. Specializes in identifying weekend escapes from these five metropolitan areas. Just enter where you want to escape from and where you want to escape to, and the site's search engine will identify dozens of escapes for you. Includes all kinds of interesting romantic, adventure, tranquil, and other types of trips. Indeed, a recent escape to Long Island, New York (Air Combat USA) cost $895 per person and involved a 40-minute flight and basic flight training, complete with a video of your successful downing of the enemy, for experiencing a real "Dogfight in an Attack Aircraft" – great for relieving stress!

Site 59   **Quick Trippers**
www.site59.com

Would you love to get away to a U.S. city for the weekend? Includes weekly specials for eight major U.S. cities – Baltimore, Boston, Dallas, Houston, Los Angeles, Philadelphia, and Washington, DC – as well as other cities, such as Jacksonville, West Palm Beach, Charleston, and San Francisco. A recent weekend special included a romantic weekend for $494 per person which included roundtrip air from New York (LaGuardia), a 3-night stay at the Charleston Place Hotel (ranked in 1999 by *Condé Nast Traveler* as the 7th top property in the U.S.), and an Avis rental car.

Travel Zoo   **Quick Trippers**
www.travelzoo.com

This site specializes in sales and specials – airlines, vacations, lodging, car rentals, and cruises. It also includes a very nice shopping feature – a weekly "Top 20 Travel Deals on the

Internet" and last minute specials that appear on many other websites such as Travelscape, Moment's Notice, Delta Air Lines, Travelocity, 11th Hour Vacations, and Bid4Vacations. For example, TravelZoo recently found a "Christmas Shopping in Paris" deal from New Frontiers – 5 nights accommodations, 5 daily continental breakfasts, 3 days metro pass, shopping discount cards, free fashion show at Le Printemps, and round-trip air (Corsair) from Los Angeles for only $559! Fly Continental Airlines and the deal goes for $599; Air France is $729.

11th Hour Vacations   **Quick Trippers**
www.11thhourvacations.com

The useful site for anyone who does last minute travel planning. So you have a three-day weekend next week and would love to go somewhere, especially if the price is right. Just go to this site and use the search engine to specify your departure city or vacation destination. Or maybe the site's "Today's Deals" and "Cruise Deals" appeal to you. For example, a recent last minute cruise deal involving seven days in the Southern Caribbean was going for $399. Not all deals seem to be such good deals. Includes another one of those irritating "Punch the Monkey" games at the bottom of the site.

Away.com   **Quick Trippers**
www.away.com

Essentially an adventure and lifestyle travel site flush with venture capital – doing lots of advertising – and loaded with travel content from several travel guidebook publishers which it generously uses as well as resyndicates to other websites. Away.com includes creative ideas for weekend escapes through its Getaway USA, 1001 Festivals, and Ideas Generator sections. Its rich number of channels and travel content can keep you busy for hours dreaming about your next perfect trip. Sign up for its e-zine and you'll receive details on a new destination each day – the ultimate way to spam yourself with travel content!

Women

Women constitute one of the fastest growing segments of the travel industry. While some travel alone, others travel with female companions or significant others. Business women (40 percent are the sole or primary household wage earner) in particular have a great deal of purchasing power; they tend to spend a lot on hotels, restaurants, transportation, and tours. Indeed, it's estimated that 50 percent of all business travelers are now women. Many of their travel interests and needs are being met by websites that focus on women travelers. Issues such as handling business situations, traveling and dining alone, packing properly, dressing smart in Islamic countries, jogging and trekking safely, saving money, getting responsive service, extending a business trip into a pleasure trip, dealing with challenging restrooms, shopping, and replenishing travel essentials are of special interest to women.

JourneyWoman	Women
www.journeywoman.com	

Designed specifically for women travelers, this popular and innovative site is rich with information and resources. Includes a free newsletter with informative articles; female-friendly city sites; travel tales; ecoadventures; book reviews; and tips on everything from what to wear to solo dining. It includes spa recommendations, travel classifieds, learning vacations, tours for women, accommodations, and much more. Its popular cyberboard has been discontinued but resurrected in the form of an innovative new website, *HERmail.com* (see next entry). Both of these sites are "must bookmark" sites for women.

HER Mail	Women
www.HERmail.net	

Here's a wonderful travel concept for women. This relatively new site, which is actually Journey Woman's sister site (grew out of the overwhelming success with its cyberboard) is a welcome addition to the world of travel for women. Based on the concept of connecting traveling women around the world, it functions as a directory or network for fellow women travelers. If, for example, you live in Chicago and are planning a trip to Moscow, just enter your destination and the HERmail database will generate at least two email addresses of women who live in Moscow who have registered with HERmail.net. Send them an email and hopefully you will soon be making two new friends in Moscow who can assist you during your stay. This site also includes useful travel tips, links, and articles.

Women Business Travelers — Women
www.womenbusinesstravelers.com

Operated by Wyndham Hotels and Resorts for female "Road Warriors", this site includes many useful travel articles, a women's forum, book club, special offers, and travel tips. The travel tips section is one of the best organized and informative sections we've encountered on any travel website. The site also conducts opinion polls and reports and archives results. For example, a resen poll indicated that 49% always connected to the Internet when traveling; 36% did so occasionally and 15 percent never connected on the road. Occasionally this site includes interesting studies of women travelers. For example, a recent study conducted by Wyndham Hotels and Resorts and New York University's Center for Hospitality, Tourism, and Travel Administration found that women were twice as likely as men to order room service while traveling alone on business (because of self-indulgence rather than safety or loneliness considerations), and women were more likely than men to incorporate some leisure time (mainly shopping) in their business trips.

Womens Travel Club — Women
www.womenstravelclub.com/index.html

This is the largest adventure and cultural tour operator in North America that is focused solely on women travelers. Costing $35 a year, membership gives you access to trip specials and a newsletter. The site also includes numerous travel tips, suggested readings, frequently asked questions, and recommended linkages.

Adventure Women	**Women**
www.adventurewomen.com	

Designed for the adventure woman over 30 (average age is 50), this site promotes a wide range of exotic travel adventures for women – no smokers and no guys – who want to experience an out of the ordinary trip! Most groups are small with activity levels ranging from easy to moderate and high energy. Includes a listing of trips for the year, weather conditions, high adventure series, and recommended travel links.

Other websites relevant to women travelers include:

www.100topwomensites.com/Women/travel/100/113k
www.budgettravel.com/women.htm
www.debbieguide.com
www.dfait-maeci.gc.ca/travel/consular/16009-e.htm
www.ivillage.com/travel/
www.maiden-voyages.com
www.o2simplify.com/fun_travel/travel/
www.poshnosh.com
www.seniorwomen.com (see page 72)
www.vagabunda.com
www.women.com/travel/
www.womentours.com
www.women-traveling.com
www.yahoo.com/Recreation/Travel/Women
www.wildwomenadv.com
www.woman-kind.com
www.womanlinks.com
www.travelingsafe.com
www.gordonsguide.com/womenstravel/index.cfm
www.exploretravel.com
www.women-networking.com/travel

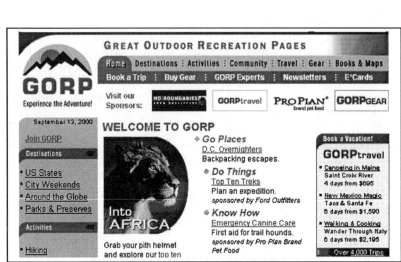

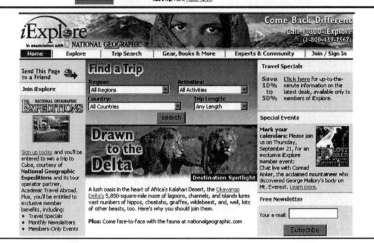

6

Special Travel Interests and Activities

MANY TRAVELERS ARE INTERESTED IN A PARTICU-
lar type of travel activity or experience. Many of these
activities relate to favorite passions, hobbies, sports, or
stress-reducing experiences. Indeed, many people organize
their travels around a special category or categories of travel: adventure,
diving, ecotourism, education, golf, luxury, mountain biking, outdoor,
shopping, skiing, or spas.

The Internet is rich with specialty travel sites that promote a
particular type of travel activity or experience. In this chapter we review
a few of the most interesting such sites, with a decided emphasis on one
of the fastest and most popular travel areas – adventure and outdoor
travel. Chapter 12 includes several specialty tour directories and groups
related to many of the interests and activities outlined in this chapter.

Adventure and Outdoor Travel

Adventure and outdoor travel, whether it's called ecotourism or active
vacations, are big businesses these days. Looking for something different from the typical history and sightseeing tour? This type of travel
requires the active involvement of participants. If, for example, you go
whitewater rafting, you're expected to carry your gear and work like a
dog in navigating your inflatable raft downstream. If you go mountain
climbing, you're expected to be physically fit and familiar with the use
of special equipment. If you join a bicycle tour, you're expected to keep

up with the group which can be a very grueling pace. If you go trekking, you can expect to spend exhausting days walking and climbing in search of your final destination. Many people love this type of travel because it is usually physically challenging and because they meet many other interesting like-minded travelers. In fact, many of these travelers become addicted to this style of travel as they become repeat adventure and outdoor travelers.

The good news is that some of the best travel sites focus on adventure and outdoor travel. Backed by tons of venture capital and developing numerous affiliate relations, such adventure-travel portal sites as *Gorp.com, iExplore.com,* and *Away.com* have evolved into terrific sites for adventure and outdoor travelers. Indeed, these three sites may cover most of your travel needs! Jampacked with content and services, use these sites to review relevant travel articles, book tours, purchase travel gear, share experiences, review bulletin boards, and search for the perfect trip to some fabulous location. These

> *Some of the best travel sites focus on adventure and outdoor travel. Many are backed by venture capital to develop as major travel portals.*

are big and well-financed sites, with full-time staffs of 100 or more specialists.

Gorp   **Outdoor**
www.gorp.com

This is the oldest and most popular outdoor travel site. Jampacked with content, community discussions, travel experts, destination information, travel tools, feature articles, and travel gear, books, and maps, Gorp focuses on these major outdoor travel activities: hiking, biking, fishing, paddling, wildlife viewing, skiing/snowsports, birding, driving/RV's, camping, climbing, caving, ecology, hunting, horseback riding, and water sports. Includes a "Top 10" section that identifies the most popular destinations for a variety of travel activities (African safaris, caving, epic bike rides, epic canoe camping, family canoe trips, global fly fishing, reef diving, sea kayaking, scenic driving, shark viewing, spring birding, summer wildflowers, unknown trout fisheries, and whale watching.

Away.com	Adventure
www.away.com	

This is an awesome travel site for adventure travelers. Backed by tons of venture capital, and representing the merger of two major adventure travel sites *(www.greentravel.com* and *www.adventurequest.com*) as well as the recent acquisition of Outdoor Adventure Online (the primary adventure travel resource on AOL), this site has quickly become a one-stop-shop for adventure and outdoor travel. Viewing itself as a combination travel agent, integrated library, outfitter, and café with lots of chat, *Away.com* is a site all adventure travelers should visit and revisit. It includes numerous related travel channels such as adventure, cultural, nature and ecotravel, families, couples and solo traveler; activities such as beaches, biking, birdwatching, climbing, diving, horseback riding, safaris, sea kayaking, trekking, walking and hiking, and whitewater rafting; regional and country-specific destinations; and search engines. The site is jam-packed with lots of useful information and travel tours, from a trip planner and finder to message boards, travelogues, specials, and a marketplace. Includes affiliate relations with *Expedia.com* and numerous travel guidebook series that provide a ton of content, which is then resyndicated, for this site. Sign up for Away.com's free email newsletters and you'll get daily and weekly features on specific destinations and announcements ("Your Daily Escape" almost gets the award for being self-inflicted spam!).

iExplore	Adventure
www.iexplore.com	

This is another aggressive award-winning adventure-travel portal site backed by tons of venture capital. Launched in late 1999, it recently announced that National Geographic will acquire a 30% stake in the company. This new alliance means that *Nationalgeographic.com* will begin using iExplore's search database of 5,000+ adventure trips in 152 countries. iExplore, in turn, will include National Geographic Expeditions trips in its database and contribute to the content of National Geographic's magazines, television, and website. Accordingly, iExplore's mission is to become the world's leading source of adventure and experiential travel, including products, information, and services. If you are interested in any of the following activities, this site is for you: bicycling, birding, food and wine, hiking and trekking, history and culture, horseback riding, mountain biking, mountaineering, rafting and kayaking, rainforests, safari, sailing and yachting, and scuba diving. Key site features include travel tools (destination and activity guides, trip search, custom trip questions, my iExplore, gear, and books); iExplore Community of experts, travelers' tales, and travelers' reviews; and a variety of information and services, such as travel advisories and health tips. Includes a price guarantee on their adventure and experiential tours. Much of the site's destination content is limited to the Lonely Planet guides. Given the rapid growth of the site, expect to see even more great features in the future. Offers a free monthly newsletter, special offers, and a hot list of the most popular trips. Includes live travel experts to answer questions. Expect to see this site rapidly expand as the major adventure-travel portal competitor to *Gorp.com* and *Away.com*.

Gordons Guide   **Adventure**
www.gordonsguide.com

This is a handy site for quickly finding tour operators that specialize in 32 different categories of adventure travel, including such activities and places as:

- Canoeing
- Charter Boating
- Dog Sledding
- Dude and Guest Ranches
- Ecotourism
- Fishing Lodges
- Heli-Skiing
- Hiking and Trekking
- Mountain Climbing
- Outdoor Skills Training
- Safaris
- Sculling Camps
- Ski Areas
- Snowmobile Lodges
- Whitewater Rafting
- Women's Travel

The site also includes feature articles, travel gear, and linkages to numerous adventure magazines, books, catalogs, giveaways, hotel and airline information, tourism bureaus, and youth summer camps.

Adventureseek	Adventure
www.adventureseek.com	

Don't know what you want to do and where you want to go? This site will help you identify and compare adventure travel options. If you're interested in identifying particular adventure activities in a specific country, use this site's nifty search engine to identify your options and compare different trips. Also includes a community section with message boards, newsletter, and a photo gallery (you can share your photos here). Adopting the concept of Frequent Flier Miles to this site, users can earn AdventureMiles™ (join, send a photo, share an experience, purchase a trip) which can be redeemed to purchase products or contribute to environmental charities through this site. Also includes FAQs and sweepstakes.

Travelon	Adventure
www.travelon.com	

This one-stop travel agency for vacation travel includes an adventure travel channel. Its search engine allows you to search by activity (from 4WD tours, ballooning, beer tasting, and bungy jumping to jungle exploration, llama trekking, and safaris), destination, departure month, and price range per person. A quick and easy way to uncover many specialty tours for adventure travelers. Explore the site's other channels to discover family, romance, resort, ski, sports, learning and culture travel as well as golf vacations, and cruises.

Ecotourism

Ecotourism continues to be a hot travel activity. Indeed, many Third World countries report a dramatic increase in the number of ecotourists who come to visit their national parks, forests, lakes, rivers, reefs, and beaches. Ecotourism is often lumped into the general category of adventure travel or responsible travel (although ecotourists still disturb the environment). However, individuals interested in ecotourism have a particular orientation to travel – preserving the environment. Many are associated with such non-profit environmental groups as the Sierra Club, Conservation International, and Zero Population Growth.

About.com/Ecotourism	Ecotourism
www.ecotourism.about.com/travel/ecotourism	

This informative site includes several useful articles on ecotourism as well as destinations, activities, and related sites on *About.com*.

Green Travel Network	Ecotourism
www.greentravel.com	
(*www.away.com*)	

Recently merged and renamed *Away.com* (see above), this site includes a "Nature & Ecotravel" channel which includes content from the Sierra Club, Conservation International, and Zero Population Growth. Includes a recommended trip section called "Nature Observation and Ecotourism" which generates a listing of more than 200 related trips. Also includes books, travel gear, and responsible tour operators dealing with ecotourism. Its "Eco Talk" section incorporates a message board and hosted chats with ecotourism experts. For travel ideas, go to the "Top Eco Inspirations" section where you will find lists of the top 10 diving destinations, top 10 birding destinations, and top 10 African safaris.

Islands, Beaches, Surfing, and Diving

If you love water sports and traveling to idyllic fantasy islands that also offer great beaches, surfing, and diving opportunities, you should examine the following websites. They are devoted to tropical paradises, sunny beaches, the big waves, and incredible diving spots from

Southern California, Hawaii, Tahiti, and Australia to Bali, the Maldives, Sinai Peninsula, and the Caribbean.

Islands	Islands
www.islands.com	

This is the website of the popular *Islands Magazine*. The site includes a destination search engine along with selected articles online, a gallery, boutique, classifieds, and travel tools. The travel tools section allows you to find a limited number of luxury resorts by region and country, vacation rentals, and travel information on the Caribbean islands.

Surfline	Surfing
www.surfline.com	

Check out the surf before you plan your next surfing adventure by using the search engine of this site. More than 100 local reporters provide current updates on surfing conditions as well as offer travel tips on surfing from California to Bali. Includes photos of surfers and surfing conditions. Offers a store for purchasing videos, books, photography, surf art, and surf gear.

Diver Planet	Diving
www.diverplanet.com	

Anyone interested in diving adventures should definitely bookmark this site. A division of *Ticketplanet.com*, this site includes a trip search engine and sections on different vacation types (dive trips, adventure tours, dive resorts) and dive destinations. It also includes online polls of the top five dive spots (Micronesia and Fiji are one and two) and the top five dive resort spots (Tahiti and Bali are one and two). Includes sections on inexpensive airlines (reservations available through *www.ticketplanet.com*), hot deals, dive news, travel resources, and destination guides (all content provided by Lonely Planet).

DAN   Diving/Insurance
www.diversalertnetwork.org

We've included this site not so much because it provides useful information on diving. Rather, it represents one of the best kept secrets for travelers in general – inexpensive evacuation insurance. Rather than pay hundreds of dollars for such insurance (it's a good idea to have such insurance – could cost over $7,000 to be evacuated abroad because of illness or accidents), for $35 you can join Divers Alert Network (DAN) and become a card-carrying member with up to $100,000 evacuation insurance coverage (covers air evacuation and transportation). You'll also receive a copy of DAN's monthly magazine on diving.

Sports

All types of sports are well represented in the travel industry. You'll find everything from sports clinics for improving skills (especially tennis and golf) to spectator (attend the Olympics, Superbowl, golf, or soccer tournament) and participant (canoeing, mountain climbing, skiing) sports. Many business travelers are especially interested in golf. Many budget travelers enjoy bicycling. And many upscale travelers are into skiing and sailing. The following websites highlight several popular sporting activities.

Golf

Golfonline   Sports/Golf
www.golfonline.com/travel/

If you're looking for golf courses in North America and abroad, use this site's handy search engine to locate some great places for planning your next great golf adventure. Includes informative articles, such as the 100 U.S. and world golf courses, tours, news, FAQs, community forums, and related links.

Golf-Travel	Sports/Golf
www.golf-travel.com	

This site functions as a directory to golf travel with links to the world's best golf courses, resorts, schools, travel agencies, and related travel services. While the sidebars are difficult to read, nonetheless, they yield lots of useful references, such as the top 100 U.S. golf resorts, the top 100 U.S. courses, and the top international courses. Includes a destination section.

Bicycling

Cyber Cyclery	Sports/Biking
www.cycling.org/	

This is the gateway site to the world of bicycling. It offers everything from mailing lists, directories, and forums to website links and bicycle shops. Includes an important set of linkages to companies offering bicycle tours around the world, bicycling magazines, and organizations, associations, clubs, and teams of bicycle enthusiasts.

Mountaineering

Mountain Zone	Sports/Mountains
www.mountainzone.com	

Mountain sports encompass everything from climbing, hiking, and skiing to biking, caving, and snowboarding. If any of these activities tweak your travel interests, be sure to visit this site which maintains special channels for these travel activities. It includes many informative articles, news, photo gallery, links to other sites, forums, and a marketplace. It also includes an online radio program. Special features include following the progress of mountain expeditions and providing ski updates.

Skiing

GoSki	Sports/Skiing
www.goski.com	

This site identifies over 2,500 ski resorts in 37 countries. It includes a travel store for ski gear, forums, news, weather, and online travel planning (vacation packages, lodging, car rentals, and local travel services). Its handy index identifies over 100 important ski subjects relevant to travelers.

SkiNet.com	Sports/Skiing
www.skinet.com	

Operated by leading ski publications (*Ski, Skiing, Freeze*), this site is jam-packed with useful information for skiers: resorts, ski snow calender, news, instruction, competition, chat, and a ski shop. It also includes online discounts. You also may want to visit its related sites: *www.skimag.com*, *www.skiingmag.com,* and *www.freezeonline.com.*

Honeymooning

Most people who get married plan a honeymoon to somewhere, be it Las Vegas, the Bahamas, the Virgin Islands, Jamaica, Hawaii, Acapulco, Tahiti, Paris, Italy, or Bali. Some look for exotic locations while others just want a great resort with lots of beautiful beaches and sunsets. And others are looking for special wedding and honeymoon packages and tips on planning the perfect honeymoon and suggestions on what romantic things to do in an unfamiliar place. If you're planning that important trip of a lifetime, you might start with these sites:

Honeymoons.com	Honeymooning
www.honeymoons.com	

This is a comprehensive honeymoon-planning site. It includes useful sections on destinations, services, and tips.

Honeymoon Travel	Honeymooning
www.honeymoontravel.com	
www.honeymoontravel-htr.com	

Both of these sites are jam-packed with information, advice, and services for honeymooners. They cover sunshine, adventure, and global destinations as well as provide services such as a registry (*www.honeymoontravel-htr.com*), FAOs, related links, and discounted wedding and honeymoon packages (*www. honeymoontravel.com*).

Luxury Travel

If your idea of "roughing it" is having to call room service twice, then you are in luck with these websites! Many of today's travelers have graduated from those backpacking days when travel was really cheap and close to the road – they've become more affluent with age and increasingly upgrade the quality of their travels as they look for more and more creature comforts offered by top hotels, resorts, and tour groups. If you like to travel in style, you'll find numerous websites that will cater to your travel desires. However, luxury is a very relative concept – for a commercial website it usually means whatever "deals" they can negotiate with hotels and resorts that will eventually get classified as "luxurious" on their website. Anyone familiar with the luxury end of the travel business, will find many glaring deficiencies in such self-proclaimed luxury travel sites. This is not surprising given the nature of sales with this high-end travel market. Keep in mind, for example, that the truly luxurious hotels and resorts tend to have a class-based attitude – being "old fashioned", they see themselves as "exclusive" or "special" and thus often refuse to lower themselves to the commercial discounting and commissions that

> *Luxury travel on the Internet is usually less than what it appears to be. Truly luxurious properties don't need the Internet – their exclusive clientele knows how to find them.*

are the bread and butter of the mass travel industry. You definitely won't find such properties on Internet auction sites! As a result, luxury travel on the Internet is usually less than what it initially appears to be. Luxury yes, or maybe, but not necessarily the best of the best. Truly luxurious properties don't feel they need the Internet to market themselves given their exclusive clientele that already knows how to find them (usually by word-of-mouth). In fact, many luxury properties offer their high profile clients the greatest luxury of all – exclusivity and privacy. When Donna Karan and Barbra Streisand stay at the fabulous Begawan Giri in Bali, for example, they want privacy – not celebrity attention. These places are "special." You'll need to access them through other means, like going directly to their home pages.

If you literally want to travel in the lap of luxury – and keeping the above mentioned caveats in mind – check out these sites:

Luxury Travel   Luxury
www.luxurytravel.com

Devoted to uncovering luxury hotels and resorts in the best locations, this site includes a search engine that is capable of accessing over 2,000 such properties worldwide. Includes feature articles on properties, guides to major cities, and romantic destinations. However, this site doesn't really represent the best of the best in luxury. For example, its selections for Bali tend to be good but by no means excellent or outstanding. Bali's top resorts, such as Begawan Giri, Four Seasons, Ritz-Carlton, The Legian, and the three Amanresorts (Amandari, Amanusa, and Amankila) – some of the top properties in the world – do not appear on this site. Use this site knowing that there are a lot more luxury hotels and resorts than are represented in this site's limited database.

Luxury4less   Luxury
www.luxury4less.com

Claiming to be the most luxurious destination on the Internet, this is a useful site for doing some initial luxury travel research. Somewhat slow, dark, and hard to read (loves to use reverses with tiny print), the site includes some of the most exclusive tours, such as around-the-world-in-22-days by private luxury jet for $39,500 per person. The site also includes spas around the world, great hotels and resorts, luxury cruises, private yachts, and grand tours. However, the selections are often very limited and not representative of the best of the best (for example, it only lists the Peninsula in Bangkok, which is a fine hotel, but it misses other top properties – the Oriental, Shangri-La, Regent, and Sukhothai; the Cairo selection is on target – the new Four Seasons – as is the La Mamounia in Marrakesh, although the fabulous new Amanjena is absent; the Park Royal in Sydney is very questionable given Sydney's current stock of fine luxury hotels and the presence of two award-winning Ritz-Carlton properties). One of the nice things about this site is that you can speak to a live travel consultant at any time (between 9am and 5pm). The site also includes a concierge section for assisting you with any special needs. Use this site for doing some initial luxury travel research, but you also may want to contact your traditional travel agent or do some travel guide-book research (for hotels and resorts, try *Fodor's Guides* or visit their website – *www.fodors.com*).

Three other excellent luxury travel sites worth visiting include:

Luxury Link Traveler:	*www.luxurylink.com*
LuxeLife:	*www.luxelife.com*
Harper's Hideaway Report:	*www.harperassociates.com*

Luxury travelers in search of fine hotels and resorts may do better by going directly to the websites of various luxury properties, such as:

Leading Hotels:	*www.lhw.com*
Small Leading Hotels:	*www.slh.com*
Preferred Hotels:	*www.preferredhotels.com*
Design Hotels:	*www.designhotels.com*
Four Seasons:	*www.fourseasons.com*
Ritz-Carlton:	*www.ritzcarlton.com*
Amanresorts:	*www.amanresorts.com*
Venice Simplon-Orient:	*www.orient-expresshotels.com*
Rosewood Hotels & Resorts:	*www.rosewood-hotels.com*

They also should check out the top tour groups (also see complete listing on page 217) that especially appeal to upscale travelers:

Abercrombie & Kent:	*www.abercrombiekent.com*
Tauck World Discovery:	*www.tauck.com*
Travcoa:	*www.travcoa.com*

Shopping

Shopping is the top leisure activity for business travelers and an important one for many other travelers. However, most guidebooks provide little information on shops beyond some very general product information. As a result, many travelers are at the mercy of advertisements and tour guides who take them shopping in exchange for commissions from shops. When it comes to specifying great shops for travelers, most travel guidebooks shy away from shopping or consider shopping a travel sin – except for our Impact Guides which focus on the best of the best in shopping (*The Treasures and Pleasures of [country]: Best of the Best*) and the *Born to Shop* series. We've also created a new travel-shopping site (*www.ishoparoundtheworld.com*) to help travelers better handle this great sport! A few other sites, such as *www.novica. com* and *www.eziba.com*, try to sell products directly from producers around the world – a kind of cyber-travel approach to shopping from your home. And, of course, you'll find thousands of sites trying to sell products online.

---

iShopAroundTheWorld   **Travel-Shopping**
www.ishoparoundtheworld.com

This is our baby. Rich in shopping content, which is based on our *Treasures and Pleasures of . . . Best of the Best* guidebooks on Asia, South Pacific, Middle East, North Africa, Europe, the Caribbean, and South America, the site provides lots of shopping and traveling tips along with information on products and destinations. Features some of the best of the best shops around the world. Includes travel tools, a community forum, FAQs, and a reservation system for booking airlines, hotels, cruises, cars, restaurants, and tours.

Novica.com   Cyber-Shopping
www.novica.com

Backed by lots of venture capital, this unusual, informative, and visually appealing site has developed a novel idea – cut out the middleman and buy directly from artists and craftsman from a select number of regions and Third World countries. The site features lots of different products as well as specific artists and craftsman from whom you may be purchasing items. The individuals usually have interesting comments about their backgrounds and current skills and products. You can purchase items online with the producer packing and shipping your item. If nothing else, this site will whet your appetite for shopping in many exotic places where you can meet the artists and crafts-men and purchase items directly from them. Offers a 100% satisfaction guarantee and includes a monthly *NOVICA.com Journal* with many adventure stories and artisan highlights. A great research site for exploring shopping around the world and a nice place to revisit and perhaps shop after coming home (we just hope they can deliver the goods without having to exercise the guarantee!).

eZiba.com   Cyber-Shopping
www.eziba.com

Like Novica.com, you don't need to take trips abroad to shop. Viewing itself as the premier online catalog and global bazaar, this site offers handcrafted items from around the world: arts, artifacts, crafts, apparel, furniture, home furnishings, garden items, tableware, foods, toys, gift items, and much more. Includes interesting feature articles and some video on the making and sourcing of products. A recent article, including photos, featured the co-founder of eZiba.com, Amber Chand, shopping for various products in the ancient medina and souks of Marrakesh. The site also includes ongoing auctions for a variety of featured products. In March 2000 Amazon.com invested $17.5 million in eZiba.com (part of $70 million in first round venture capital funding) as part of its strategy to introduce Amazon's 20 million customers to the handcrafted items offered by eZiba.com.

Other shopping sites – most of which allow you to shop online for travel-related items such as clothes, backpacks, luggage, clocks, straps, security devices, lights, electrical converters and adapters, umbrellas, translators, organizers, and travel pouches – are examined in Chapter 7, pages 144-146, under "Travel Gear."

Spas

Welcome to the body shops! Like adventure travel, spas are extremely popular with both business and leisure travelers today. Indeed, the number of spas is expected to more than double within the next four years. Many five-star hotels and resorts are developing spa centers in order to meet the increasing demand for such self-indulgent body services. Many are attached to the traditional health and fitness centers and include a variety of spa activities lasting from 30 minutes to 8 hours! Others are separate entities and function as specialty spas. If you are a spa lover and wish to plan your next trip around some wonderful spa experiences (try the spa at the Oriental Hotel in Bangkok), here are some key sites to plan for that special experience:

Spa Finder   **Spas**
www.spafinder.com

Looking for that perfect spa at home or abroad? Here's the site that makes it easy to search by destination and category. Classifies spas into several appealing categories: retreats, resorts, luxury, adventure, weight management, wellness retreats, holistic retreats, spas abroad, and spas at sea. Includes a keyword search engine for locating spas around the world. The site also allows you to search by interests and includes sections on shopping, cuisines (includes recipes), and featured specials. Users can use a toll-free number to call vacation spa consultants and make reservations. Includes a network of day spas and a gift certificate program. The database only includes some spas – some of the world's best cannot be found through this site. Also publishes *Spa Finder Magazine*.

Spa.com	Spas
www.spa.com	

This site is jam-packed with useful information on the world of spas. Indeed, you should start your spa research with this site. Working with a network of 23 partner spas, this site allows you to book a spa online. The site includes detailed information on over 500 spas. It includes a spa finder, feature articles, a shop, a reservation system, gift certificates, giveaways, incentives, a community section, and much more.

Other spa-related sites worth visiting include:

About.com:	*www.spas.about.com*
Healing Retreats:	*www.healingretreats.com*
Healthy Travel:	*www.healthytravel.net*
Royal Spas:	*www.royal-spas.com*
Spa Magazine:	*www.spamagazine.com*
Spa Only:	*www.spaonly.com*
Spa View:	*www.spaview.com*
Spa Wish:	*www.spawish.com*
Yoga Site:	*www.yogasite.com*

Theme Parks

You'll find lots of theme parks throughout North America as well as some in Europe and Asia. However, the granddaddy of theme parks, and one of the most popular vacation destinations in the world, are the Disney family of theme parks.

Disney	Theme Parks
www.disney.go.com	

Explore the world of Disney through the company's main site. It includes information on Disney park (Walt Disney World) and resort (Disneyland) vacations. You also can book vacations and buy tickets to the park and resort. The site also includes the Disney cruise line (can book cruises and review specials) and links to Disney's three international parks and resorts – Disneyland Paris, Tokyo Disneyland, and Tokyo DisneySea. A special section reviews favorite places and special attractions.

Work, Study, Education, and Volunteer

Many travelers are into education, volunteer, and study tours as well as international work experiences, or what some call experiential, responsible, or soul-driven travel. They enjoy going to places where they have a chance to meet the local people, learn about the local culture, and perhaps study the local language. Many join work-study tours, such as an archeological dig, or attend a two-week language class in a foreign country. Others look for homestays where they can live with a local family and learn about life in a foreign country. And still others look for short-term work experience, such as teaching English, working as a ski instructor, waiting on tables at a resort, or volunteering to help build roads, clean up the environment, construct shelter, take care of children in a daycare center, or resettle refugees. Several websites are devoted to this type of responsible and socially conscious travel. While many such travelers are young students, others are retirees who are interested in engaging in socially meaningful travel. Here are some of the useful websites for this type of travel:

Transitions Abroad   **Work/Study**
www.transitionsabroad.com

This is one of our favorite organizations, publications, and sites. Operated by work-study-travel abroad guru Clay Hubbs, who for years has promoted the concept of "responsible travel", this is the online extension of his wonderful bimonthly magazine for students and lifelong learners – *Transitions Abroad* – who are interested in responsible travel which focuses on learning about other cultures by meeting the people, speaking the local language, and working short-term (and avoiding the tours and tourists). Like the companion magazine, this site is jam-packed with practical information and advice for anyone interested in work, study, travel, and living abroad. It includes a search engine as well as an overseas planner and profiles of programs and resources.

Global Volunteers
www.globalvolunteers.org

Volunteers

Global Volunteers is devoted to helping establish mutual understanding between the peoples of many different cultures. It stresses the concept of "Service-Learning" – travel that feeds the soul. It annually coordinates more than 150 teams of volunteers who participate in short-term human and economic development projects throughout the world with special emphasis on the U.S. Africa, Asia, the Caribbean, Europe, Latin America, and the Pacific. The site features special programs, outlines program options, includes frequently asked questions, and provides an online application form.

Go Abroad
www.goabroad.com

Work/Study

This student-oriented site is designed for anyone interested in study abroad, language schools, overseas internships, international volunteer positions, teaching abroad, jobs abroad, and ecotourism. The site includes a study abroad directory, travel guides, and travel tools. It also includes a store, reservation system, free newsletter, and linkages to other useful sites, such as *InternAbroad.com, Volunteer Abroad.com, TeachAbroad.com, JobsAbroad.com*, and *USUniversities.com*. A well-done and attractive site that keeps getting better.

Global Exchange
www.globalexchange.org

Work/Study

This site is devoted to promoting environmental, political, and social justice around the world. Somewhat difficult front page to read (dark and bad type style), the site includes a "Reality Tours" section for those who want to meet community leaders in Cuba, Haiti, South Africa, or Ireland; visit environmentally sustainable farming projects in Cuba; or learn about the arts and religions of Haiti, Thailand, Palestine, and Israel. Country tours include the USA (California), France, Iran, Palestine/ Israel, Costa Rica/Nicaragua, Haiti, Ireland, South Africa, Cuba, India, Mexico, and the US-Mexico Border. Issue tours cover everything from community development and human rights to ecology, education, and race.

CIEE   Work/Study
www.ciee.org

Known as the Council on International Educational Exchange, this is one of the oldest and most respected international student groups. It's especially well known for issuing international ID cards that help students get travel discounts. CIEE sponsors tours, promotes exchanges, and operates international study programs. Primarily oriented to high school and college students, its travel section focuses on airfares, railpasses, international ID cards, travel gear, hotels, hostels, tours, travel insurance, language courses, study abroad, work abroad, and volunteer experiences. It includes an airfare search engine and a travel store.

Escape Artist   Work
www.escapeartist.com

The name of this site says it all! Yes, it's designed for people who want to escape from home and travel or live abroad – especially those with a bad case of wanderlust. Indeed, the site is designed to promote overseas living "for international job seekers, expatriates, and tax exiles." Representing a goldmine of information, this is one of the richest sites for all types of international linkages. Indeed, you can spend days getting lost in the fascinating web of URLs uncovered by this site which take you into specific countries. While the site is especially oriented to helping people relocate and live abroad, there's lots here to explore for anyone interested in short-term work, travel, and study abroad. You'll find channels on living overseas, Offshore Investing, Country Destinations, Magazine on Living Overseas, and Expatriates Reference Pages. We consider this to be one of the key gateway sites for international job seekers. You'll even find links on how to acquire a second passport. Affiliated with the popular living abroad and investment newsletter *International Living* as well as publishes the popular *Escape From America Magazine*.

iAgora.com	Work/Study
www.iagora.com	

This is another one of our favorite sites. Essentially a community of young travelers interested in work, study, and travel abroad, this site is very content rich. It includes a very active community of travelers who exchange information and advice with special emphasis on short-term work abroad.

Learning	Study
www.learn.unh.edu	

See page 71 for details.

Travel Learn	Study
www.travelearn.com	

See page 71 for details.

Elderhostel.org	Study/Seniors
www.elderhotel.org	

See page 70 for details.

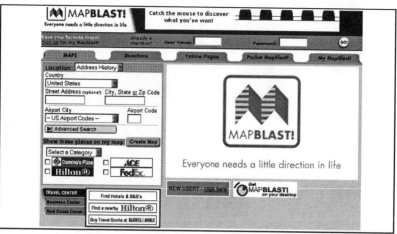

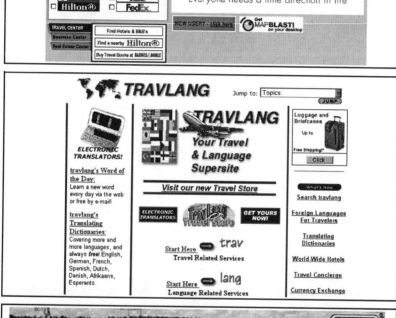

7

Travel Basics and Tools

T RAVELERS HAVE MANY QUESTIONS RELATING TO the travel process in general and to their destinations in particular. Often referred to as "travel basics", these questions range from exchange rates, time zones, Internet connections, health, maps, money, and passports to safety, time zones, Customs regulations, travel information, complaints, and the weather. Appearing repeatedly on travel websites as a separate section called "Travel Tools", several of these categories – especially currency calculators, the weather, time zones, embassies, and distance calculators – provide basic travel information.

In this chapter we identify numerous websites that deal with travel basics. Many of these sites should be incorporated into your pre-travel checklist. Taken as a group, these sites constitute a handy travel tool kit or arsenal of information and services that you can refer to again and again as you plan all of your travels.

Airline Basics and Issues

Concerned about flight schedules, seating arrangements, frequent flier miles, consumer rights, and airline safety and security? Do you have a complaint you would like to air in the hopes that someone will take action? Here is a set of airline-related sites that will answer many of your questions as well as raise many new questions about flying that you may never have thought about. For a good overview of major issues relating to air travelers, you may want to visit this rather aging site which still offers an electronic version of Mark Kantrowitz's *The Air Traveler's Handbook*:

www.cs.cmu.edu/afs/cs/user/mkant/Public/Travel/airfare.html

Airline Schedules and Airports

OAG *www.oag.com*	Airline Schedules Airports

Travel agents and other professionals use the OAG constantly for checking flight schedules. This online version of the massive *OAG Directory* lists most flights around the world. Currently operated by Reed Business Information Group, which also is trying to sell the OAG, the search engines for this site allow users to find flights for various times, destinations, and airlines as well as check flight status and survey airports. It includes global information on airports and useful destination information such as language, electricity, dialing codes, driving, business hours, public holidays, emergency services, climate, clothing, and more. If you're concerned about airport locations, transportation, terminals, restaurants, shops, taxes, and services, this site should answer most of your airport questions. It also includes separate destination sections on health, passports and visas, customs, and for general travel information. A rich resource on flights, airports, and travel.

AirWise *www.airwise.com*	Airline Schedules Airports

Focused on flight information and airports, this site provides the latest news on airlines, airports, and the aviation industry. It includes a flight arrival section that allows users to check flight details for major airlines; an airport guide section which also identifies the world's top 50 airports; a reservation section for booking flights and hotels, renting cars, and purchasing travel insurance; travel resources (ATM location, airline and web sites, currency converter); weather checker; discussion forums; and features such as airport shopping and low cost airlines. A well done and useful site.

SkyGuide	Airlines
www.sky-guide.com	Airports

Hosted by American Express, this site is loaded with information on airlines, airports, and ground transportation. Includes sections on weather, airport tips, airlines, ground transportation, safety and troubleshooting, general travel tips, and business travel resources. The airline section covers airline websites, baggage handling, tickets, inflight food service, and plane configurations. The airport section looks at hub cities, ground transportation, business services, Internet access, security, and shopping. Also includes a subscription-based section ($69 for 12 months) that provides detailed information on flight options, including airlines, departures, arrivals, connecting flights, flight numbers, and more.

Air Safety

AirSafe	Air Safety
www.airsafe.com	

If you have any questions or concerns about airline safety, be sure to visit this air safety site for the traveling public. Using NTSB data, the site identifies the record of air fatalities by airline and aircraft model, the top 10 fatal events, and fatality ratings of aircraft and airlines (Did you know in North America AirTran and Midwest Express have the highest number of fatalities per 1,000 passengers?). The site also includes information on passenger air rage, fear of flying, safety links, and advice on a host of travel issues, including how to complain effectively to the airlines and/or government (includes addresses of relevant agencies). Includes a travel store.

| **Federal Aviation Administration** | **Airlines** |
| *www.faa.gov/passinfo.htm* | **Airports** |

This government (FAA) site is designed for airline consumers with special emphasis on airline safety. It includes useful articles, frequently asked questions, and a wealth of linkages to other sites on a variety of safety and travel topics: weather related delays at major U.S. airports (updated every 5 minutes), child safety seats, cabin safety, passenger security, travel advisories, U.S. Customs regulations, world times, and causes of aircraft accidents. It also includes linkages to airlines, airport codes, and U.S. and international airports.

| **RulesOfTheAir** | **Airlines** |
| *www.rulesoftheair.com* | |

This site has a very clever query engine – just identify an airline from a extensive pull-down list and link it to another pull-list of categories, such as double bookings of reservations, and you'll get a summary of airline policies and practices, i.e., the rules of the airline. The site also includes sections on travel advice, destination tips, and frequently asked questions. You also can make airline and hotel reservations and reserve a car through this site.

| **ACAP** | **Safety, Security,** |
| *www.acap1971.org* | **Health** |

Founded by Ralph Nader in 1971, the Aviation Consumer Action Project (ACAP) represents thousands of air travelers, pilots, flight attendants, air traffic controllers, air safety experts, air disaster victims, and government officials who want to improve air safety and security while protecting consumer rights. This site includes aviation news, industry links, members' links, membership information, publications, and online surveys of complaints.

Passenger Rights and Complaints

PassengerRights **Rights**
www.passengerrights.com

Are you ticked off but not sure what to do? Do you have a horror story with an airline you would like to share with the world? Do you want to laugh or cry yourself silly with travel horror stories? Here's some great help in getting your voice heard. This site is dedicated to uncovering horror stories (everything from being trapped onboard for six hours or jettisoning sewage into someone's backyard to peanut allergies, ruined honeymoons and anniversaries, and an airline losing a motorized wheel chair), voicing one's opinion, and whistle blowing (actually has separate sections focused on these topics). It also provides practical advice on how to file complaints with a high probability of getting action, including a useful electronic complaint form and seven tips on how to complain. Includes sections on travel secrets, hot topics, and questions. But not everything is negative here. The bright side of this site is its electronic form to register good experiences with a travel provider which are then forwarded to someone who would love to read it! The site also includes a newsletter. A great site for abused and disgruntled passengers who can sound off in the right direction.

Air Travel Complaints **Complaints**
www.airtravelcomplaints.com

Complaining against bad airline behavior keeps getting easy with online automated search and complaint systems. From lost luggage, bumped flights, and rude flight attendants to lousy food, snippy gate agents, and delayed flights, this site reveals it all. Devoted to cataloging complaints and helping abused passengers complain effectively, this site has a clever complaint engine. It allows you to select an airline from a pull-down menu, enter your flight number, date of flight, and reservation/confirmation number, select a complaint category (includes 18 complaint categories), and write and transmit a complaint automatically. Another section allows you to review existing complaints by searching by 50 complaint categories. If you're thinking of flying United, American Airlines, TWA, or Southwest Airlines, for example, just find these airlines on the pull-down menu and select any of 19 complaint categories to review what people are saying.

Other sites for disgruntled airline passengers include:

Untied:	*www.untied.com*
NorthworstAir:	*www.northworstAir.org*
Airlines Suck:	*www.airlinesuck.com*

Frequent Flyers

WebFlyer	**Frequent Flyer**
www.webflyer.com	
www.insideflyer.com	

These two URLs will take you to the same place – the largest and most extensive website that dispenses information on frequent flyer programs. Headed by frequent flyer guru Randy Peterson, this site is designed to service the frequent flier community with numerous products and services. It includes sections on frequent flyer programs, message boards, travel tools and tips, linkages to related sites, and a frequent travel horoscope. Conducts online surveys and offers a newsletter.

Mileage Workshop	**Frequent Flyer**
www.mileageworkshop.com	

Trying to accumulate more frequent flyer miles but you're having difficulty doing go by flying or making more credit card purchases? This site is designed to help users acquire frequent flyer miles online by nontraditional means – free mileage deals from phone companies, completing surveys, entering contests, or special offers to students and seniors. Identifies new options as well as provides links to sites making such offers.

Other useful sites focusing on frequent flyer miles include:

Frequent Flier:	*www.frequentflier.com*
Selling miles for cash:	*www.smartflyer.com*
Guest deals:	*www.moremiles.com*
United Kingdom:	*www.ukflyer.com*
Canada:	*www.eliteflyer.com*

For information on airline ticketing, including discounts, consolidators, air couriers, and travel agents, see Chapter 12 on the middlemen and their suppliers.

Complaints and Settlements

In addition to websites devoted to complaining about airline service (*www.airlinecomplaints.com* and *www.airtravelcomplaints.com*), other websites help travelers complain about any and everything relating to travel, from tour groups to hotels, car rentals, and restaurants. Some, such as TravelProblems, also negotiate settlements for travelers:

Travel Problems	**Complaints/**
www.travelproblems.com	**Settlements**

Too busy to complain? Feeling frustrated and powerless in the face of a large corporation whose customer service really sucks? Here's help. Perhaps better than hassling directly with a lawyer, Small Claims Court, or an ineffective ombudsman, this "complaint management service" takes the pain out of complaining and reaching a beneficial settlement – it will do everything for you. If they accept your case, for a flat fee of $30, TravelProblems will attempt to negotiate a settlement of up to $200 on your behalf. If the settlement is for more than $200, the fee is $55 plus a 20% commission. These fees cover all of their correspondence, telephone calls, faxes, and emails. A settlement may result in a cash refund, credit, upgrades, free travel, or frequent flyer miles/points. The clever site includes a handy online Airline Complaint Form and Cruise Line Complaint Form on which you include all complaint information and specify your preferred type of settlement: cash refund, credit, free air ticket or cruise, frequent traveler points, or upgrade. Enter your credit card number and hit "Accept Terms and Submit" and you may soon have a representative from TravelProblems "getting even" for you. An innovative concept and service that truly uses the power of the Internet to get the critical voice of consumers heard by corporations. This site also includes a directory of travel links.

Customs Regulations

Some of most frequently asked questions we get from our readers and users concern U.S. Customs regulations. How much duty must one pay on purchases from abroad, especially for jewelry, clothes, art, and antiques? Is the General System of Preferences (GSP) on or off again? Must you pay duties by cash or can you use credit cards and a personal check? These are important questions for shoppers who would like to know their total costs before making large purchases that could result in onerous Customs duties. Unfortunately, each year the U.S. Congress plays politics with the GSP system as part of the annual appropriations process. The result is one of the craziest travel games around – you may literally pay

Each year the U.S. Congress plays politics with the GSP system as part of the annual appropriations process. The result is one of the craziest travel games around.

$10 in duties on an item which normally is covered by GSP because the U.S. Congress temporarily suspends GSP during budgetary negotiations; once the budget is passed, GSP is reinstated and you will get a refund check because the reinstated GSP is usually applied retroactively. Customs officials shake their heads in acknowledging such a stupid waste of taxpayer's money – for the $10 duty paid the Customs official took 30 minutes to complete the paperwork to make the assessment and then six months later the U.S. Treasury cuts you a refund check for the $10! Given this situation, you may want to research Customs regulations before you travel abroad by going directly to this site:

U.S. Customs   **Customs**
www.customs.ustreas.gov/travel/travel.htm

Learn all about how the U.S. Customs system works – and doesn't work – for travelers. This section of the U.S. Treasury site includes lots of useful information relating to restricted/prohibited merchandise; medications and drugs; business travel; mailing goods to the U.S.; frequently asked questions; pets/animals; arriving by private boat, plane or car; the inter-agency Border Inspection System; U.S. Customs requirements in brief; government, military personnel, and crew member exemptions; and traveler alerts. Under "Travelers Alerts" you'll learn, for example, that Cuban cigars are still a threat to the U.S. and thus are prohibited from entering the country. A useful but sometimes depressing site. Includes an online version of the popular brochure "Know Before You Go" which is jam-packed with information on duty-free exemptions, gifts, personal belongings, household effects, paying duties, shipping goods to the U.S., duty-free shops, prohibited and restricted items, and customer service programs. If you have questions about Customs regulations, start with this site.

Culture

Are you interested in learning about other cultures before you depart on your adventure? Are you concerned about how to behave in certain business and social situations and how your behavior might be inter-preted in another culture? Here's a site that provides some help with those potential cross-cultural communication problems:

Web of Culture   **Culture**
www.webofculture.com

This site focuses on providing useful information to businesses about different cultures. It includes articles – both instructive and hilarious – on such topics as Global Marketing Mistakes, 10 Success Factors for Globalizing, and Gestures Around the

World. Its reference channels include everything from consulates, currency, and embassies to languages and weather.

Currency Calculators

One of the most ubiquitous features found on many travel websites is the currency calculator. Use these calculators to find out what the daily exchange rate is for the currency you will soon be acquiring and even have the currency delivered to your home address the day before you leave on your adventure.

Oanda.com   **Currency**
www.oanda.com

The most popular online currency converter, this site is loaded with useful information and services. Using the automated currency converter, just enter your currency and the one you need to convert to, and you get the latest exchange rate. Includes useful articles on exchange rates as well as offers an extensive line of FX products. Also includes travel advisories and a newsletter. Its FX Delivery™ system will even deliver foreign currency and traveler's checks (between $200 and $1500) to your home – an ultimate pre-trip planning service!

Universal Currency Converter   **Currency**
www.xe.net/ucc

Similar to *Oanda.com*, this site allows you to quickly convert any of the world's currencies. Just enter the type of currency desired and the currency you wish to exchange. Presto! You'll get an accurate bank exchange rate for the day.

Distance Calculators

So you don't know how far it is to your next destination but would like to find out quickly without having to consult maps and books. You're in luck with the Internet. A few websites specialize in calculating the distance between locations. Start with this excellent site and you probably won't need to go anywhere else except for some maps at MapBlast (*www.mapblast.com*) and MapQuest (*www.mapquest. com*):

Indo.com *www.indo.com/distance/*	Distance

This is one of our favorite websites – but for visiting Bali, Indonesia! However, it offers a wonderful automatic distance calculator for figuring distances anywhere in the world. The service uses data from the U.S. Census Bureau and a supplementary list of cities around the world to find the latitude and longitude of the two locations and then calculates the distance. Just enter the destination you are leaving and the destination you desire to reach, and the software will quickly generate the distance in miles as well as in kilometers and nautical miles. For example, you learn the distance between Washington, DC (east-northeast, 72.5 degrees) and Casablanca, Morocco (west-northwest 297.0 degrees) is 3798 miles (or 6112 kilometers or 3300 nautical miles). After calculating the distance, the site also provides direct links to two useful sites: MapBlast (*www. mapblast.com*) for driving distance and directions and Xerox PARC (*pubweb.parc.xerox.com/map*) for a destination map.

Electricity, Phones, and Computers

International travelers who are used to packing their electrical appliances, phones, computers, and hand-held devices often need information on electrical power and outlet configurations, telephone connections for modems, the use of cell phones, and special equipment. While many major travel sites occasionally provide tips on these subjects, one in particular is devoted to these topics:

Kropla *http://kropla.com*	Electricity Phones

Operated by Steve Kropla, this site provides useful information on a variety of subjects relating to modems, electrical power, electrical outlet configurations, sources for purchasing telephone and electrical travel accessories, international dialing codes, and television broadcast standards. The site also includes a list of useful travel links.

Roadnews   **Computers**
www.roadnews.com

This site is devoted to helping road warriors – those travelers who don't leave home without their computers/notebooks. For more details, see our discussion on page 121 under Internet Access.

Laptop Travel   **Laptops**
www.laptoptravel.com

This site includes lots of articles and product profiles for the mobile computing community. Includes features on wireless products (cables, modems, phones, and phone services), PDA's and handheld computers and accessories, palmtop, and laptop products and accessories. A separate section focuses on international travel – worldwide connectivity and power conversion products (adapter plugs, voltage conversion, surge protectors, global modems, and pulse noise filters).

If you want to keep abreast of rapidly changing developments in web-based travel – including the marriage of wireless technology and travel (Internet access on airlines at 30,000 feet) and the introduction of e-books by airlines – be sure to visit these two related sites:

Web Travel News:	*www.webtravelnews.com*
PhoCusWright:	*www.phocuswright.com*

Embassies and Consulates

Many travelers need to contact embassies and consulates for visas, travel, and business information. Here are the key sites that generate such information with a quick click of your mouse:

| Embassy Page | Embassies |
| www.embpage.org | Worldwide |

Includes a comprehensive listing of diplomatic posts world-wide – a database of over 50,000 addresses, phone numbers, and email addresses. The site also includes linkages to other international sites, world news, open forums, frequently asked questions, and a newsletter. It also hosts sponsored linkages on adventure travel, foreign currency, recruiters, meeting planning, and Internet news.

| Embassy World | Embassies |
| www.embassyworld.com | Worldwide |

This site includes a directory of embassies and consulates worldwide. Just select a country and all the embassies in that country are listed. Includes a separate section on U.S. embassies abroad, United Nations permanent missions, and special search tools, such as an international telephone directory, an international voltage directory, and visa requirements.

| Embassy.org | Embassies |
| www.embassy.org | In U.S. |

If you're only interested in locating foreign embassies located in Washington, DC, go to this online directory for names, addresses, telephone/fax, and email numbers, and URLs. The site also includes business directories for diplomats, Americans living abroad, foreign visitors, and educators.

Events and Festivals

Do you want to know what's going on in Paris in April? What about New York City, Chicago, Toronto, Los Angeles, Hong Kong, and Singapore? Any chance you might be making a scheduling mistake because of holidays? Here are three sites that summarize upcoming events in various communities:

What's Going On   Events
www.whatsgoingon.com

This site loves festivals. If you're searching for what to do anywhere in the world, especially for festivals, races, fairs, sports events, and national day celebrations, try this site's event search engine. Just enter the city, state, and time frame or search by categories or keywords and the database will list upcoming events in your desired location. The international event search engine covers 47 major cities, from Amsterdam to Vienna. The site includes several interesting features, such as The Coolest Place on Earth Today, The Month's Top 10 Events, and The World's Top Destinations for Events and Celebrations. The site also offers message boards, a free newsletter, and will take reservations for standard and consolidator airfares. It's well worth adding this site to your arsenal of travel planning sites.

On the Road   Events
www.ontheroad.com

Promoting itself as the tactical destination guide for business travelers, this growing site now covers 15 major North American destinations, London, and 15 cities in Asia and Europe. It includes a database of 1,000 Insider Tips, 1,500 restaurants, 15,000 entertainment, sports, and business events, and 400 business services, all independently selected by its editorial staff. Includes checks on Business Events, Fine Dining, and Art of the Deal. Its innovative Art of Deal section identifies three top restaurants in each city where you are well advised to go to negotiate your best business deals. Since the site does not accept advertising, it views itself as one of the more objective travel sites on the Internet which also boasts one of the most talented staffs of international and travel writers.

World Public Holidays   **Events**
www.tyzo.com/tools/holidays.html

Use this database to identify public holidays that might affect your travel schedule. Indeed, you may discover the particular shop, museum, or restaurant you hoped to visit in Istanbul will be closed because you're scheduled to be there on a major public holiday! Includes handy pull-down menus of countries, cities, and dates. The site also includes useful travel planning linkages (directories, magazines, health and safety), travel tools (language, maps, weather, time zones), travel supplies (airlines, cruise lines, hotels, trains, travel agencies), and linkages to different categories of travelers (adventure, women, seniors, students, budget, business, family, disabled, gay/lesbian).

Other useful sites for checking out events and festivals include the following:

Festival Finder:	*www.festivalfinder.com*
Festivals:	*www.festivals.com*
Fest Pass:	*www.festpass.com*
Film Festivals:	*www.filmfestivals.com*
Pollstar:	*www.pollstar.com*

Health

There's nothing worse than getting ill while traveling – an otherwise wonderful trip can easily turn into the "trip from hell". Because health is such an important issue for travelers, and many illnesses are not well understood by many travelers, several websites provide useful information on staying healthy while traveling. They include a combination of health advisories, feature articles on travelers diseases, and preventive measures to stay healthy. While you should visit these sites prior to departing on a trip abroad, you might also want to visit them on the road should you take ill. Many of the sites offer useful advice on handling one of the most common travel illnesses – traveler's diarrhea. You should find the following websites especially useful in addressing the whole issue of health and travel.

Medicine Planet   **Health**
www.medicineplanet.com
www.travelhealth.com

Wow! If you only have time to visit one medical site relevant to travelers, make sure it's Medicine Planet. This very informative travel medical site has it all. It includes separate health centers for travel health, women's travel, children's travel, seniors' travel, and adventure travel which are jam-packed with informative articles and advice. A destination section allows users to specify countries from a pull-down menu. Each country is examined in terms of its entry requirements and most common health problems for travelers. Each health risk, such as rabies, malaria, and hepatitis B, is explained in full from description, transmissions, and significance to travelers to symptoms, diagnosis, treatment, and prevention. Using this site is like having a doctor in your house and on the road. The site also includes a "Medicine Translator" and "Ask the Experts" section as well as areas for travel health news, tools, products, and insurance opportunities. You also can register for a free membership which gives you access to "Ask the Experts" and email alerts on relevant health news in your countries of interest.

Center for Disease Control   **Health**
www.cdc.gov/travel/

This is one of best health sites for travelers – the place you initially go to for travel health information. If, for example, you plan to visit Saudi Arabia or Bangladesh, you'll learn about recent outbreaks of meningococcal disease among travelers returning from the Hajj in Mecca, Saudi Arabia (April 2000) and dengue and dengue hemorrhagic fever in Bangladesh (August 2000). It includes a "to do" health checklist for travelers, travel health news, reference materials, and information on a wide range of health and travel subjects, from outbreaks, traveling with children, special needs travelers, to diseases, safe food and water, vaccinations, cruise ships and air travel. Its search engine includes a pull-down menu that takes you directly to specific countries where you learn about their current health and disease situations for travelers. Includes links to related sites – Department of State, Division of Quarantine, National Center for Infectious Diseases, Pan American Health Organization, and World Health Organization.

HealthLink Travel Medicine   **Health**
healthlink.mcw.edu/travel-medicine

Sponsored by the Medical College of Wisconsin Physicians and Clinics, this site provide lots of useful information on a variety of health problems while traveling abroad. It includes discussions on such topics as traveler's diarrhea, traveling with children, typhoid fever, sunburn and sun protection, respiratory infections, malaria, altitude sickness, cholera, dengue fever, giardiasis, hepatitis A, lyme disease, meningitis, motion sickness, and rabies. A very useful site for better understanding some of the most important illnesses encountered while traveling abroad – and possible preventive measures.

Travel Health Online   **Health**
www.tripprep.com/index.html

This useful site includes three major sections – destination information, traveler health information, and travel medicine providers. Use the destination finder for country health profiles. The traveler health information section includes an inventory of illnesses, health and safety tips, and information for special needs travelers (diabetics, disabled, heart disease, pregnant travelers). The Travel Medicine Providers includes a list of medicine providers in the U.S. and 27 countries.

Healthy Flying   Health
www.flyana.com

This is a terrific site for travel health information relating to airlines. Also known as the "Healthy Flying With Diana Fairchild" site (she's author of the book *Jet Smarter: The Air Traveler's Rx*), it includes a collection of articles by Diana Fairchild on a variety of important airline health and related topics: airline air, air and pilots, airline meals, air rage, complaints, crew fatigue, dehydration, ear pain, fear of flying, first class, flight attendants, jet lag, oxygen, pesticides, phobias, radiation, skypoxia, sleeping, smoking, stress, and toxins. You'll discover many things about health and flying your never thought existed. For example, you'll learn about poor air quality for airline passengers; indeed, airline pilots get 10 times more oxygen than economy passengers!

International Society of Travel Medicine   Health
www.istm.org

If you are traveling and need to find a health clinic or health practitioner, go to this site which covers 38 countries. It includes a search engine to find health clinics and practitioners worldwide that are members of the International Society of Travel Medicine. This site also includes links to the latest news from the Center for Disease Control and the World Health Organization.

Other useful health sites for travelers, which deal with everything from airborne diseases to jet lag and ear pressure, include:

No Jet Lag: *www.nojetlag.com*
WebMD: *www.webmd.com*
Dr. Koop: *www.drkoop.com*

Insurance

While you may have excellent medical, home, auto, and personal insurance back home, chances are it does not provide much coverage outside your country. Given the many unpredictable situations you may find yourself in when traveling abroad – from accidents, diseases, and dental care to trip cancellation, lost luggage, rental car damage, and theft, you should seriously consider acquiring a separate insurance policy that covers possible problems encountered while traveling. What, for example, would happen if you are in a serious car accident or have a heart attack while on safari in Kenya? Chances are you'll want to be flown back home ("evacuated") as soon as possible for medical care. And it won't be a cheap flight home, especially if you come on board on a stretcher and with IVs stuck in your arms. You need special care in the air which will be much more expensive than a first-class ticket. You are well advised to have emergency evacuation insurance just in case you must be airlifted, alive or dead (transporting your body in a coffin costs more than excess baggage). The cost of an emergency evacuation can run more than $10,000. Since your current medical insurance most likely does not cover such situations, you need to get a special medical evacuation policy which may or may not be expensive, depending on where you shop for such insurance. Check out some of these sites for travel insurance options as well as use search engines to find other online companies offering travel insurance:

World Travel Center   **Insurance**
www.worldtravelcenter.com

If you need special travel insurance, this may be the place to start shopping for the best coverage and deals. The site specializes in providing 24-hour worldwide medical coverage by offering these popular products: travel insurance, international medical insurance, travel protection, emergency evacuation and repatriation, and assistance services. It includes single trip, multi-trip, and group plans. Its Policy Picker™ system allows users to specify the type of insurance they need for how long, get an online quote, and then purchase the insurance. You can examine insurance options with four different insurance providers: International Medical Group, UNICARD Travel

Association, 1Travel Insurance, and MEDJET Assistance. Other sections of this site, which is largely set up as partnership relationships and affiliate programs, include travel planning, travel advisories, news, weather, travel stories, currency converter, and FAQs.

Divers Alert Network (DAN)   **Evacuation**
www.diversalertnetwork.org

All international travelers should carry evacuation insurance, just in case they are in an accident or become seriously ill and need to be evacuated for special medical care. While such short-term insurance can be very expensive if acquired through an insurance company, DAN is one of the best kept secrets for acquiring inexpensive evacuation insurance. Join this organization for $35 and you'll also get evacuation insurance coverage. See page 95 for more details.

Council Travel   **Insurance**
www.counciltravel.com/travelinsurance

This site offers travel insurance for student travelers that covers several important areas: accident medical expense, sickness medical expenses, emergency evacuation and repatriation of remains, accidental death and dismemberment, baggage and personal effects, baggage delay, trip cancellation and interruption, trip delay. Underwritten by AIG, premiums run $48 for 1-7 days, $68 for 8-15 days, $118 for 1 month, and $578 for 12 months. You'll need to have an International Student Identification Card (acquired through the Council Travel) to qualify for such insurance. The remainder of the Council Travel site includes lots of useful travel information and services for student travelers, including cheap airfares, rail passes, travel gear, hotels and hostels, tours, language courses, study abroad, work abroad, and volunteer experiences.

Global Travel Insurance   Insurance
www.globaltravelinsurance.com

This site belongs to one of the major travel insurance companies. It includes online travel insurance quotes for a variety of insurance plans: short term single trip medical travel insurance, multi-trip travel protection plan, expatriate long term insurance plans, and group travel insurance plans. Its Patriot Plan includes everything from medical, evacuation, trip cancellation, lost luggage, sudden recurrence of pre-existing condition, and emergency dental. This site also includes a lot of additional travel information and services, from weather, news and travel tips to travel resources, web links, and travel gear.

Travel Insurance Services   Insurance
www.travelinsurance.com

Representing the Travel Underwriters Group of Companies of Canada, this site offers trip cancellation/interruption and emergency excess hospital/medical insurance for both single trip and multi-trip travelers. It provides online quotes.

Several other websites offer travel insurance information and services. The first three companies – Travelex, Access America, and Travel Guard – are three of the top U.S.-based travel insurance companies that work with many travel agencies:

Travelex:	*www.travelex.com*
Access America:	*www.accessamerica.com*
	www.etravelprotection.com
Travel Guard:	*www.travelguard.com*
Travel Secure:	*www.travelsecure.com*
Travel Protect:	*www.travelprotect.com*
Global Cover:	*www.globalcover.com*

Internet Access For Road Warriors

If you're a road warrior who frequently travels with the assistance of a computer and the Internet, getting connected to the Internet with the right equipment can often be a challenge. If you like to stay connected to the Internet while traveling – especially for email purposes – be sure to check out several of the following free email sites. Most travelers interested in using the Internet on the road have three major concerns. First, can they conveniently and inexpensively access their current email account while traveling outside the free dial-up area of their ISP? Second, how can they set up a special email account they can easily access when traveling. Third, where can they get access to the Internet – with or without using their laptop? What about new wireless connections?

> *Finding an Internet connection is relatively easy in countries such as the U.S., Canada, Australia, Finland, and Sweden. However, it can be problematic in digitally-deficient countries such as Vietnam, Kenya, Tanzania, Russia, and Cuba.*

Unless you are traveling to places that provide inexpensive telephone connections to an ISP with an international presence, such as AOL, CompuServe, and Microsoft Network, you may need to set up a special email account that can be accessed anywhere in the world. Several websites, such as Hotmail, YahooMail, AltaVista, Lycos, and iVillage, offer free email accounts that can be accessed through their sites from any computer. This means you may need to have someone back home check your regular email account and forward any important messages to your special travel account. Alternatively, you may be able to access your main email account by using such sites as MailStart, ThatWeb, and WorldRoom – but only if your ISP mail account is a POP3 (most are) and it uses standard Internet mailbox access protocols that allow these sites to access your account by email address and password. Finding an Internet connection while traveling is relatively easy in highly wired countries such as the U.S., Canada, Australia, Finland, and Sweden. However, it can be problematic in such countries as Vietnam, Myanmar, Kenya, Tanzania, Russia, and Cuba which have very few cybercafes (also called

Internet cafes) and Internet wired hotels. But this situation is rapidly changing as more and more of the world's digitally-deficient countries enter the 21st century where communication technology tends to separate the "haves" from the "have-nots".

Free Email Accounts for Travelers

HotMail	**Email**
www.hotmail.com	

Hotmail is the favorite free email account for travelers and others. Indeed, over 40 million people have Hotmail accounts. It's easy to set up and use. In fact, many cybercafes around the world include a Hotmail icon on their computer screens because it's such a favorite site for travelers who primarily use the Internet café to access their Hotmail account. Operated by Microsoft Network, the site can be navigated in seven languages. While the email program has some limitations (sets a quota of messages you can receive each mouth – this is not designed for heavy business usage), overall it's the perfect account for most travelers. Hotmail even allows you to retrieve messages from up to four other email accounts (a similar function to MailStart and ThatWeb). However, expect to receive lots of junk mail as a Hotmail account holder – many spammers, from get rich quick schemes to purveyors of porno, target these accounts. Hotmail does have an Inbox Protector for automatically dumping all junk mail into a separate Bulk Mail folder from which you can easily delete undesired messages or which automatically dumps such messages every 30 days and thus helps keep you under your account quota. The site also includes news, chat, special offers, white pages (street addresses and phone numbers), email lookup, and a Hotmail Member Directory to locate others who use Hotmail accounts.

Numerous other websites offer free email accounts which can be great temporary set-ups for travelers:

Yahoo:	*www.yahoomail.com*
Excite:	*www.excite.com/info/inbox/welcome.html*
Lycos:	*http://comm.lycos.com*

AltaVista: *http://tools.altavista.com*
iVillage: *www.ivillage.com*

Accessing Your Regular Email

MailStart   **Email**
www.mailstart.com

This site allows travelers to access their regular email account
for free and thus eliminate the need to set up a separate global
email account such as Hotmail. Just go to this site, enter your
email account and password, and wait for your account to come
up. If it works, you'll have instant access to your email anywhere in the world. MailStart only works with email accounts
that use standard Internet mailbox access protocols and those
that are not behind a firewall. For example, MailStart does not
work with Hotmail accounts. Before you plan to access your
email on the road through MailStart, make sure you try it out.
It will probably work with your ISP. However, you may
discover it does not support your account and thus you may
need to set up a global email account.

Two other sites also enable users to access their email account:

ThatWeb: *www.thatweb.com*
WorldRoom: *www.worldroom.com*

Locating Cybercafes

CyberCaptive   **Internet Access**
www.cybercaptive.com

Discover where to find a cybercafe anywhere in the world by
using this site's search engine. Enter the name of a city, state,
or country and CyberCaptive searches its database of more than
5,000 cybercafes in generating a listing. Each listing includes
the name, address, telephone number, and web address of the
cybercafe. This also includes cybercafe forums, visitors sur-

veys, public Internet access points (Internet kiosks and terminals in airports, hotels, malls, and restaurants), resources for
computer-equipped travelers, and information on how to start
your own cybercafe.

Netcafe   **Internet Access**
www.netcafes.com

This site is jam-packed with news for travelers. Use the search
engine to identify cybercafes in 164 countries. The current
database includes 4,200 cybercafes. Includes cybercafes news
as well as sections on regional news, travel, and entertainment.
The site is rich with links to other major news and travel
providers.

Traveling With a Laptop/Notebook

RoadNews   **Laptops**
www.roadnews.com

This site is designed for frequent travelers, especially road
warriors who travel with or who often need access to a
laptop/notebook computer. It gives advice on trip planning,
selecting hardware, learning about various telephone and
power adapters, where to find a local ISP, and how to adjust
your communication software as you travel the globe. Includes
discussion groups, articles on fax and web-based email
services, list of in-flight laptop services by airline, foreign
exchange rates and time zones, world weather on the Internet,
and possible road hazards (safety and health).

Laptop Travel   **Laptops**
www.laptoptravel.com

See page 112 for discussion of this useful site.

Language and Free Translations

While you can't learn every language, you should at least try to learn a few words of a local language. It will help you get around as well as communicate that you are a friendly and considerate traveler. Indeed, one of the best ways to meet people is to speak a few words of their language. At the same time, you may need to translate correspondence or send correspondence in a foreign language. A few Internet sites can help you deal with language challenges. Our favorite site is *www. travlang.com*:

Travlang   **Language**
www.travlang.com

What a neat site – one you could get hooked on for hours! If you need to learn a word or phrase or translate something, just go to the foreign language section and select the language you speak and the language you want to learn, and presto, the search engine delivers numerous alternative words and phrases by category (places, restaurants, shopping, numbers, directions). It also includes an audio component so you can hear the correct pronunciation of each word. The site includes numerous linkages to each language and country so you'll have a better understanding of your destination. It also includes a message board, travel store, currency exchange rates, worldwide hotels, travel concierge, and translating dictionaries.

Other excellent sites that offer free translations over the Internet, as well as linkages to other relevant sites, include:

Free Translation:	*www.freetranslation.com*
Translate-Free:	*www.translate-free.com*
AltaVista:	*www.babelfish.altavista.com/ translate.dyn*
Research-It:	*www.itools.com/research-it/research-it.html*

Maps and Route Planners

While many men don't like to ask for directions, they will probably enhance their questionable street smarts by going to several websites that give them answers to their mapping and geographic orientation problems. Several sites include detailed maps of cities and regions. Other sites are more interactive in that users receive actual directions to specific locations. Remember those great TripTiks the American Automotive Association (*www.aaa.com*) prepares on paper for its members? They still do them – even deliver them to your door – but they also can send them to you electronically. Many other companies also offer routing information online.

Maps

MapQuest	Maps
www.mapquest.com	

This is the "best of best" website for map information and directions. While the core of this site is focused on providing maps and driving directions in the U.S., Canada, and Europe, the site also includes live traffic reports (with traffic cams), yellow and white pages (find businesses and people), travel guides (restaurants, hotels, travel deals), city guides, message boards, and wireless services. Its Express Lane search engine results in specifying driving directions – just enter your "going from" destination (address or intersection, city, state/province, country) and your "going to" destination and it gives you directions. One feature of this site is its related linkages – once it gives you directions, it includes lots of information on the destination, such as area traffic reports, message boards, yellow pages, related maps, and city guides (courtesy of DigitalCity).

MapBlast	Maps
www.mapblast.com	

This an another excellent mapping site which begins with the quote *"Everyone needs a little direction in life."* The site provides maps by entering an address or telephone for the area. It also generates directions by entering both "From" and "To" addresses. The site also includes travel, business, and real estate centers, and Yellow Pages.

Maps On Us   **Maps**
www.mapsonus.com

This site enables users to create a map of their desired location as well as plan a route. It also includes the Yellow Pages, an Address Book, message boards, and frequently asked questions.

Several other sites also include online maps and related mapping resources:

Expedia:	*www.expediamaps.com*
Excite:	*maps.excite.com*
Maps:	*www.maps.com*
Xerox:	*pubseb.parc.xerox.com/map*
National Geographic:	*www.nationalgeographic.com/ maps/index.html*
CIA:	*www.odci.gov/cia/publications/ factbook/ref.html*
University of Texas:	*www.lib.utexas.edu/Libs/PCL/Map_ collection/Map_collection.html*
University of Texas:	*www.lib.utexas.edu/Libs/PCL/Map_ collection/world_cities.html*

Route Planners

Freetrip   **North America**
www.freetrip.com

If you want to quickly calculate your distance and driving time, be sure to visit this user-friendly site. Just enter your destination, along with preferences for routes and services, and Freetrip will calculate the total distance and driving time, identify selected facilities (advertisers on site), and a summary of driving directions which includes both accumulated and remaining miles and times. This site also includes travel tips, frequently asked questions, and information on leisure, business, family, RV travel, getaways, trucking, and special deals.

Yahoo Maps	North America
www.maps.yahoo.com	

Covering the geography of both Canada and the United States, this easy to use site generates driving directions, along with a routing map and destination map, once you enter your starting address and destination address. A personalization section allows you to store directions for your favorite destinations. An excellent uncluttered site that focuses on its main mission – dispensing directions with maps.

Expedia Maps	North America/Europe
www.expediamaps.com/DrivingDirections.asp	

This useful site generates maps for many locations in North America and Europe and includes a helpful route planner. Once you locate a map, the site also includes additional information on the destination, such as flights, hotels, and car rentals which are part of Expedia's extensive commercial database, as well as provides driving directions. You can print out the map, save it to your "My Maps & Routes" file and/or email it to someone else.

CW Lease Routeplanner	Europe
www.cwlease.com/cwlint/selection.html	

If you're planning to drive in Europe, be sure to check out this useful site. It calculates distance, fuel consumption in both kilometers and miles, and fuel costs.

Other useful route planners for Europe include:

Easy Tour: *easytour.dr-staedtler.de/*
                          routenplanung_engl.asp
Reiseroute.de: *www.reiseroute.de/route_uk.htm*
Mappy.com: *www.iti.fr*

Luggage and Packing

Selecting luggage and packing are two "essentials" all travelers face. They also are the two activities that often get left to the last minute and result in doing "too much" or "too little". Here are a couple of useful sites that can assist you in making those all important luggage and packing decisions:

Compleat Carry-On Traveler   **Luggage/Packing**
www.oratory.com/travel

This site provides a wealth of practical information and advice on the art of living out of one carry-on bag! Operated by packing guru Doug Dyment, it addresses one of the biggest mistakes travelers make – overpacking. Focusing on traveling light, the site includes separate sections on what to take, how to pack, resources, travel library, and travel links. It includes good advice on how to minimize wrinkled clothes that make you look like you're living out of a suitcase. Especially great tips for budget travelers and those who don't plan to do much shopping while traveling – just a change of clothes, please!

SkyGuide   **Luggage/Packing**
www.sky-guide.com/html/travelresources/index.html

This comprehensive travel site by American Express includes under its "General Travel Tips" section articles on selecting the appropriate luggage to travel with (hard versus soft-sided, leather, fabrics, handles, wheels) and savvy packing tips, such as bundling and interweaving techniques.

Money Matters and ATMs

Money concerns go far beyond figuring out local exchange ranges through such currency conversion sites as *www.oanda.com* and *www.xe.net/ucc*. For many travelers, some of the most important money matters deal with finding an ATM when traveling (over 600,000 available worldwide) or acquiring traveler's checks and using credit cards. Here are some sites that assist travelers with such money matters:

MasterCard	ATMs
www.mastercard.com/atm/	

This ATM finder site includes two search engines for finding ATMs closest to you. If you're looking for an ATM in North America, just put in an address (must include street, city, and state/province) and hit the "Find ATMs" button to get results. If you are traveling outside this area, go to the Worldwide ATM Locator section and select a country. You also can select countries by region.

VISA	ATMs
www.visa.com/pd/atms	

This is one of the best sites for locating more than 627,000 ATMs in 120 countries. Just select a region of the world and then go to a specific country where you can view ATM locations near a specific address. The site also includes safety tips in using ATMs, procedures for reporting a lost Visa card, contact phone numbers for acquiring traveler's checks abroad, safety tips, location of airport ATMs, and tips on traveling abroad. And, of course, the site allows you to apply for a Visa card.

Passports (U.S.)

If you need to get a U.S. passport or are concerned about your passport expiring within the next six months, visit this site for all the information you need to take care of your passport needs:

Department of State   **Passports (U.S.)**
http://travel.state.gov/passport_services.html

There's much more to this site than what initially meets the eye. This relatively unadorned site is jam-packed with useful information about U.S. passports and the 4,500 passport acceptance facilities nationwide (probate courts, post offices, libraries, county and municipal offices). It summarizes several passport services: where to apply, passport agencies, fees, applications, processing time, National Passport Information Center, and frequently asked questions. The site also explains how to apply in person, apply for passport renewal, replace a lost or stolen passport, get a passport quickly, add extra pages, change your name in your passport, and obtain copies of passport records. The site includes other useful travel information: top 10 tips for travelers, visa and foreign entry requirements, where to get a copy of your birth certificate, press releases, and links to many related offices and services. A rich site for answering most of your passport questions and linking to the whole international complex within the federal government, including travel warnings, diplomatic posts worldwide, U.S. Customs Search, foreign embassies in the U.S., the Centers for Disease Control and Prevention, and much much more.

Restaurants, Dining, and Food

Let's face it, you've got to eat when you travel. But it's about more than just eating. Food and dining can be one of the great pleasures of travel, especially when visiting the United States, Mexico, Brazil, France, Italy, Morocco, Turkey, Thailand, Singapore, Hong Kong, and even Australia! While finding food is usually no problem, finding a really good to outstanding restaurant in an unfamiliar place can be a challenge – but not if you use the right resources and network with the right people, such as a seasoned hotel concierge at a top hotel. At the same time, many travelers have special dining needs, especially Jewish travelers seeking kosher foods and vegetarians looking for good vegetarian restaurants.

The good news is that many websites now focus on identifying the best restaurants throughout the world as well as focus on special dining needs. Some sites, such as *Fodors.com*, are closely tied to a popular travel guidebook series noted for its reliable restaurant recommendations. Other popular sites, such as *Citysearch.com, Digitalcity.com, Worldroom.com*, and *Washingtonpost.com*, include restaurants as one channel in a larger community, city, or regional destination site. Travelers to Southeast Asia, for example, can go into the *Worldroom. com* site to locate the latest in restaurant recommendations, conducted by local journalists and food critics, in the major cities they are visiting. However, the restaurant recommendations on many websites are often suspect because the content providers are known to cannibalize each other – few do original research by actually visiting the restaurants and sampling the cuisine. Indeed, Fodor's and other travel guidebooks, which occasionally do major updates (no series does a 100% update) are frequently used as the basis for restaurant recommendations and summaries, even though their restaurant data is often dated and inaccurate. The truth of the matter is that it is extremely difficult to stay current and accurate on the restaurant scene. After all, the restaurant business is one of the most volatile businesses affecting travelers. The restaurant that was popular last year may be closed this year or its award-winning chef was recently hired by the competition or started his

> *The restaurant recommendations on many websites are often suspect since the content providers are known to cannibalize each other – few do original research by actually visiting the restaurants and sampling the cuisine.*

or her own restaurant. In the end, the best source for accurate restaurant information is usually a local food critic or a well informed concierge at one of the top hotels – he usually knows the current "in" spots, those places his top guests come back from with rave reviews. In fact, if you have ever used the concierges at the Regent and Four Seasons Hotels, as well as at the Ritz-Carlton Hotels, you know you are dealing with experts; they know their guests and usually recommend the best of the best in the dining department. Guests at other hotels may not be as fortunate since at some establishments people behind the concierge sign function as bellboys and troubleshooters rather than dedicated information and service experts.

Assuming you don't have the immediate services of a Regent concierge and you know many restaurant recommendations on community websites are dated, inaccurate, and quirky, you might want to visit the following sites that specialize on restaurants and compare and contrast their reviews and recommendations:

Restaurant Row	**Restaurant**
www.restaurantrow.com	

This is one of the best restaurant sites that really uses the capabilities of the Internet to both identify the top restaurants and allow users to make reservations online. The site includes a database of more than 110,000 restaurants in 7,000 cities worldwide. You can search by restaurant name, city, or zip code. In the case of many restaurants (but not all), you can view a menu, see photos, view a map, get directions, read reviews, and email a friend. It includes a "10 Best" feature for each city as well as a "Top Table" instant reservations feature. The site continues to add new features such as sections dealing with food, wine, and dining out. A recent exclusive article appeared on this site entitled "The Truth About Wine" authored by Julian Niccolini, co-owner of the famous Four Seasons Restaurant in New York City. Keep your eye on this site. It could become your favorite online research tool for dining, especially in the U.S. Its global coverage remains limited for now, but this should expand soon.

Zagat	**Restaurants**
www.zagat.com	

Bookmark this one! For travelers in the United States, this website is a welcomed addition to online restaurant recommendations. The publishers of the popular and reliable Zagat restaurant guides now include restaurant reviews on more than 20,000 restaurants, bistros, cafes, coffeehouses, diners, hotels, and takeout joints in the United States, Toronto, Vancouver, London, Paris, and Tokyo. Each review comes with ratings and average costs. Just click onto the menu of states and cities and search for restaurants by name or browse reviews by neighborhood, by cuisine, or alphabetically. The site also lists the most popular places to meet and eat in each city.

CuisineNet   Adventure
www.cuisinenet.com

This site taps into a large database of restaurants for 11 major metropolitan areas in the United States. Just select a city and search by restaurant name, location, type of cuisine, and desired price range and amenities. Many of the restaurants are rated according to food, service, ambience, and overall. The site also identifies the most popular restaurants in each city; summarizes the top picks for several categories of restaurants (cozy, late night, brunch, vegetarian, soup, healthy, Jewish/ kosher); offers tips on dining etiquette; and operates an online gourmet market and club. While Zagat has a reputation for reliability because of its highly respected annual publications, it's unclear who operates this site or how restaurants get selected and rated. Some strange recommendations appear for our area, Washington, DC, in the case of Italian restaurants, but the site is fairly accurate in the case of Thai restaurants.

Fodor's   Restaurants
www.fodors.com

This is one of the few sites that includes recommended restaurants for various countries and cities around the world. Indeed, most guidebook series, such as Lonely Planet, do not recommend restaurants on their websites. The Fodor recommendations also appear in the offline guidebooks and are generally reliable which is why this site is worth visiting. If you are planning to travel to a country for which there is a Fodor's travel guidebook, check the restaurant section of this website for current recommendations. Not all country guidebooks are represented on the site. For example, Fodor's publishes a guidebook on Morocco, but the site at present does not include hotel and restaurant information found in the guidebook on Casablanca, Fez, or Marrakesh. The search engine is easy to use. You can search restaurants by either name, criteria (price, cuisine, or location) and destination. The best restaurants are highlighted with a red asterisk.

Frommer's   **Restaurants**
www.frommers.com

If you go deep into the destination section of this rich site, you'll find restaurant recommendations for numerous cities worldwide. Includes many of the best restaurants for each destination.

A few other sites also yield information on various types of restaurants. Several of these sites include restaurants in many countries and cities and enable users to review menus and make reservations online:

Dine (North America):	*www.dine.com*
Epicurious:	*http://food.epicurious.com*
Epinions (U.S.):	*www.epinions.com*
Food and Wine:	*www.foodandwine.com*
Foodline:	*www.foodline.com*
Gayot:	*www.gayot.com*
Jewish/Kosher (Global):	*http://shamash.org/kosher*
	www.jewishtravel.com
	www.kosherdine.com
Menus On Line (U.S.):	*www.menusonline.com*
Opentable:	*www.opentable.com*
Sushi (Global):	*www.sushi.infogate.de*
Vegetarian (Global):	*www.veg.org/veg/Guide*
	www.vegdining.com

Safety

Safety in the air, on a cruise ship, or on the ground remains an important travel issue today. While terrorism, assaults, and robberies aimed at travelers are not frequent occurrences in most countries, nonetheless, they do happen. Consequently, it is incumbent upon the traveler to take care of his or her safety by being prepared. The following government site can assist with such preparation:

Travel Warnings   **Security**
http://travel.state.gov/travel_warnings.html

If you're concerned about the safety situation in any particular country, be sure to visit this site. This is the U.S. Department of State's official travel warning site. It includes current travel warnings as well as a database of countries, listed alphabetically, which includes information on the safety and security situation for travelers. For example, on September 1, 2000, the U.S. State Department issued a travel warning for Philippines – avoid all travel to the southern and western areas of the Island of Mindanao because of increased incidents of terrorism and violence aimed at tourists. The site also includes information on road conditions overseas and offers an email service for receiving the latest travel safety announcements.

Shipping

While many travelers may pack lightly, they also enjoy discovering new things which often don't fit into their suitcase(s), such as a lovely framed painting or a large piece of furniture. Indeed, some travelers pack according to the single-bag advice of *www.oratory.com/travel* and then they discover they either need to buy more bags or arrange to have their loot shipped home by air or sea. Not surprisingly, many travelers may be reluctant to buy large items they cannot hand-carry home; some decide to leave lovely treasures behind because they don't know how to handle shipping. Although it can be expensive if you air freight heavy items, shipping is relatively easy to arrange; it also can be relatively inexpensive, especially if you have a large sea shipment. Whatever the case, to do it right, you need to know whom to talk to or call about shipping your goods. While many shops will arrange for shipping, and you can use them to consolidate other purchases, you may want to find your own shipper through the recommendations of your hotel concierge or business center. You also can go online to find shippers, especially international air services such as UPS, FedEx, Emery, and DHL. The following site includes links to the major international air shippers:

www.businesstravel.com/reference.asp

In many countries these shippers have offices in the capital city. You can find information on their services and locations by going directly to these websites:

Air Express International:	*www.aeilogistics.com*
Airborne Express:	*www.airborne-express.com*
BAX Global:	*www.baxworld.com*
DHL Worldwide Express:	*www.dhl.com*
Emery Worldwide:	*www.emeryworld.com*
Federal Express:	*www.fedex.com*
TNT Worldwide Express:	*www.tnt.com*
United Parcel Service:	*www.ups.com*

For information on reliable sea freight shippers, you'll need an offline approach. We recommend contacting your hotel concierge or business center, asking for recommendations from top shops, and/or contacting expatriates who know reliable shippers who regularly work with embassies and the expatriate community.

Time Changes and Zones

Many travelers need to know the differences in times as they plan their itineraries, especially if they need to make long distance phone calls. While many travel sites include this element as part of their "Travel Tool Kit", you can go directly to sites that primarily focus on time differences. Some of these sites operate like currency converters – they convert your present time to the destination time as well as show the differences in world time zones. Other sites summarize time differences for each country and provide telephone information, such as area codes, for each country:

Time Zone:	*www.timezoneconverter.com*
World Time Server:	*www.worldtimeserver.com*
White Pages:	*www.whitepages.com.au/time.shtml*

Tipping Practices

Tipping is an important concern amongst travelers who are used to tipping service providers but not sure what to do in different situations and cultures. What is the local custom on tipping? Who expects to receive a tip? How much should I tip? Answers to these and many other questions concerning tipping are nicely compiled in these sites:

Tipping   **Tipping**
www.tipping.org

If you ever had questions about tipping, this site will probably provide the answers. It includes a useful Excel Spreadsheet that summarizes appropriate tipping behavior, complete with re-commended percentages and amounts, for a variety of service providers: airport sky caps, barbers, beauty shop workers, wait-ers/waitresses, casino workers (dealers, drink waiter/ waitress, slot machine changers), cruise ship personnel, deliveries (pizza, furniture, floral), disc jockeys, hotel personnel, parking atten-dant, restaurant personnel, taxi driver, and train personnel. The site also includes discussion groups and links to sites such as TipRate Calculator, TableManners (by CuisineNet), world tipping behavior, novel tipping cards, tip jars for websites, and creative tipping approaches.

Talesmag   **Tipping**
www.talesmag.com/links/traveler.html#Tipping

This section of the Talesmag site provides a quick overview of tipping practices and advice for tipping abroad and on cruises as well as tips and rates in the U.S., Middle East, Africa, North America, South America, Asia, Australia, and Europe. Also includes an interesting article on the history of tipping. For example, you'll learn that a Cornell University student found that servers who initially introduced themselves by name to dinners received a 53% higher tip than those that did not; waiters who squat next to your table, and thus improve eye contact, usually increase their tips by 18%; and those friendly female waitresses who draw friendly faces on the back of your check receive a 18% higher tip (male waiters actually end up getting a 3% decrease in tips for engaging in such behavior!). And waiters and waitresses who casually touch you receive a 42% increase in tips. Whoever said tipping was strictly a mathematical calculation to fulfill cultural obligations!

Tourist Offices and Convention Bureaus

One of the best sources for travel information are the tourist bureaus of each country. While many of these organizations have a reputation for primarily mailing out brochures and maps and answering questions about travel to their destinations, with the advent of the Internet, many of the organizations now provide a wonderful array of information and services, from information about visa requirements, articles about various aspects of their country, and frequently asked questions to message boards, newsletters, restaurant and hotel reviews, and linkages to a host of organizations (travel agents, tour groups, government agencies, hotels, restaurants, and shops).

> *One of the best sources for travel information are tourist bureaus. Many offer a wonderful array of on-line resources, from articles and message boards to linkages to key local resources.*

However, the extent to which each country uses the Internet to publicize its travel attractions varies dramatically from one country to another. Some countries still do not have websites for promoting tourism. On the other hand, two of the best government tourist organizations in the world are the Hong Kong Tourist Association (*www.hkta.com*) and the Singapore Tourist Board (*www.newasia-singapore.com*). If you compare these two sites with those of most other countries, you'll see this difference between well organized tourist bureaus versus ones that are struggling to get a presence online. Some tourist bureaus, such as the Australia Tourist Commission (*www.australia.com*), have a strong commercial orientation. Other tourist bureaus, such as the one sponsored by the Egypt Tourist Authority (*www.touregypt.net*), are more oriented toward presenting informative articles, providing linkages, profiling communities, and promoting distinct travel communities. Regardless of their orientations, most websites of tourist bureaus are good gateway sites into their country's history, culture, economy, news, and travel. For your future reference, we include the URLs for most tourist bureaus in the chapter on great destinations, Chapter 13.

The following sites will give you quick access to the tourist bureaus in the United States and many other countries:

USA City Link	**United States**
www.usacitylink.com	

Wow! This site claims to be the Internet's most comprehensive listing of U.S. states and cities with information on travel, tourism, and relocation, which is probably true. As such, use it as a gateway to wherever you want to go in the United States. If, for example, you are interested in traveling to Florida, just click onto Florida and you'll get a page with relocation services, discounted online reservations (air, hotel, car), and links to state tourism sites, major city websites, and city information. It even links to a site on The Everglades and Ten Thousand Islands (*www.florida-everglades.com*).

Tourism Offices Worldwide Directory	**Global**
www.towd.com	

This is the best of the online directories to state tourism offices in the U.S. and national tourism offices throughout the world. Just use the pull-down menus to find your U.S. state or country and the search engine instantly displays essential contact information: name, address, phone and fax number, website URL, and email address. Both the website URL and email address are hot-linked to the offices so you can conveniently contact them. The information on this site is much more complete than other sites dealing with national tourist offices.

Tvlon.com   Global
www.tvlon.com/International.html

This well designed site is literally in your face – countries are listed on the front page in alphabetical order. Once you click onto your selected country, the site gives you the address, phone, and fax number as well as the URL and email address whenever available. However, this list is incomplete since many countries, such as India have had well developed websites for a few years (*www.tourindia.com* and *www.tourism india.com*). In other words, the fact that a URL does not appear for the tourist office does not necessarily mean it does not have a website. Most likely this site remains incomplete or has not been updated. For your convenience, all URLs appearing in the database are hot-linked to the tourist office's website. If you prefer visiting tourist offices or bureaus online before contacting them by other means, this is the site for you!

Convention Bureaus   Global
www.conventionbureaus.com

This one-stop gateway site, which is especially useful to event planners, identifies convention and visitors bureaus throughout the world. It includes separate channels on North America, South America, Europe, and Asia. Just click onto a region and then a country and city and you'll get a list of relevant organizations. The site also includes linkages to various related organizations, such as industry associations, event planning websites, *ExpoWorld.net, MajorExhibitHalls.com,* and *Find SpeakersandBureaus. com.*

Arm Chair   Global
www.armchair.com/bureau/inttb.html

Here's a quick way to find international tourist offices and bureaus. Just click onto the letter of a country and you'll get a list of tourism offices and bureaus with addresses, phone, and fax numbers. Unfortunately, the site does not include URLs or emails which are more important to many of today's wired travelers who prefer not to phone, fax, or mail.

Travel Facts and Information

If you're looking for basic travel facts on international destinations, try these websites. The first is brought to you courtesy of the U.S. Central Intelligence Agency (CIA) which is very knowledgeable about every country in the world and which has been in the travel business ever since it was transformed from the OSS (Office of Strategic Services) into the CIA in 1947!

CIA World Factbook   **Travel Facts**
www.odci.gov/cia/publications/factbook/index.html

What better place to get your travel facts and information than from the CIA? After all, the 25,000+ employees of this agency are seasoned travelers – be it on the road or via satellite and cyberspace – and for decades they have traveled to some of the most interesting and dangerous places on earth. They also have a tremendous database of information on destinations. Since 1971 the CIA has published an unclassified version of *The World Factbook* in print form; in 1975 the book first became available to the public through the U.S. Government Printing Office. Representing one of three types of finished intelligence (basic versus current and estimative), this country directory examines the background of each country, with lots of useful information on the history, geography, government, economics, communications, transportation, military, and major transnational issues. Within the past few years the CIA has made the print version of this book available online through this site. If you want some background information on a country, including maps (in both JPEG and PDF formats), you might want to start with this informative site. Ironically, some country sites refer to the CIA handbook for background information on their country!

Web Travel News   **Travel Facts**
www.webtravelnews.com
www.phocuswright.com

While this site (actually two related sites) is of most interest to travel professionals who track changes in web-based travel developments, it also includes information of interest to many travelers. Recently acquired by *Phocus Wright.com*, an association of online travel professionals, this site is loaded with interesting travel information. For example, it recently included news on *Inflightonline.com* which is now offering a high-flying Internet service – on flights at 30,000 feet – which represents the new marriage between wireless and travel.

The major sources for travel facts and information, with an emphasis on specific country and city destinations, will be the many travel guidebooks, magazines, and newsletters identified in Chapter 9.

Travel Gear

When it comes to packing those bags, make sure you're taking everything you need for the trip. If you're into adventure travel, you may need to take special equipment. Take, for example, a safari. You should include a hat, rainwear, sweaters, long-sleeve shirts, and shorts. International travelers need to consider packing an electrical adaptor, hairdryer, language translator, security devices, money belt, organizers, and special luggage accessories and straps. While some of these items may be difficult to find in your local shopping mall, they are readily available over the Internet. Consider visiting these two websites for all your travel gear, from luggage to first aid kits:

Magellans   **Travel Gear**
www.magellans.com

This is a wonderful one-stop shop for all of your travel gear. It includes luggage, electronic appliances, safety devices, trip planners, clothing, packing aids, binoculars, toiletries, insect protection, water bottles and purifiers, and gifts for travelers. But it's more than just an online catalog. It includes many useful travel tips on packing, carry-on limits, business travel electricity, jet lag, malaria, modems, water purification, and women's issues. Its country directory section is especially informative for deciding on travel gear. For example, if you're planning a trip to Cuba, click onto the "Travel Guides" section and again on "Country by Country Database" for "Cuba". Here you'll learn about health risks, water quality, security concerns, weather, electronic standards, and modem/phone use in Cuba. You are well advised to pack UltraThon repellent because of the presence of Dengue Fever and a security wallet because of potential pick-pockets. Cuba also uses three-prong grounded electrical plugs as well as rounded two-prong ungrounded electrical plugs (includes photos on site).

TravelSmith	Travel Gear
www.travelsmith.com	

This popular direct-mail catalog house is well known for its innovative quality travel gear, especially clothes, footwear, luggage, and accessories for men and women. Includes recommended packing lists for different types of travel adventures – business travel, cruises, hiking and trekking, water travel, rafting and whitewater, safaris, Northern Europe, Mediterranean, and tropics. Includes an extensive alphabetical listing of recommended tour companies in a section entitled "The Best Travel Companies Directory" (Unique Journeys). Its Travel Center also includes free on-line mini guides from Fodor's, tourism offices, travel insurance, passport and health information, U.S. Customs and duties regulations, five-day forecasts, packing lists, weather, currency rates, and a U.S. Embassy directory.

Several other websites also offer a good selection of travel gear, with special emphasis on adventure, outdoor, or active travel, as well as include numerous travel and packing tips. These online stores are well worth visiting:

Patagonia:	*www.patagonia.com*
Eaglecreek:	*www.eaglecreek.com*
World Travel:	*www.worldtravel.com*
Travel Supplies:	*www.travelsupplies.com*
Warrior:	*www.warrior.com*
Le Travel Store:	*www.letravelstore.com*
Road Warrior Gear:	*www.roadwarriorgear.com*
Things4Travel:	*www.things4travel.com*
Road Trip Store:	*www.roadtripstore.com*
REI:	*www.rei.com*
Altrec:	*www.altrec.com*
MountainWoman:	*www.mountainwoman.com*
Mountainzone:	*www.gearzone.com*
PlanetOutdoors:	*www.planetoutdoors.com*

Travel Tips, Advice, and Experts

Most major travel sites include a section variously called "Travel Tips", "Tips and Advice", or "Experts". Behind each of these sections is usually a list of several 1-2 page articles on everything from shopping for airline tickets and packing to renting a car and reporting lost luggage. Many sites also have a "FAQ" section that performs a similar function – dispenses travel advice in a Q&A format.

While you will find thousands of travel tips in the advice, experts, and FAQ sections of the many sites outlined in this book, the following two sites take travel tips and expert advice to a new level:

FreeTravelTips   **Tips**
www.freetraveltips.com

This is a very straight forward site – includes hundreds of useful tips on a variety of important travel subjects: before you go, packing, airlines, rental cars, hotels, cruise lines, foreign travel, kids traveling, theme parks, restaurants, research, and road trips. The site also includes a "to go" checklist, travel tools, and a travel store. Answers numerous questions you might have about travel.

All Experts   **Tips and Advice**
www.allexperts.com/travel

This is a wonderful site for communicating directly with professional and amateur travel experts who are referred to as "Intrepid Travelers". If you have a question concerning a particular destination or travel issue, just click to the appropriate section, review the bios and evaluations of the various expects, and ask your question. For example, Marcia Selva who operates one of the leading specialty travel agencies on Vietnam, Cambodia, Laos, Thailand, and Burma (Global Spectrum in Falls Church, Virginia) serves as a community resource on her countries of expertise. Just ask her a question and she'll quickly reply. This is a free service that should result in useful information. A special feature involves evaluations of the experts on the basis of knowledge, timeliness of response, clarity of response, politeness, general prestige, and number of questions asked. In fact, you can select an expert based upon the scores they receive on these criteria. The site includes an inventory of previously asked questions, a message board, and information on how you can volunteer to become an online expert with this site. And if you can't find an answer to your question, the site recommends going to their partner site, About.com (*http://searchabout.com/full search.htm?=travel*).

---

12 Degrees   **Experts**
www.12degrees.com

This novel site introduces a new approach to travel planning for independent travelers – customize an overseas vacation with the assistance of leading travel guidebook writers and destination specialists. Consisting of a cadre of 30+ guidebook writers organized by destination, you can click on to their bios and consider whether or not you want to work with them. By "work" we mean contracting them for their services (primarily arranging a customized itinerary) on an hourly rate. For example, if you are interested in visiting Thailand, your expert will be bestselling travel writer Joe Cummings, one of Lonely

Planet's first writers, who has written more then 35 guidebooks, phrase books, maps, atlases, and photographic books on Thailand and other Asian destinations. You would contact Joe to custom-design a trip to Thailand for you. Local travel specialists (called Destination Specialists) who are linked with 12Degrees will, in turn, make all travel arrangements. The site includes a list of trip ideas, with sample itineraries, to help inspire and motivate the traveler in the process of planning a customized trip. If you decide to consult directly with an author/expert, the typical charge is $75-$100 per hour, with most consultations lasting 1-3 hours. You'll receive a quote from the author/expert, who estimates how long it will take to complete the consultation, before the consultation actually begins and before you prepay with a credit card. The author/expert then completes a detailed itinerary for your review and approval. Once finished, a 12degrees travel coordinator will call you to confirm the itinerary and assign a 12degrees destination specialist to book your itinerary. The site claims it's cheaper to book through them (they arrange special discounts) than to go elsewhere to arrange your trip. If you are an independent traveler, you may want to first check out this site's "Trip Ideas" section (*www.12degrees.com/region/world. thtml*) for ideas, inspiration, and motivation. After all, they are developed by individuals who have a passion for travel!

Weather Please

Travel and weather seem to go hand in hand. Whether you want to determine the best times to travel or just check a local weather forecast, several websites can assist you. These two interactive sites generate a wealth of weather information for travelers:

Weather.com   **Weather**
www.weather.com

Wow! You never thought the weather could be such an involved subject. This is the premier online weather site which is operated by cable TV's Weather Channel – probably the only one you really need to visit. One of the most popular websites on the Internet, which gets more than 40 million hits a month, it's a favorite resource of Internet users. Its slick interactive feature allows users to access five-day weather forecasts around the world. Just enter your city and click to get the latest in weather information. The site also is jam-packed with other weather-related information including weather maps, headline weather news, tropical updates, storm watch, travel-related weather, and bulletin boards, chat groups, and audio and video weather forecasts. Travelers find the flight arrival section useful – just enter the flight departure and arrival times and click for information on the flight which also comes with weather information on the destination. Users also can customize weather information they wish to receive from this site.

CNN	Weather
www.cnn.com/WEATHER/	

As you might expect from CNN, this site is both slick and thorough when it comes to the subject of weather. Use the search engine to generate a five-day forecast for your desired destination in the U.S. and abroad. The site also includes many informative articles, weather maps, a storm center, allergy reports, and a business traveler's advisory. Includes linkages to weather emergency sites, such as Disaster Relief (*www.disaster relief.org*) and NOAA Weather Radio (*www.nws.noaa.gov/ noaa radio.shtml*).

Other useful weather sites, many with interactive elements and linkages, include the following:

Intellicast:	*www.intellicast.com*
USA Today:	*www.usatoday.com/weather*
Weather Images:	*www.weatherimages.com*
World Climate:	*www.worldclimate.com*
Weathersite:	*www.weathersite.com*
Yahoo:	*www.weather.yahoo.com*
Severe Storms:	*www.nssl.noaa.gov*
WMO:	*www.wmo.ch*

In a hurry?
text express

search

destinations

theme guides

ADVENTURE. AWARENESS. AMOEBIC DYSENTERY.

what's on your planet this week
15-17 September, <u>Inkslinger's Ball</u>, Hollywood, California
Where the gurus of tattoo needle you

<u>Destination Monaco</u>

With its glamorous lifestyle and tax-free income, Monaco is the playground of Europe's elite. Get cleaned out by lady luck at the casino one day and put on the Grimaldi's guest list the next.

8

Travel Guidebooks
and Bookstores

ANY TRAVELERS LITERALLY PLAN AND LIVE BY
the book – they seek out the best travel guides on destinations to formulate dreams, acquire insights and tips, and plan detailed itineraries. Americans in particular, whether traveling independently or as a group, are famous for carrying their favorite travel guide(s), and they often religiously follow guidebook recommendations – a kind of personal travel advisor or best friend for sleuthing the local travel scene. They also identify their class of travel – you are what you read – by the guidebooks they carry: Lonely Planet, Frommer's, Fodor's, Moon, Rough, Let's Go, Insight, Knopf, Eyewitness, Footprint, Michelin, or Impact. Budget travelers and backpackers debate the merits of planning their trip with a Lonely Planet, Moon, Rough Guide, or Let's Go guidebook. Higher-end travelers prefer Fodor's, Michelin, and Impact. And somewhere in between, travelers debate the merits of the flashy picture guidebooks, such as Insight, Knopf, and Eyewitness, or the detailed Frommer's and Footprint Handbooks.

We tend to be Fodor's and Frommer's travelers who often throw in a Lonely Planet or Moon guidebook for good luck in dealing with the details of history, culture, and sightseeing. We rely on the former guidebooks for uncovering the best hotels and restaurants. We use the later guidebooks for unique insights on the local travel culture, including many how-to tips on navigating from one location to another, or if we want historical and cultural details.

Choices, Choices, and More Choices

Travel bookstores and many superstores (Barnes and Noble, Borders, and Books-a-Million) with large travel sections and cafes have become favorite hangouts for inveterate travelers. Indeed, visit popular specialty travel bookstores in San Francisco, Chicago, New York City, and Washington, DC and you'll often see the aisles crowded during lunch time, in the evenings, and on weekends with travel wannabees, and those struck with wanderlust, in search of the perfect guidebooks for planning their next trip. Some people hang around these stores for hours, flipping through the richly illustrated picture guidebooks in the hopes of stimulating new travel interests or narrowing down their travel choices – dreaming where next to explore the world. Many simply become overwhelmed with the many guidebook choices for each destination. With a wall of over 100 guidebooks on France and another 50 guidebooks on Paris to choose from, what is one to do? Which guidebooks yield the best travel information and would be the perfect "fit" for your style of travel? Maybe ask an employee who really knows this business, especially if you are patronizing a specialty travel bookstore where employees supposedly love what they sell. When in doubt, buy several such books in the hopes that you have really covered all of your travel ground!

Online Content Providers

Travel guidebook publishers play one of the most important roles when it comes to travel planning on the Internet. Indeed, they are one of the major sources for much of the travel content that appears on the Internet. Examine most any travel site and you'll quickly discover they are "content poor" as well as redundant – lack original travel content beyond some breaking travel news and general travel tips; many sites acquire their destination content from similar sources.

Since most travelers are primarily destination-oriented (see Chapter 13), they look for information about their favorite destinations: entry requirements, transportation, hotels, restaurants, sightseeing, shopping, history, culture, sports, entertainment, and assorted travel basics (see Chapter 7). Because of this situation, many travel sites turn to travel magazine articles, freelance travel writers, and major travel guidebook publishers, especially Lonely Planet and Frommer's, to acquire travel content for specific destinations. Some content is acquired free of charge (through partnership arrangements or promises of good PR "exposure") while other content is leased by travel publishers (see discussion in Chapter 13). One of the best examples of this syndicated content approach is the popular adventure travel site Away.com. Not surprisingly, many travel writers are disgruntled with the common practice of offering them free "exposure" in exchange for their content. The trend is to either buy or lease travel content directly through travel guidebook publishers or through syndicated services such as our own *www.contentfortravel.com* site.

Guidebook Publishers on the Net

The good news for many travelers is that several guidebook publishers include some of their content online, operate useful travel websites, and offer books online. Like many other travel websites, these sites include travel forums, travel tips, newsletters, and excerpts from guidebooks. Some, such as Lonely Planet, become travel lifestyle hangouts for travelers and relevant guidebook users who often exhibit serious cases of wanderlust. And one publisher, Rough Guide, has even gone so far as to put the complete texts of their guidebooks online for free viewing. They claim that doing so has actually increased offline and on-line bookstore sales. So, if you want a free read of any budget travel Rough Guide, including their wonderful Inter-net guide (*Rough Guide to the Internet*, see pages 18 and 156) just go to their colorful site and select your destina-

> *Several guidebook publishers operate useful websites with travel forums, tips, newsletters, and excerpts from their guidebooks. Rough Guide even puts the complete texts of books on-line for free.*

tion: *www.roughguides.com*. Six of the best online travel sites are operated by guidebook publishers and authors: Frommer's, Fodor's, Lonely Planet, Rough Guide, Insiders' Guides, and Rick Steves. Frommer's and Rick Steves brand their sites, as well as their travel series, around the author's names. Several of the following websites function as gateway content sites for dozens of "content poor" travel sites:

Frommer's   Guidebooks
www.frommers.com

You've come to the source for a great deal of useful travel content on over 100 major worldwide destinations. This very popular site (usually ranks at the top of travel sites), which is also very bright and cluttered, is designed to promote budget travel guru Arthur Frommer as well as his popular magazine (*Arthur Frommer's Budget Travel*) and guidebook series as well as budget travel in general, an approach to travel that was pioneered by Arthur Frommer more than 40 years ago but taken to new lows and highs by other travel publishers. The destination section (a small "Destinations from Frommer's Travel Guides" search box on the upper left) of this site is jam-packed with useful travel information ranging from planning a trip, accommodations, and dining to attractions, nightlife, shopping, side trips, and walking tours. This content comes from the regularly revised Frommer's guidebooks. It's also this content that is syndicated to many other travel websites. This site has many nice interactive features normally not included on other sites. For example, if you are searching for a restaurant in a particular city, you can do so based upon the following selection criteria: price, neighborhood, and type of cuisine. This is a great site to use for both pre-trip planning and on the road. Also check out this site's many other valuable features and resources – daily newsletter, advice, vacation ideas, tips and resources, budget magazine, message boards, travel store, specials, booking services, and Arthur's "Tip of the Day" and his "Soap Box".

Fodor's   Guidebooks
www.fodors.com

Fodor's travel guidebooks have long been noted for their reliable listings of top quality accommodations and restaurants. This sleak and clean looking site (not the typical jumble of bars, buttons, photos, and flashing elements) continues that tradition along with adding additional value not found in the guidebooks, such as open and hosted forums. The two main features on this site are the search engines for locating Fodor's many annotated restaurants and accommodations. The site allows you to search by name, criteria (price, cuisine, location), and destinations. For example, if you're going to Bangkok, just click onto Asia and go directly to Bangkok where you will get a listing of numerous recommended restaurants. The "best of the best" Fodor recommendations are indicated with a red asterisk. Other interesting sections on this site include news and features, forums, top stories, a daily travel poll, online reservation system, and travel tips. The site also allows users to create their own miniguide. For example, if you are only planning to visit three cities on your next trip (say London, Paris, and Rome) and only want information on dining (usually good to excellent) and shopping (usually very limited), you can clip and paste relevant sections from Fodor's three country volumes to create your own customized miniguide. If you're traveling abroad to any of Fodor's destinations, this site is well worth visiting both before and while you are traveling.

Lonely Planet	Guidebooks
www.lonelyplanet.com	

This is "budget traveler and backpacker central" with a decided emphasis on young world travelers who have traveled to just about every conceivable place on earth. Many have been hopelessly stricken with wanderlust and are constantly feeding Lonely Planet with insightful travel tips and updates on destinations. In fact, the Lonely Planet guidebooks are the most widely branded travel guidebook series in the world. They have almost risen to a cult status amongst budget travelers and backpackers who sometimes argue over the relative merits of packing a Lonely Planet versus a Moon Handbook (Lonely Planet usually wins out except in the case of Indonesia which still belongs to Moon founder and Indonesia guru writer Bill Dalton). This is a sometimes quirky site with strange labels on sections which should be more obvious and descriptive of content (What, for example, lies behind these sections: The Thorn Tree, The Scoop, eKno, Postcards, Propaganda, and SubWWWay?). Go directly into "Text Express" to find out how to translate such unclear and convoluted buttons. Most of the destination information is very general – good for an overview – but does not include many travel essentials, like accommodations and restaurants. You'll have to buy the guidebook to get such "inside" information and recommendations. Other useful sections include a lively bulletin board, weekly travel news and features, and tips, warnings, and stories by readers. This is a good site to survey what Lonely Planet travelers, who represent many nationalities, are saying about the reality of various destinations, especially the sections on travel tips, warnings, scams, yarns, fables, and anecdotes (go to the "Postcard" section) – information that is often absent in travel guidebooks. The eKno section (*www.ekno.lonely planet.com*) provides low cost integrated communication services (phone, voicemail, email, faxmail, travel documents). Lonely Planet also has launched its CitySync service which enables travelers to download abbreviated versions of their guidebooks on PDAs using either a CD-ROM or an online connection.

Rough Guides   **Guidebooks**
www.roughguides.com

This popular budget travel guide publisher has gone that extra step – put all of their guidebooks online, including a wonderful how-to Internet guide. Thank you, Rough Guides! With lots of patience and possible eye strain, you can read more than 60 country books (incorporates more than 14,000 destinations) free of charge. The site also includes several other useful sections: music, Internet links, news from the road, and travel insurance. Since Rough Guides is the publisher of the popular *Rough Guide to the Internet*, which we recommended on page 18 as a "must have" book for home and on the road, you can access the complete text of this useful guide on this site. It includes all the hotlinks to the thousands of sites found in the book. So why buy the book for $9.95 when you can get it online and in a handy electronic format? Because it's a neat little book to have at your side. Our recommendation: bookmark this section of the Rough Guide site so you can instantly access any of the recommended websites appearing in the book. Just go directly to this section of the site to read, and use, the book:

www.roughguides.com/internet/directory/index.html#tools

If you just want to access the travel section, which is somewhat limited in scope, go directly to this URL:

www.roughguides.com/internet/directory/travel.html

Insiders' Guides   **Guidebooks**
www.insiders.com

The Insiders' Guides represent some of the best guidebooks on over 60 destinations in the United States and Bermuda. They are very well written and insightful. This is a simple, no-nonsense combination destination-bookstore site – delivers lots of useful content about particular destinations and then offers the relevant book for sale. Just click onto the site map and select your desired location. The result will be a wealth of information on each city or area – history, transportation, accommodations, bed and breakfasts, restaurants, nightlife, shopping, attractions, day trips, parks and recreation, and real estate (for those interested in relocation). You also can purchase the book online through its sister company, Falcon Books. Since the owners of both companies, Landmark Communications, recently sold these publishing firms to the third largest travel publishing house in the United States, Globe Pequot Press, we may be seeing some changes in both websites in the near future or perhaps these well designed sites will improve the Globe Pequot Press (*www.globe-pequot.com*) travel site. But for now, the Insiders' site is one of the best travel guidebook sites for providing content on major destinations in the United States and Bermuda.

Rick Steves   **Guidebooks**
www.ricksteves.com

While Rick Steves is no Arthur Frommer, nonetheless, he has a similar knack for self-promotion. Indeed, travel branding around a single travel expert has reached new heights with this highly personalized travel site that also delivers lots of useful content. Unlike other travel guidebook websites, this one is designed by the author of the Rick Steves' guidebook series (now published by Avalon) and videos on Europe. It primarily promotes Rick Steves (*Europe Through the Back Door* as well as over 10 other destination and language guidebooks) as a travel expert as well as his budget travel publications, videos, and tour services on Europe. While singing the praises of independent budget travel, this site is not a Lonely Planet do-your-own-thing-avoid-the-tours-and-tourists travel site. Indeed, the site heavily promotes several group budget tours led by Rick Steves and his associates, which is one of the central business models underlying this site. The Rick Steves travel emphasis and style tends to be budget transportation, accommodations, and restaurants with a great deal of travel time devoted to learning about local history, culture, and language as well as sightseeing in museums, taking walks, and visiting historic buildings. The site does not include much on restaurants, hotels, and entertainment. However, it does provide a wealth of information for independent travelers on several European destinations. It includes many travel tips, travel links, frequently asked questions, message board, travel store, a free rail guide and newsletter, and a list of upcoming Rick Steves' tours to Europe.

Several other travel publishers operate their own websites. While many of them, such as Falcon, Footprint, Hunter, and Globe Pequot are primarily online catalogs and bookstores that only showcase their titles, other sites, like the ones we've just outlined, also include useful travel information and interactive elements. However, if you are looking for lively message boards and discussion groups, focus your attention on the sites we just described. The following travel guidebook publisher sites represent some of the best travel writing available:

Moon Handbooks:	*www.moon.com*
Footprint:	*www.footprint-handbooks.co.uk*
Globe Pequot:	*www.globe-pequot.com*
Columbus Publishing:	*www.wtg-online.com*
Let's Go:	*www.letsgo.com*
Fielding:	*www.fieldingtravel.com*
Insight Guides:	*www.insightguides.com*
Falcon:	*www.falconoutdoors.com*
Lanier Publishing:	*www.travelguides.com*

Impact Guides:	*www.impactpublications.com*
Travelers' Tales:	*www.travelerstales.com*
Hunter Publishing:	*www.hunterpublishing.com*
Michelin:	*www.michelin-travel.com*
Gayot/Gault Millau:	*www.gayot.com*
Ginkgo Press:	*www.ginkgopress.com*
Intrepid Traveler:	*www.intrepidtraveler.com*

Online Bookstores

We're unabashed fans of bookstores, whether they be found online or offline. There's nothing like a really good bricks and mortar bookstore to whet your travel appetite. Indeed, we've done some of our best travel planning in the travel guide aisles of bookstores. And we are not alone. Visit a good bookstore, especially one of the superstores (especially Barnes and Noble or Borders), with an extensive travel section or a travel bookstore, and you'll often (especially on weekends) discover the aisles crowded with "travel planners" in the process of either stimulating their travel interests or putting the final touches to their current travel plans.

Given the rapid changes in the bookstore business, as well as the rise of online bookstores such as Amazon.com, you can easily shop for travel books and maps online. While it's not as much fun nor informative as hanging out in bookstore aisles and experiencing serendipity as you pick up one travel guide after another, online travel bookstores are at least open 24-hours a day and many offer discounts and quick delivery. Like using online booking services (Chapters 10-12), many travelers use online bookstores only after they have decided exactly where they want to go and have already done their travel research.

Most bricks and mortar bookstores also have an Internet presence. The largest online bookstores with an extensive travel section include:

Amazon:	*www.amazon.com*
Barnes and Noble:	*www.bn.com*
Fatbrain:	*www.fatbrain.com*
Borders:	*www.borders.com*

Barnes and Noble and Borders superstores usually have a good basic travel book section and an atmosphere that encourages you to browse their resources. The good news is that many of these bookstores are open until 11pm cach day and have coffee bars and cafes where you can further browse through your alternative guidebooks. These bookstores also have their own websites which include reader reviews of travel guides and recommendations based upon similar travel interests and buying behavior. Their search engines usually generate a comprehensive listing of titles. For example, if you are looking for books on London, Amazon.com generates a list of 11,242 books that either directly or indirectly have something to do with London! Indeed, visiting Amazon. com, BarnesandNoble.com, and Borders.com is like having an electronic version of *Books in Print* for generating information on subjects, titles, and authors and includes book descriptions, reviews, prices, publication dates, and ISBNs.

Several bookstores only specialize in travel books and other related travel resources, such as maps, videos, CD-ROMs, and travel gear (backpacks, compasses, light weight apparel, luggage locks, straps, money belts, personal alarms, and safety devices). While all of the following travel books have an online presence, some of them are major bricks and mortar travel bookstores, such as Rand McNally, Powell's, Book Passage, World Wide Books and Maps, Savvy Traveller, Distant Lands, and The Travel Store. Others, such as the Literate Traveller and Forsyth are primarily direct mail and online travel bookstores. We have not included what we call "travel shell bookstores" – those which function as Amazon.com or Barnes and Noble affiliates. Such Internet bookstores operate as hotlinks to Amazon and Barnes and Noble. In other words, when you see the Amazon or Barnes and Noble logo on their site, this indicates they do nothing other than operate as a hotlink to these sites in exchange for a 10-15% commission on everything you purchase. We, instead, recommend that you support "real" travel bookstores – those that actually work for their customers either offline or online and play a vital role in travel planning. These bookstores maintain inventory and offer customer service. They are in the business of promoting and supporting travel. Here are some of our favorite travel bookstores which more or less have an online presence:

Rand McNally:	*www.randmcnally.com*
Adventurous Traveler:	*www.adventuroustraveler.com*
Literate Traveller:	*www.literatetraveller.com*
Powell's:	*www.powells.com*
Book Passage:	*www.bookpassage.com*
Travel Bug:	*www.swifty.com/tbug*

World Wide Books & Maps:	*www.travelbooksandmaps.com*
Easy Going:	*www.easygoing.com*
Magellan Travel:	*www.magellantravelbooks.com*
Forsyth Travel:	*www.forsyth.com*
Map Guides:	*www.map-guides.com*
Distant Lands:	*www.distantlands.com*
Savvy Traveller:	*www.thesavvytraveller.com*
iShop Books n' More:	*www.ishoparoundtheworld.com*
Travel Books:	*www.travelbooks.com*
Passenger Stop:	*www.passengerstop.com*
Traveler's Pack:	*www.travelerspack.com*
Pacific Travellers Supply:	*www.pactrav.com*
Omni Resources:	*www.omnimap.com*
Travelden:	*www.travelden.com*
The Traveler:	*www.thetraveler.com*
The Travel Store:	*www.travelitems.com*
Explore, Inc.:	*www.toexplore.com*
Books For Travel:	*www.booksfortravel.com*
Galley Slaves:	*www.galleyslaves.com*
Curious Cat:	*www.curiouscat.com/travel*
Global Corner:	*www.globalcorner.com*
Discover Store:	*www.discover.com*
National Geographic Store:	*www.nationalgeographic.com*
Sierra Club:	*www.sierraclub.com*
PBS:	*www.shopPBS.com*
Excursionist:	*www.travel-books.com*
Phileas Fogg's:	*www.foggs.com*
Things4Travel:	*www.things4travel.com*
Hit the Road:	*www.roadtripstore.com*
Travel Reference:	*www.travreflib.com*
WordsWorth Books:	*www.wordsworth.com*
Booksmith:	*www.booksmith.com*

You'll also find other excellent travel bookstores which do not have an Internet presence, such as the Travel Books and Language Center in Washington, DC and The Complete Traveller in New York City.

If you are looking for an independent bookstore near you, go to this website and search for it by location:

www.bookweb.org

9

Major Travel Media

THE TRAVEL MEDIA IS A LARGE AND GROWING BUSI-
ness which provides essential information to travelers. It
includes a host of major media players: newspapers, magazines, newsletters, radio, television, and Internet. If you enjoy
following current events in different destinations, reading about the
latest travel trends and news, and learning about many aspects of travel,
you'll want to visit several websites identified in this chapter. The sites
outlined here are largely operated by a combination of media and travel
professionals who collaborate in disseminating travel information to the
widest audience possible.

International News

Many international travelers are used to tuning into CNN International
and the BBC in their hotel rooms or reading the *International Herald-
Tribune* and *Economist* to keep up with the latest in international news.
For the latest international news, visit these key media sites which are
known for their quality reporting:

CNN	International News
www.cnn.com/CNN	

It's tough to rival CNN in the international news arena. CNN
maintains a variety of sites, but CNN International serves as a

gateway to CNN's many specialized world channels: Q&A With Riz Khan, World Beat, Insight, World Sport, World Weather, World Business Today, World Report, and CNN Hotspots. It also links to CNN's main site as well as CNN Europe, CNN Financial News (CNNfn), CNN Sports Illustrated (CNNSI), CNN Airport Network, and CNN Radio. The site also includes video on demand. This is a rich international news site which you may want to visit again and again as part of your trip preparation as well as while traveling on the road. If you're primarily traveling in North America, you will probably want to focus on CNN's main site: *www.cnn.com.*

BBC World Service   **International News**
www.bbc.co.uk/worldservice

The BBC (British Broadcasting Corporation) remains one of the most respected international media groups and rivals CNN in many respects. Indeed, many international travelers, especially business travelers, would love to watch BBC and CNN simultaneously. This site, which is available in 43 different languages as well as in audio, is jam-packed with the latest BBC news and feature articles. If you want to know what's going on in the real world – rather than just focus on history, culture, and sightseeing that commonly dominates leisure travel – you'll want to visit this site frequently. Includes favorite websites ("Electric Journeys"), extensive sports coverage, news bulletins, special programs, and related BBC sites. This site even includes an innovative section on learning English for non-English speaking visitors! For information on the United Kingdom, including the nations of England, Northern Island, Scotland, and Wales, be sure to visit the BBC's main site: *www.bbc.co.uk.*

International Herald-Tribune   **International News**
www.iht.com

Published by *The New York Times* and *The Washington Post*, edited in Paris, and printed in several locations around the world, the *International Herald Tribune* features the top international news accompanied with the quality reporting expected of two top daily newspapers in the U.S. In many respects, this is one of the few international daily newspapers (*USA Today* would be its major competitor). This site summarizes the material found in the newspaper that is widely distributed in major hotels and newsstands around the world. It includes features on fashion, food, art, music, and theater as well as articles on travel, money, and financial markets. Its search engine allows users to review the previous six days of the publication by various keywords. The online articles tend to be short and thus make for quick reads.

USA Today	International News
www.usatoday.com	

USA Today can rightly claim to be one of the major international newspapers by the mere fact that its printing and distribution is truly global. Visit almost any city in the world and you are likely to find a recent copy of *USA Today*. While the newspaper focuses a great deal on news in North America, it does have strong international coverage. This site is organized like the newspaper – into five major channels: news, sports, money, life, and weather. It's loaded with lots of news on everything from stocks and sports scores to careers and travel. For travelers, it includes a flight tracker and city guides (courtesy of an affiliate relationship with DigitalCity). Like most of the newspaper, much of what you read is in the form of quick and easy snapshots or sound bites. The focus here is on the snappy headlines and easily digestible news summaries.

Economist	International News
www.economist.com	Magazine

The *Economist* is simply one of the finest international news magazines. Authoritative, well written, and with many in-depth analytical articles, it provides some of the best coverage of the international scene. This site puts much of the magazine content online. It also includes an archived section from which you can access past issues of the magazine since 1995. Very strong on international political and economic news. A favorite of many international business travelers.

Other online magazines with a heavy emphasis on international news coverage include *Time* and *Newsweek*:

Newsweek: *www.newsweek.com* (links to MSNBC)
Time Magazine: *www.time.com*

While both magazines provide excellent international news coverage, *Time* really shines when it comes to providing online regional news coverage through its special editions on Asia, Europe, and Canada.

Online Travel Magazines

Almost every major travel magazine now has an online presence. The following magazines represent diverse treatments of travel for everyone from budget to business and luxury travelers and from physicians to women and CEOs. Most of these sites represent magazine publishing companies that print paper versions of their magazines. On the other hand, a few sites, such as *Journeywoman* and *Ticked Off*, are strictly online magazines. Salon, another online magazine, used to have a lively travel section which was finally put to rest in June 2000 when it terminated its staff as part of its new survival strategy; however, you can still read its many archived travel articles by going to *www.salon.com*. Major travel magazine sites include:

Travel-Holiday *www.travelholiday.com*	**Travel Magazine**

This site is based on the print version of *Travel-Holiday Magazine* which is popular with many travelers interested in quality travel, interesting destinations, and well written, compelling articles. This easy to navigate site includes lots of useful travel tips, feature articles, and a bulletin board for questions as well as special sections on destinations and cruises. Like the print magazine, the emphasis throughout this site is on providing interesting travel articles.

Concierge	Travel Magazine

www.concierge.com

This is the website for the popular upscale *Condé Nast Traveler* magazine. There is much more to this site than what initially appears on the front page. Most of the goodies are hidden behind some rather bland buttons, especially "Advice", "Features," and "CN Traveler". The most original sections are "CN Traveler", which takes you to the many featured articles, photos, and lists appearing in the print magazine, and the forum or "Discussion" for asking questions. The "Features" section includes several useful reference tools (currency calculator, worldwide airport guide, U.S. b&b finder, world's best hotels), travelers' aids (ask the experts, travel deals, horror stories, disputes, and Q&A), and get aways (islands, cruises, family, hotels, restaurants, monuments, spas, skiing, golfing, romantic places, honeymoons, and rooms with a view). The site provides a full range of travel information and services by including affiliate relationships with other sites. City destination information, for example, is provided by Fodor's Travel Publications (go directly to *www.fodors.com* for more complete listings). Its booking services are linked to Expedia.com and it offers travel books through BarnesandNoble.com. Its related sister site includes Epicurious (*http://food.epicurious.com* which covers *Bon Appétit* and *Gourmet* magazines with many destination articles). An excellent online resource from one of the major media players in the travel industry. For individuals interested in quality travel to some of the world's best places.

Travel and Leisure	Travel Magazine

www.travelandleisure.com

Published by American Express, the monthly *Travel and Leisure* magazine remains one of the most popular travel publications with lots of great articles on interesting destinations. The results of the magazine's annual World's Best survey of its readers (published in the September issue) are of special interest to the travel industry and travelers in search of the "best of the best" in travel. In addition to its many informative articles, the site also includes interactive bulletin boards, chat, feedback, and an advanced search engine. It also includes booking services through American Express Travel and Travelocity and links to its network of American Express travel sites: *Travel and Leisure Family* (*www.tlfamily.com*), *Travel and Leisure Golf* (*www.tlgolf.com*), *Skyguide* (*www.skyguide. com*), *Food and Wine* (*www.foodandwine.com*), and *B. Smith Style* (*www.bsmithstyle.com*).

Frommer's	**Travel Magazine**
www.frommers.com	

While this site is a major center for all types of information and services for budget travelers, it also includes articles from the popular monthly *Arthur Frommer's Budget Travel Magazine*. Just click on the magazine section which is usually featured front and center on this busy site. You also can request a free trial issue of the magazine as well as subscribe to it online. For more information on the architecture of this site, see our description on page 154.

These and several other travel magazines with websites include the following:

Adventure Travel:	*www.bluemagazine.com*
	www.escapemag.com
	www.mungopark.com
	www.actionasia.com
	www.outpostmagazine.com
	www.travelroads.com
	www.roadstoadventure.com
Airline Magazines:	*www.hemispheresmagazine.com*
	www.americanair.com/away
	www.delta-sky.com
	www.swaspirit.com
Alternative Travel:	*www.transitionsabroad.com*
	www.tripsmag.com
Arizona:	*www.arzhwys.com*

Budget Travel:	*www.bigworld.com*
	www.frommers.com
	www.bedandbreakfast.com
Business Travel:	*www.businesstraveller.com*
	www.btonline.com
	www.meetings-conventions.com
	www.sky-guide.com
Caribbean:	*www.caribbeantravelmag.com*
Cruising:	*www.porthole.com*
Discount Airfares:	*www.bestfares.com*
Islands:	*www.islands.com*
Luxury Travel:	*www.ceotraveler.com*
	www.luxurious-adventures.com
National Geographic	*www.nationalgeographic.com/traveler*
Magazines:	*www.nationalgeographic.com/ adventure*
	www.nationalgeographic.com/ngm
	www.nationalgeographic.com/world
National Parks:	*www.npca.org/magazine*
Physicians/Medicine:	*www.diversionmag.com*
	www.istm.org/jtm.html
Spas:	*www.spamagazine.com*
Texas:	*www.texashighways.com*
Ticked Off Travelers:	*www.ticked.com*
Travel and Leisure:	*www.travelandleisure.com*
Travel Terrific:	*www.travelterrific.com*
Travel Weekly:	*www.twcrossroads.com*
Where Magazines:	*www.wheremagazine.com*
Women:	*www.journeywoman.com*
	www.maidenvoyages.com

Newsletters

Many travel websites include e-zines and newsletters for those who volunteer their email address. But the many traditional print travel newsletters, most of which also have an Internet presence, are subscription-based; they require prepayment before you can access them online or receive their print version by mail. For example, *Andrew Harper's Hideaway Report* is a monthly newsletter aimed at relatively sophisticated travelers in search of small and enchanting vacation retreats; it costs $135 per year. The *Educated Traveler* is published bimonthly and costs $48 a year. The monthly *Consumer Reports Travel Letter* costs $39 a year. While many of the newsletters are aimed at independent travelers, others are designed for travel professionals, such as WebTravelNews. Some of the major travel newsletters include:

Andrew Harper's Hideaway Report:	*www.harperassociates.com*
CEO Traveler:	*www.ceotraveler.com*
Consumer Reports Travel Letter:	*www.consumerreports.org*
Educated Traveler:	*www.educated-traveler.com*
Emerging Horizons – Accessible Travel:	*www.candy-charles.com*
Entree News:	*www.entreenews.com*
Have Children Will Travel:	*www.havechildrenwilltravel.com*
Interactive Travel Report:	*www.garrett-comm.com/nls/ itrhome.shtml*
International Living:	*www.internationalliving.com*
	www.escapeartist.com
Network for International Living:	*www.liveabroad.com*
Thrifty Traveler:	*www.thriftytraveler.com*
Travel Smart:	*www.travelsmartnews.com*
Upscale Traveler:	*www.upscaletraveler.com*
Web Travel News:	*www.webtravelnews.com*
	www.internettravelnews.com

For an online guide to over 5,000 newsletters, including 185 specializing on travel, visit this useful site:

www.newsletteraccess.com

Newspapers

If you're planning to visit a destination, you may want to access the local newspapers for information on local news. With thousands of daily newspapers published worldwide, it can be a daunting task trying to find online versions of such publications. But it's easy to do so if you use the following gateway sites that serve as search engines and directories of newspapers worldwide:

News Directory:	*www.newsdirectory.com*
Newspapers:	*www.newspapers.com*
Concentric:	*www.concentric.net/~stevewt*
Newslink:	*www.newslink.org/news.html*
Internet Public Library:	*www.ipl.org/reading/news*

Several major newspapers publish separate travel sections in their Sunday editions as well as maintain a travel section on their main website. These sections may include sponsored forums and online chats. The following newspapers are well known for their travel sections:

Atlanta Journal:	*www.accessatlanta.com*
	www.ajc.com
Baltimore Sun:	*www.sunspot.net*
Boston Globe:	*www.globe.com*
Chicago Tribune:	*www.chicago.tribune.com*
Christian Science Monitor:	*www.csmonitor.com*
Dallas Morning Star:	*www.dallasnews.com*
London Telegraph:	*www.the-planet.co.uk*
Los Angeles Times:	*www.latimes.com/travel*
Miami Herald:	*www.herald.com/travel*
New York Post:	*www.nypostonline.com*
New York Times:	*www.nytimes.com*
San Francisco Chronicle:	*www.sfgate.com*
San Francisco Examiner:	*www.examiner.com*
Seattle Times:	*www.seattletimes.com*
St. Louis Dispatch:	*www.stlnet.com*
USA Today:	*www.usatoday.com/life/travel*
Washington Post:	*www.washingtonpost.com*
Wall Street Journal:	*www.travel.wsj.com*

Radio

Very few radio programs do travel features. However, one program on National Public Radio focuses solely on travel:

www.savvytraveller.com

Hosted by travel commentator Rudy Maxa, the hour-long program reaches nearly 200 public radio stations. It usually features a couple of guests each week who talk on a variety of travel subjects. If you miss the radio program, you can go directly to the Savvy Traveller website to view a synopsis of the program as well as listen to an online audio version of the interviews. Since the site archives its programs, you can review many of its program segments which aired during the past three years. The site includes travel tips. Rudy Maxa also contributes a weekly travel column to MSNBC's website – *www.msnbc.com/news/ trav-main_front.asp* or *www.msnbc.com/news/TRAV-MAXAARCHIVE_ Front.asp.*

Television

Similar to radio, very few television networks, stations, or programs focus on travel. However, three do special travel programs as well as include a great deal of travel information on their related websites:

CNN Travel:	*www.cnn.com/TRAVEL/*
Discovery Channel:	*www.discovery.com*
The Travel Channel:	*www.travelchannel.com*

Since Discovery Communications owns both the Discovery Channel and The Travel Channel, there are basically two players when it comes to travel on television – CNN and Discovery.

The Travel Channel *www.travelchannel.com*	**Television**

If you receive The Travel Channel on cable TV (it's one of our favorite channels, along with CNN and c-Span), you may want to visit this website which includes a complete program schedule for many days in advance. You can even specify which programs you wish to see several days in advance and the program should automatically send you email reminding you of the program time (you need to join the free "My Discovery" program to get the email reminders). Much of the program content is currently provided by Condé Nast Traveler, Lonely Planet, and other travel video companies. It includes such regular programming as Adventure Bound, Amazing Destinations, Destination Style, Exotic Islands, Great Vacation Homes, Incredible Vacation Videos, Travel Channel Secrets, and The Tourists, as well as specials which seem to run regularly – World's Most Dangerous Places and Journeys to the Ends of the Earth. But this site is much more than just about television programming and video clips. Designed as a complete travel resource, with several interactive elements, the site also is loaded with many travel features to assist travelers – trip planner/ideas; live cams; reservation system for air, hotel, car, and cruises (through Gorp.com); travel tools and tips (maps, weather, converters, health); travel forums; crossword puzzles; family travel; the world's best; and a travel store (books, videos, expedition wear, and travel gear).

CNN Travel	**Television**
www.cnn.com/TRAVEL	

This site includes travel-related news stories, city guides, and information on its popular travel show, "CNN Travel Now". The site also archives transcripts from recent (8 months previous) travel shows. Some of the best features of this site include a currency converter, travel adviser, message board, web handbook (linkages), driving directions, language translator, and an online travel poll. You can easily miss these sections if you don't look carefully at the small print.

Discovery	**Television**
www.discovery.com	

While not strictly a travel site, the Discovery website is rich with adventure and nature information for kids and adults alike. Its travel section is directly linked to its sister site, The Travel Channel. Discovery has basically become what the National Geographic Society (*www.nationalgeographic.com*) wishes it would have become on television and online. Left in the dust a few years ago by more entrepreneurial Discovery Communications, National Geographic is playing catch-up by partnering with such adventure websites as iExplore.com (Discovery and

The Travel Channel have partnered with the competition –
Gorp.com). If you have kids, you'll probably want to have them
explore this fun and informative site which includes lots of
information on animals, pets, and school. The danger of such
exposure, of course, is that your youngster may develop a bad
case of wanderlust – just like the millions of young people who
have marveled at the photographs, videos, and television
specials produced by the National Geographic Society for more
than 50 years. The site also promotes the Discovery Store
which includes everything from videos, scale models, and cute
stuffed animals to CD-ROMs, jewelry, and travel gear.
Discovery.com is available in several regional and country
versions, such as Discovery Asia, Discovery Japan, Discovery
India, Discovery Canada, Discovery Channel Middle East, and
Discovery Europe. This is a very fine site that is well worth
exploring for all types of travel and adventure information.

Two major television networks also maintain travel sections on
their sites which primarily feature travel news, city and country profiles,
and travel tips and tools:

ABC: *www.abcnews.go.com/sections/travel*
MSNBC: *www.msnbc.com/news/ trav-main_front.asp*
                    (Includes articles from travel columnists
                    Peter Greenberg and Rudy Maxa)

10

Air, Sea, and Land
Transportation

OMEHOW YOU'VE GOT TO GET THERE BY AIR, SHIP,
car, rail, bus, or some other conveyance. And once you reach
your destination, you have to get around from place to place –
car, taxi, bus, subway, or pedicab. But how are you going to get
everything arranged? Should you call your travel agent for assistance,
use an Internet booking site, or contact the transportation provider
directly? Chances are you will be doing all three, depending on your
mode of transportation and your willingness or unwillingness to be
involved in the details of the ticketing process.

Looking and Booking Online

Each year millions of travelers spend billions of dollars on transportation. Indeed, the single largest travel expenditure on the Internet is for
airline tickets. The largest Internet travel sites, such as Travelocity and
Expedia, primarily issue airline tickets – by far their largest revenue
stream. In fact, recent studies show that by July 2000 nearly one-third
of all airline passengers acquired their tickets over the Internet. This
number could well surpass 90 percent within the next five years. This
mass movement to purchasing airline tickets over the Internet is not
surprising since airlines have been deliberately pushing travelers onto
the Internet to purchase air tickets and away from travel agents who
only a few years ago issued over 90 percent of all airline tickets.
Through a combination of incentives and disincentives – major airlines
decrease commissions to travel agents and travel agents respond by
charging clients $10 to $20 to issue airline tickets – more and more

travelers are turning to the Internet to make airline reservations. Airlines also have encouraged travelers to bypass their travel agents and book online with them by making the whole online booking experience relatively quick and easy and by enticing them with special offers such as extra miles or discounts. Just take a quick look at United Airlines' website – *www.ual.com* – and you'll see how informative and convenient this whole process can be, from checking flight schedules and finding fares to entering Mileage Plus numbers to get credited toward accumulated flight miles.

Renting a car over the Internet also can be quick and easy. Many travel sites include a car rental section where you can reserve a car from most major car rental firms at competitive prices.

On the other hand, booking cruises still is not a prevalent online experience. Cruises are still primarily arranged through traditional travel agents who work closely with cruise lines. Because of the close sales and marketing relationships between cruise lines and travel agents, many cruise lines encourage travelers to book directly through their travel agent. As a result, most individuals interested in cruise travel use the Internet to research alternative destinations and cruise lines, but in the end they do the actual booking through a travel agent.

In Chapter 12 we will examine the major online booking and reservation sites, from mega sites and online travel agents to discount specialists, consolidators, and reverse auction sites. There we will look at all the different games being played with airline tickets and what online services may make the most sense, including dollars and cents, for you.

This chapter primarily identifies the websites of the major transportation companies. For a quick worldwide directory of all airlines, airports, rental car companies, cruises, trains, and hotels, be sure to bookmark this useful site:

www.airwebtravel.net

If used in conjunction with Chapter 12, this chapter will serve as become the chapter from which to launch your research for examining different transportation providers whom you may or may not choose to book with directly. This is especially true in the case of most cruise lines which do not allow you to book online; they encourage you to examine their sites for information – and ostensibly for motivation – but then see your travel agent to purchase cruise services.

Airlines and Their Incentives

During the past 10 years airlines have been in intense competition for customer loyalty by offering frequent flyer programs that provide financial incentives, such as free trips and upgrades, for maintaining repeat business. During the past three years, airlines have been trying to eliminate costly middlemen – travel agents – in the whole ticketing process as well as attract a whole new class of traveler – the cyberbuyer. Giving travel agents a 10 percent commission on each ticket sold costs airlines billions of dollars in lost revenue each year. Since sophisticated software and Internet applications now allow airlines to deal directly with customers through quick and easy online booking engines, it made good financial sense – however wrenching for travel agents – to eliminate these expensive middlemen. Not surprising, many travel agents have been up in arms and very anti-Internet because the airlines and their new best friend, the Internet, have threatened their livelihoods. Having gone from denial to acceptance of the Internet, and now accepting the fate of their traditional ticketing roles, many traditional travel agents have gone out of business as more and more of their customers have migrated online to do their own ticketing. In fact, by the year 2001, over 50 percent of all airline passengers are expected to acquire their tickets online rather than through travel agents.

> *During the past three years, airlines have been trying to eliminate costly middlemen – travel agents – in the whole ticketing process as well as attract a whole new class of traveler – the cyberbuyer.*

Attempting to recover lost revenue, many travel agents now charge their customers service fees ($10 to $20) to issue airline tickets; this is still workable with an older generation of traveler that may not be too Internet savvy, but it probably provides an incentive for more Internet savvy travelers to go online to do their own ticketing.

Before deciding how you plan to purchase your airline tickets, you may want to visit the websites of various airlines to see what online travel services, including destinations and timetables, they provide. Also, look for special deals, discounts, and vacation packages. U.S.-based airlines in particular are offering all types of special promotions and incentives to lure more and more customers online to purchase tickets and plan their trips. Some airlines, such as Continental, offer free newsletters that alert registered visitors to airline and car rental specials that are only available by booking through their online sites. Others, like Northwest Airlines, entice travelers with special online promotions, such as double and triple miles, for booking certain flights during low traffic periods. And still others, like United Airlines, Continental, Delta, Air France, and Thai Airways, offer special vacation packages that compete very favorably with tours offered by travel agents. Hong Kong-based Cathay Pacific offers special all-Asia passes for 16- and 30-day periods as well as encourages visitors to become registered *Cyber-Travelers* who are eligible to receive a newsletter, notices of special fares, the Internet All Asia Pass, seat auctions, contests and other promotions that are not available to the general public. Accordingly, online buyers of tickets with such Internet savvy airlines are being treated as a special class of privileged customers – similar to members of frequent flyer clubs.

Several websites function as gateways to the airlines by listing their home pages. One of the most convenient sites is the OAG which provides an alphabetical listing of all airlines as well as includes useful information on aircraft, timetables, and airports. You can directly access the airlines and timetables by going to this URL:

www.oag.com/search_and_links/airlines

Other useful sites that also function as gateways to airlines include:

Airline Contacts:	*www.washingtonpost.com/wp-srv/ travel/toolbox/airlinecontacts.htm*
Air Web Travel:	*www.airwebtravel.net*
Airlines of the Air:	*www.flyaow.com*
Airline Finder:	*www.air.findhere.com*
Airlines of the World:	*www.chicago.com/air/carriers*
Airline Homepages:	*www.dove.net.au/~davemac/airlines*

Each of these gateway sites are more or less complete. For your quick reference, here are the English language homepages of 55 major international and U.S. domestic airlines, including their toll-free numbers (international reservation number in the case of international airlines), in North America. This list represents less than 20 percent of all airlines functioning in more than 200 countries:

Aer Lingus:	*www.aerlingus.ie/usa*	1-800-223-6537
Aeroflot:	*www.aeroflot.org*	1-888-340-6400
Aeromexico:	*www.aeromexico.com*	1-800-237-6639
Air Canada:	*www.aircanada.ca*	1-800-776-3000
Air China:	*www.airchina.com/cn/english*	1-800-982-8802
Air France:	*www.airfrance.com*	1-800-237-2747
Air India:	*www.airindia.com*	1-800-223-7776
Air Jamaica:	*www.airjamaica.com*	1-800-523-5585
Air New Zealand:	*www.airnz.com*	1-800-262-1234
AirTran:	*www.airtran.com*	1-800-247-8726
Alaska:	*www.alaskaair.com*	1-800-426-0333
Alitalia:	*www.alitalia.it*	1-800-223-5730
Aloha:	*www.alohaair.com*	1-800-367-5250
America West:	*www.americawest.com*	1-800-235-9292
American:	*www.aa.com*	1-800-433-7300
Ansett Australia:	*www.ansett.com*	1-800-442-9626
ANA:	*www.fly-ana.com*	1-800-235-9292
Asiana:	*www.flyasiana.com*	1-800-227-4262
Austrian:	*www.aua.com*	1-800-843-0002
British Airways:	*www.british-airways.com*	1-800-247-9297
Cathay Pacific:	*www.cathay-usa.com*	1-800-233-2742
Continental:	*www.flycontinental.com*	1-800-231-0856
Delta:	*www.delta-air.com*	1-800-241-4141
Egypt Air:	*www.egyptair.com.eg*	1-800-334-6787
El Al Israel:	*www.elal.co.il*	1-800-223-6700
Finnair:	*www.us.finnair.com*	1-800-950-5000
Frontier:	*www.frontierairlines.com*	1-800-243-6297
Garuda:	*www.garudausa.com*	1-800-342-7832
Gulf Air:	*www.gulfairco.com*	1-800-528-3130
Hawaiian:	*www.hawaiianair.com*	1-800-367-5320
Iberia:	*www.iberia.com*	1-800-772-4642
Icelandair:	*www.icelandair.com*	1-800-223-5500
Japan:	*www.japanair.com*	1-800-525-3663
KLM:	*www.klm.com*	1-800-374-7747
Korean Air:	*www.koreanair.com*	1-800-438-5000
Lufthansa:	*www.lufthansa-USA.com*	1-800-645-3880
Malaysian:	*www.malysia-airlins.com.my*	1-800-552-9264
Mexicana:	*www.mexicana.com*	1-800-531-7921
Midway:	*www.midwayair.com*	1-800-446-4392
Midwest Express:	*www.midwestexpress.com*	1-800-452-2022

Northwest:	*www.nwa.com*	1-800-225-2525
Qantas:	*www.qantas.com*	1-800-227-4500
Sabena:	*www.sabena.com*	1-800-955-2000
SAS:	*www.flysas.com*	1-800-221-2350
Singapore:	*www.singaporeair.com*	1-800-742-3333
Southwest:	*www.southwest.com*	1-800-435-9792
Spanair:	*www.spanair.com*	1-888-545-5757
Swissair:	*www.swissair.com*	1-800-221-4750
TAP:	*www.TAP-AirPortugal.pt*	1-800-221-7370
Thai Airway:	*www.thaiair.com*	1-800-426-5204
Transworld:	*www.twa.com*	1-800-221-2000
US Airways:	*www.usairways.com*	1-800-622-1015
United:	*www.ual.com*	1-800-826-4827
Varig Brazilian:	*www.varig.com*	1-800-468-2744
Virgin Atlantic:	*www.fly.virgin.com*	1-800-862-8621

Cruises, Freighters, and Other Adventures

So you would rather float than fly, or perhaps do both? Welcome to the wonderful and special travel world of cruising, a style of travel that captivates the attention of millions of dedicated cruise travelers each year. Cruising is big business and it keeps getting bigger and bigger each year. And cruise companies keep building bigger and hopefully better ships to create even more exciting cruise adventures.

Like budget travel, cruise travel is almost a cult form – many people only want to travel by cruise ship; it's their way of seeing the world, meeting new people, having a good time, and avoiding the many hassles associated with other forms of travel, like airports and luggage. Just check into your cabin, unpack, and enjoy the rest of your trip which will be taken care of by others. At the same time, today's cruise ships keep getting bigger and bigger to accommodate a traveler that continues to expect bigger and better cruise ships.

If you love to cruise, chances are you will be working with a travel agent in putting together a cruise package and paying for the cruise. With the exception of Renaissance Cruises, which during the 1990s ran afoul of angry travel agents by trying to sell cruises directly to the public (they have now come in from the cold, literally begging still angry travel agents to put them back on their radar screens), most cruise lines are very agent-friendly. Indeed, cruise lines are highly dependent upon travel agents for filling their ships. Given the current glut of cruise ships, with the launch of several new 3,000+ passenger super cruise ships, the cruise lines are more dependent than ever on the services of travel agents to fill their ships.

So where does that leave you and the Internet in relation to cruise lines? When it comes to the cruise business, it's mainly about comparing services, cruise styles, itineraries, and prices. In other words, you are encouraged to use the Internet to research alternative cruises and cruise lines, but when it comes to booking a cruise, most cruise lines draw a very delicate line; they encourage you to see a travel agent who will take care of all the details in exchange for at least a 10 percent commission from the cruise line. While you can do some online booking of cruises, in most cases you must call a toll-free number where you will actually talk to a cruise booking agent, which in effect is a travel agent at the other end of the phone. The good news is that all cruise lines have their own websites from which you can do a great deal of research before seeing your travel agent.

Cruises and cruise ships come in all cruising schedules and floating forms. You can take a day-trip up a river or spend 60-180 days cruising around the world in everything from barges, river boats, tall ships, and 40-foot sailboats carrying six people to huge 1200-foot long floating cities capable of handling more than 3,000 passengers – and everything in between (barges, river boats, ferries, tall ships).

Many adventuresome budget travelers with lots of time (30 to 75 days) and who prefer the high seas often avoid the party crowds found on cruise ships. Many favor cruising by freighter which may or may not be less expensive (from $50 to $200 a day), but definitely more Spartan, than a luxury cruise ship that comes complete with floor shows, casinos, beauty salons, exercise rooms, water sports, huge dining rooms, bars, and atriums. However, cruising by freighter can be a much more exciting and more personal experience than going by luxury cruiser. It may well be the cruise of a lifetime as you get a close-up view of the ship and its personnel, visit exotic ports, and enjoy the comradery of a small like-minded group of travelers.

If you are interested in cruising by freighter, start by reviewing the *Internet Guide to Freighter Travel* which gives an inside look at freighter travel, including costs, travel tips, freighter agents, shipping companies, types of ships, pirates, seasickness, ports, and much more. The guide is available online and includes many useful linkages:

www.maxho.com/~frman

Another good overview of freighter travel is found at *www.atwtraveler.com/freightr.htm*.

For information on freighter alternatives, including booking services and agents, you should visit these sites for information on such travel:

Travltips:	*www.travlips.com*
Freighter World Cruises:	*www.freighterworld.com*
Freighter Travel:	*www.freightertravel.hb.co.nz*
Freighter Cruises:	*www.freighter-cruises.com*
Freighter Travel:	*www.freighter-travel.com*
The Cruise People:	*http://members.aol.com/CruiseAZ/ freighters.htm*
Escape Artist:	*www.excapeartist.com/unique_ Lifestyles/freighter_Travel.html*

Unlike regular cruises that are largely handled through travel agents, cruising by freighter involves contacting special agents which can be found by visiting these websites.

Assuming you like the good life on the high seas, with all the expected decadent amenities, you should start your cruise research by exploring several sites that outline cruise alternatives. Several websites serve as gateway sites to the cruise businesses. These sites in particular will help you plan a cruise and locate the major cruise lines:

Fielding:	*www.fieldingtravel.com*
Travel Page:	*www.travelpage.com/cruise*
	www.cruisepage.com
Cruise Opinion:	*www.cruiseopinion.com*
Tutto Crociere:	*www.cybercruises.com*
National Geographic:	*www.nationalgeographic.com/cruise*

Fielding   **Cruises**
www.fieldingtravel.com

Based on its bestselling cruise guidebook – *Worldwide Cruises* – the Fielding site identifies the major cruise lines by name and region, rates and compares each cruise line, and identifies the best cruises for the year. It also includes tips on choosing a cruise, getting ready, and ending a cruise. For example, you'll

learn that the highest rated cruise lines, those receiving six stars
– for *"the ultimate cruise experience"* – are:

- Crystal Cruises
- Cunard
- Radisson Seven Seas Cruises
- Seabourn Cruise Line
- Silverseas Cruises, Ltd.

Not far behind in the five-star category ("a very special cruise
experience") are:

- Carnival Cruise Line
- Celebrity Cruises
- Costa Cruises
- Cunard
- Holland America Line

This site also includes a cruise forum (Fielding's Crowsnest®)
which provides feedback from travelers who have taken various
cruises. The section called "Alternative Cruises" outlines
different types of cruises and companies:

- Adventure and eco-tourism sailings
- Adventure and eco-tour companies
- Canal barges
- European coastal cruises, ferries, and yachts
- European coastal cruises companies
- Freighters
- River cruises
- Sailing ships
- Sailing ships cruise companies

Although somewhat dated with information from its 1998
edition of *Worldwide Cruises*, nonetheless, this site provides a
wealth of information to help you identify the perfect cruise.
We highly recommend it as a good starting point for reviewing
cruise options.

Travel Page   **Cruises**
www.travelpage.com/cruise/
www.cruiseserver.net

This popular cruise site includes a wealth of information on cruising through CruiseServer, the Internet's largest database of more than 11,000 cruise itineraries and over 300 ship profiles. In addition to providing direct links to dozens of cruise lines, shipping companies, and ports, the site includes these special features:

- Our favorite cruises
- A cruise club with weekly specials
- Online reviews of over 11,000 cruises
- Specials on cruises
- Tips on getting a cruise job
- Special needs
- Internet cruise survey
- Inspection scores on ships
- Live photos from the bridges of 15 ships

The site also includes a reservation system for airlines, cruises, cars, hotels, resorts, and vacation packages; links to thousands of destinations worldwide; and public forums focused on destination talk. The site claims to offer the best Internet deals on cruises.

Cruise Opinion   **Cruises**
www.cruiseopinion.com

Okay, you've seen the fabulous ads, drooled over the glossy photos of the ultimate romantic fun and sun cruise, and listened to a travel agent talk about a wonderful getaway package. You're ready to book the cruise, but maybe you would like an "insiders" view of what really lies behind all the advertising and sales hype. If you want to know what others are saying about their cruise experience, be sure to bookmark this popular site. It includes a huge database (over 4,000) of opinions, ratings, and comments which you may find useful when considering your cruise options. Discover how others rate cruises and cruise ships and what they say about their cruise experience, both likes and dislikes. The comments can be quite revealing. Indeed, if you select a particular cruise ship, you may want to go to this site to see what previous passengers said about their experience. How, for example, did they rate the food, room service, family or senior experience, activities, ports of call, wheelchair access, medical facilities, nightclubs, shopping, cruise staff, deck service, casino, beauty salon, ship cleanliness, cabin comfort and amenities, noise levels, tender service, entertainment, air/sea program, embark/disembark, and overall cruise value. Just read a few of the reviews for what is reputed to be the world's best cruise line and ship – the Crystal Harmony – and you may come away in awe that anyone could create such a fabulous and thoroughly decadent cruise experience, enough to turn any cruise doubters into dedicated cruise travelers. It's all here on this site. You would be foolish not to peek at such feedback before you book a cruise on a ship that could well become your worst travel nightmare! Similar to TravelPage, this site allows you to book a cruise by calling a toll-free number (1-800-295-5621). The site also includes links to a few cruise lines and cruise media.

Tutto Crociere   **Cruises**
www.cybercruises.com/cruiseurl.htm

While this website primarily functions as an Internet cruise magazine (*Tutto Crociere*), it includes a very useful set of linkages to online cruise magazines, cruise databases, cruise news, forums, travel and cruise operators, cruise ports, port authorities, port associations, onboard services, cruise employment and recruiting, freighter cruises, cruise vessels, trade shows, conferences, tall ships, shopping agencies, shore excursions, land programs, and many other related cruise sites.

National Geographic	Cruises
www.nationalgeographic.com/cruise/ship	

This handy site allows you to specify your cruise criteria (location and type of cruise activities) and then search for the cruise that's right for you. The site also takes visitors through a 360 degree virtual tour of a ship (Norwegian's *Dreamward*) and includes message boards and recommended resources. Several elements on this site appear to be aging, and all do not function all of the time.

You also may want to examine several online cruise publications that offer a wealth of information on cruising:

Cruise Critic:	*www.cruisecritic.com*
Cruise Hunt:	*www.CruiseHunt.com*
Cruise Lines International Association:	*www.cruising.org*
Cruise Mates:	*www.cruisemates.com*
Cruise News:	*www.cruise-news.com*
Cruise News:	*www.romanticgetaways.com*
Cruise News Daily:	*www.cruisenewsdaily.com*
Cruise Observer Online:	*www.traveletterz.com*
Cruise Travel Magazine:	*www.travel.org/CruiseTravel*
Cruise Week News:	*www.cruise-week.com*
Get Cruising:	*www.getcruising.com/cruising*
National Association of Cruise Oriented Agencies:	*www.nacoa.com*
Porthole:	*www.porthole.com*
SNCM (Mediterranean Ferries):	*www.sncm.fr*
Tutto Crociere – the Cyberspace Cruise Magazine:	*www.cybercruises.com*

Next, go directly into the sites of the major cruise ship lines to discover what they have to offer. Most have toll-free numbers through which you can request brochures and make reservations. None allow you to directly book a cruise online:

American Hawaii Cruises:	*www.cruisehawaii.com*
Carnival Cruise Lines:	*www.carnival.com*
Celebrity Cruises:	*www.celebrity-cruises.com*
Classical Cruises:	*www.classicalcruises.com*
Clipper Cruise Line:	*www.clippercruise.com*
Commodore Cruise Line:	*www.commodorecruise.com*
Costa Cruises:	*www.costacruises.com*
Crown Cruise Line:	*www.crowncruiseline.com*
Cruise West:	*www.cruisewest.com*
Crystal Cruises:	*www.crystalcruises.com*
Cunard Line:	*www.cunardline.com*
Discovery Cruise Line:	*www.discoverycruiseline.com*
Disney Cruise Line:	*www.disneycruise.com*
Festival Cruises/First European Cruises:	*www.festivalcruises.com*
Holland America Line:	*www.hollandamerica.com*
Imperial Majesty Cruises:	*www.marineex.com*
Mediterranean Shipping Cruises:	*www.msccruise.com*
Orient Lines:	*www.orientlines.com*
P&O Cruises:	*www.pocruises.to*
Princess Cruises:	*www.princess.com*
Radisson Seven Seas Cruises:	*www.rssc.com*
Regal Cruises:	*www.regalcruises.com*
Renaissance Cruises:	*www.renaissancecruises.com*
Royal Caribbean Intl:	*www.royalcaribbean.com*
Royal Olympic Cruises:	*www.royalolympiccruises.com*
Seabourn Cruise Line:	*www.seabourn.com*
Sea Cloud Cruises:	*www.seacloud.com*
SeaEscape Cruises:	*www.seaescape.com*
Silversea Cruises:	*www.silversea.com*
Star Clippers:	*www.starclippers.com*
Windjammer Barefoot Cruises:	*www.windjammer.com*
Windstar Cruises:	*www.windstarcruises.com*
World Cruise Company:	*www.worldcruiseco.com*

Most specialized and small "boutique" cruise lines include the following companies:

Abercrombie & Kent:	*www.abercrombiekent.com*
Alaska's Glacier Bay Tour and Cruises:	*www.glacierbaytours.com*
Alaska Sightseeing/ Cruise West:	*www.cruisewest.com*
American Canadian Caribbean Line:	*www.accl-smallships.com*
Bergen Line Inc.:	*www.bergenline.com*
Classical Cruises:	*www.classicalcruises.com*
Clipper Cruise Line:	*www.clippercruise.com*
Club Med 2:	*www.clubmed.com*
Delta Queen Steamboat:	*www.deltaqueen.com*
KD River Cruises of Europe:	*www.rivercruises.com*
Norwegian Coastal Voyage Inc./Bergin Line Services:	*www.coastalvoyage.com* *www.bergin.com*
Peter Deilmann EuropAmerica Cruises:	*www.deilmann-cruises.com*
Riverbarge Excursions:	*www.riverbarge.com*
Special Expeditions:	*www.specialexpeditions.com*
Star Clippers:	*www.starclippers.com*
Swan Hellenic:	*www.swan-hellenic.co.uk*
Tall Ship Adventures:	*www.tallshipadventures.com*

For excellent deals on discounted cruises, be sure to visit Moments Notice's site and sign up for its e-zine:

www.moments-notice

You'll regularly receive by email a listing of the latest deals on cruise bargains which may represent more than 50 percent savings.

Car Rentals

Fly into most major airports around the would and you will most likely find several of the major international car rental companies presented in the arrival halls: Avis, Hertz, Budget, and Kemwel. In many parts of the world Thrifty and Dollar also are represented.

Similar to airline tickets, car rentals can easily be booked online. Indeed, most travel websites that include reservation systems usually include a button for worldwide car rentals. Convenient gateway sites for information on rental cars include:

Air Web Travel:	*www.airwebtravel.net.*
BNM:	*www.bnm.com*
	www.rentalcarguide.com
Free Travel Tips:	*www.freetraveltips.com/Cars*
Travelers Net:	*www.travelersnet.com*
Cheap Car Rental:	*www.cheapcarrental.com*
	www.travelnow.com
Rental Cars:	*www.rentalcars.com*
Traveleader:	*www.traveleader.com*
FrugalFlyer:	*www.frugalflyer.com/carrental.htm*

While you can book cars through the many travel sites appearing in Chapter 12, you also may want to go directly to the websites of the car rental companies. Most of these provide convenient online reservation systems and often include specials (Hertz, for example, maintains a "Special Offers" page with many different specials) that are only available to Internet users, including online coupons:

Ace:	*www.acerentacar.com*
Alamo:	*www.goalamo.com*
Auto Europe:	*www.autoeurope.com*
Avis:	*www.avis.com*
Budget:	*www.budgetrentacar.com*
Discount Car:	*www.discountcar.com*
Dollar:	*www.dollarcar.com*
Enterprise:	*www.enterprise.com*
Europecar:	*www.europcar.com*
Europe By Car:	*www.europebycar.com*
Hertz:	*www.hertz.com*
Kemwel:	*www.kemwel.com*
National:	*www.nationalcar.com*
Payless:	*www.800-payless.com*
Practical:	*www.practical.co.uk*

Rent-a-Wreck:	*www.rent-a-wreck.com*
Thrifty:	*www.thrifty.com*

Subways and Trains

Riding the rails remains a very popular and inexpensive way of traveling between and within cities in many parts of the world. Trains are especially popular in Europe where travelers often purchase special rail passes to inexpensively get around Europe. Subways in Paris, Madrid, Moscow, London, Singapore, Hong Kong, and Tokyo are some of the best in the world. Knowing how to use these rail systems, however, can be a challenge for many travelers.

If you want to understand how to reach various city locations by using subways in many major cities of the world, there's no better site than SubwayNavigator to prepare you for the task:

www.subwaynavigator.com

This site includes information on subway systems in 60 cities around the world (10 are in the U.S.). Just enter your departure and arrival stations in a city and the site will calculate the estimated time of the journey, provide line and station directions, and even generate a graphical map of the subway system. For each city, the site also includes linkages to other sites relevant to the particular city in question.

Several global and regional rail websites provide useful information on train travel. The following websites function as gateway sites for identifying various rail systems, purchasing rail passes, and planning a rail journey:

RailServe:	*www.railserve.com*
European Railways:	*http://mercurio.iet.unipi.it*
RailEurope:	*www.raileurope.com*
Train Web:	*www.trainweb.com*
RailPass Express:	*www.railpass.com*
European Railpasses:	*www.ricksteves.com/rail*
Rail Travel Center:	*www.railtvl.com*
Air Web Travel:	*www.airwebtravel.net*

If you are interested in exploring a specific rail system, railway, or rail company in various countries, check out these sites:

Australia:	*www.gsr.com.au*
	www.gsr.com/au/theghan
Canada:	*www.viarail.ca*
China:	*www.china-railway.com*
Great Britain:	*www.britrail.com*
	www.railtrack.co.uk
Great Train Escapes:	*www.greattrainescapes.com*
India:	*www.india-rail.com*
	www.indian-travel.com/rail2.htm
Italy:	*www.fs-on-line/eng*
Japan:	*www.westjr.co.jp/english*
London/Paris:	*www.eurostar.com*
Orient-Express:	*www.orient-expresstrains.com*
South Africa:	*www.bluetrain.co.za*
Swiss Rail:	*www.railinfo.ch*
Trans-Siberian:	*www.trans-siberian.co.uk*
	www.xs4all.nl/~hgj
United States:	*www.amtrak.com*

For luxury train travel in Europe, Southeast Asia, and Australia, check out the Orient-Express site:

www.orient-expresstrains.com

Buses and Special Passes

Bus is still the world's number one means of public transportation. Budget travelers usually save a great deal of money on local transportation by using buses between and within cities. Even within the United States, buses carry over 45 million passengers each year – nearly 10 percent more than airlines. In the case of the North America, visit Greyhound's website for information on its fleet of 2,600 buses involved in intracity transportation:

www.greyhound.com

The site includes a handy fare finder (enter your departure and arrival cities to get a fare), information on Canadian tours, special online fare promotions, travel planning, shipping services, special tours and charters (Greyhound hauls a lot of meeting and convention groups, school and church groups, and sightseers (through Hotard Motor Coach Services) to New Orleans, the Mississippi Gulf Coast, Florida, and Washington, DC). The site also encourages users to purchase the special one-price Ameripass for unlimited travel for up to 60 days; international visitors get a special International Ameripass for unlimited travel ($179 for 7 days; $269 for 15 days; $369 for 30 days; and $499 for 60 days) which can average as cheap as $8 a day when purchasing the 60-day pass.

Other bus lines and organizations in the United States include the following companies:

American Bus Association:	*www.buses.org*
Grayline:	*www.grayline.com*
Peterpan:	*www.peterpan-bus.com*
Trailways:	*www.trailways.com*

Even though you may not normally take buses, when traveling abroad you should check into the bus situation. As long as they are safe and clean, buses can be a very convenient and inexpensive way to get around locally. In fact, many cities promote bus travel amongst tourists by offering special discount passes for unlimited bus trips for 1, 3, 5, or 10 days. In many European countries, the buses are often considered better than the rail service. If you decide not to travel by rail, you might consider getting a Busabout or Eurolines bus pass. For information on bus travel in Europe, visit this site:

www.bugeurope.com/transport/bus.html

For information on unlimited travel by coach in Europe, visit the Busabout website which explains its network of 70 European cities and how to acquire a consecutive pass for 15 and 21 days or 1, 2, or 3 months or a flexipass:

www.busabout.com

Alternatively, check out Eurolines website which explains how its extensive bus network (500 cities in 25 European countries) operates when you purchase a flexible Eurolines Pass for unlimited travel for up to 30 or 60 days. It includes special discounts for young people under 26 and for senior citizens:

www.eurolines.com

all-hotels.com...has your hotel

The world's leading hotel site with 60,000 hotels worldwide

The Hotels

What's Available!

Discount

Bed & Breakfast

Join all-hotels

Member Login

Services to Hotels

Magazine

Help & Info

About Us

Try Our New Search!

Hire Cars

Flights

Vacation Packages

Currency Converter

Discount Hotels
Looking for a bargain?
Click here for great
deals in selected cities.

What's Available?
Know your dates and
destination? Click here
to book quickly.

Bed & Breakfast
Looking for a more
personal touch? Click
here for somewhere
special.

The Hotels
Gateway to over
60,000 bookable
hotels worldwide.
Click here and use our maps
to guide you to your perfect hotel.

Amazing Savings!
in the all-hotels top ten

Hotels in New York
Los Angeles
Washington DC
Venice
London

Paris
San Antonio
San Diego
Amsterdam
Toronto

Sign up Your Hotel

Advertise With Us

Become an Affiliate

THE RITZ-CARLTON®

ABOUT US · UPCOMING DESTINATIONS · WEDDINGS & HONEYMOONS
GROUP & BUSINESS TRAVEL · GIFT SHOP · CONTACT US · ASSISTANCE · THIS SITE

Welcome
How may we be of assistance?

Would you prefer to make a reservation
or explore our hotels and resorts?

Please select the destination of your choice...

SELECT A HOTEL   GO

THE RITZ-CARLTON®

The Leading Hotels of the World

Find a hotel by name   GO

Custom Hotel Search

retrieve a reservation

destination decisions

leaders club

special selections

alliance partners
Relais & Chateaux

about us

travel talk

*Nestled into country lanes,
languishing by taleum beaches, and astride
great avenues are over 300 of the world's
finest luxury hotels... hotels that have
earned the right to call themselves, Leading
Hotels. However, to find such luxury you
must know the right people and join the right
conversations. Fortunately, you've come to
the right place. After all,*

*When the conversation turns to travel,
people turn to Leading Hotels.*

11

Accommodations

INDING A PLACE TO UNLOAD YOUR GEAR AND SLEEP is always one of those necessary nuisances of travel – unless you are staying in a very special place. Accommodations are one of the advantages cruise ship travelers have over ordinary travelers who must go through the ritual of packing and unpacking several times as they go down the road to their next destination.

Depending on how you like your accommodations – from no-star to five-star – the Internet may become your best friend in finding just the right place, and at the right price, to fit your budget and travel style. You'll discover numerous sites that cater to backpackers in search of hostels, budget travelers seeking inexpensive hotels, individuals who love bed and breakfast experiences, others looking for mid-range hotels and resorts, and those in search of the best of the best in five-star accommodations. Whatever your preferences, the Internet can take you to all the right places, and hopefully at the right prices.

Booking Online Versus Offline

There remains an important debate as how to best book a room at the cheapest price. Similar to airlines that sell their seats at different prices, hotels and resorts also sell their rooms at different prices, depending with whom you make your reservation. For example, should you go through a travel agent, contact the hotel directly, call the toll-free reservation number, book online from a hotel broker or through a hotel reservation system operated by a travel website, or just show up at the front desk?

Numerous studies of hotel and resort booking practices have arrived at a similar conclusion about the best and the worst pricing on rooms. Remember, most properties have different classes of rooms and pricing structures. They offer rack rates, which are the fully published rates, as well as corporate, convention, weekend, senior, educator, minister, three-day stay, and other special discounted rates which they don't widely publicize. You'll have to ask in order to learn about these rates. The worst rate you can pay is the full rack or published rate. You almost always end up paying that rate when you use the hotel's convenient toll-free reservation number that usually connects to some distant central reservation system. When calling that number, you might ask about any specials, but chances are you will be quoted the full rack rate. The cheapest hotel rate you will get is usually when you call directly to the front desk of the hotel and ask about their special rates. You may be surprised to learn the price of your room drops 20 to 30 percent because you called directly and asked the question. Another way to save money is to book your hotel through a travel agent or hotel broker who works with blocks of discounted rooms. In many cases, they may get a better rate than you get by calling the front desk.

Just because a site says it offers discounted rooms is no reason to believe that it offers the best deals around.

So what happens to the price of a room when you book online? There is a good chance you will pay top dollar – the full rack rate for your online efforts to ostensibly save money. At the same time, you may contact an online hotel broker or surf to various travel sites that offer discounted rooms and thereby save 10 to 30 percent off the rack rate. It all depends on whom you work with online. Our advice: shop around both online and offline. Just because a site says it offers discounted rooms is no reason to believe that it offers the best deals around. You may do better by calling the hotel front desk or work through your travel agent. But do visit the websites of the hotels. Like many airlines and car rental firms that now offer online purchasing incentives, such as special discounts and coupons for Internet users only, you may find hotel and resorts enticing more and more people to book directly online rather than pay the standard 10 to 15 commissions to booking agents. Our experience is that, like so much other commerce on the Internet, online room sales are in a state of transition. Smart hotels will increasingly offer specials and discounts to individuals that directly book through their sites. In addition to offering corporate, weekend, senior, educator, and minister discounts, more and more properties will probably offer special "cyberbuyer" discounts.

Gateway and Database Sites

Many of the booking agents we identify in the next chapter operate huge databases of hotels worldwide. Three of the Internet's best hotel booking engines, WorldRes, Inc. (*www.worldres.com*), USA Hotel Guide (*www.usahotelguide.com*), and TravelWeb (*www.travelweb.com*) for example, have relationships with 50,000 to 100,000 hotels around the world. Their booking engines are used by many other websites. They, in effect, function as major gateways to the global accommodations industry; they feed thousands of hotel reservations through their system each day. Other booking engines used by such mega sites as Travelocity and Expedia have similar databases of hotels worldwide. When you access their sites, you can make hotel reservations anywhere in the world; many of their properties are part of the major hotel chains. In fact, you are well advised to do a little research by comparing these sites' online room prices; next check out an online hotel broker to see what prices they offer; and finally go directly to the hotel's website to check on their online prices and see if they offer any additional incentives or specials for cyberbuyers. But you're still not through. At this point, you need to go offline and call or fax the front desk of the hotel to get a price quote – inquire about any specials and then ask for their "best price". You might also check with a travel agent to see if there are any other special unpublicized rates.

The results of this online/offline research, while time consuming, may be both revealing and financially rewarding. You may learn your second highest price will come through the ostensibly cheap travel booking sites in Chapter 12! But, then, you may discover they have the best prices of all. You won't know until you do some basic comparative research. Whatever you do, don't assume you're getting the best price because a website says they are the cheapest. Many of them are unethical or uninformed, which is not how you want to be charged for your room!

Some of the major websites that function as gateways for booking accommodations worldwide include the following:

Accommodation Search Engine:	*www.ase.net*
Hotel Guide:	*www.hotelguide.com*
All-Hotels:	*www.all-hotels.com*
WorldRes, Inc.:	*www.worldres.com*
USA Hotel Guide:	*www.usahotelguide.com*
Hotels Travel:	*www.hotelstravel.com*
TravelWeb:	*www.travelweb.com*
Places to Stay:	*www.placestostay.com*
1Travel:	*www.onetravel.com*
Travelscape:	*www.travelscape.com*
Hotel Scope:	*www.hotelscope.com*

The two mega travel sites include accommodations as one of their major booking channels:

Travelocity:	*www.travelocity.com*
Expedia:	*www.expedia.com*

Two auction sites allow individuals to set their own prices for hotel rooms. Travelfacts Auction functions like a regular auction – individuals bid on what's available for sale. Priceline, on the other hand, operates as a reverse auction – you must give the site your credit card number before you can set your own price; if Priceline accepts your offer on a hotel room, you are automatically charged per your bid. These two sites are interesting to visit simply because of their novel approaches to pricing travel products and services:

Travelfacts Auction:	*www.bid4travel.com*
Priceline:	*www.priceline.com*

Hotel Brokers and Discounters

Hotel brokers are to the hotel industry what consolidators are to the airline industry. They work with discounted rooms, including both the budget and premium ends of the market. A room with a rack rate of $200 a night might go for $140 through a hotel broker; at the same hotel a $450 superior suite might be priced at $325 through the broker. Many room brokers claim they discount rooms from 40 to 65 percent off the rack rate, but don't believe the hype since it's actually closer to 10 to 20 percent; some of their prices may even be higher than a quote you get directly from the front desk for a weekend special or some other type of special promotion. Some brokers discount rooms by buying blocks of rooms from hotels at large discounts and then reselling them to the public at modest discounts; others specialize in discounting excess room inventories to last-minute travelers. After all, an unsold room generates zero income for a hotel; it's better to get something than nothing for those empty rooms, which is where hotel brokers play an important role in the accommodations game.

In the past, most hotel brokers operated like airline bucket shops – you called a toll-free number to get a quote. Today, they still have their toll-free numbers but they also have an Internet presence. You interface with brokers in one of two ways. First, some require prepayment for the room and give you a reservation number. Second, others give you a reservation number and you pay the hotel when you check out. Ideally, you should try to pay as you check out, although the major brokers want prepayment.

Here are some of the major hotel brokers whom you can contact on the Internet. While most focus on hotels in North America, others also include many cities around the world. The largest discount broker is Hotel Reservations Network (which also has an international presence):

Hotel Reservations Network:	*www.hoteldiscount.com*
Quikbook:	*www.quikbook.com*
Accommodations Express:	*www.accommodationsexpress.com*
1-800-USA-Hotels:	*www.1800usahotels.com*
Central Reservation Service:	*www.reservation-services.com*
1Travel's Hotel Wiz:	*www.hotelwiz.com*
Hotel Discounts:	*www.hoteldiscounts.com*

There is more to hotel discounting than just reducing the rack rate. One innovative website, Roomsaver, offers online hotel discount coupons that may be good for up to 50 percent savings on over 5,000 hotels, motels, and resorts in the United States. However, it's more likely you'll get $5 off the going rate which more often than not represents a 7 percent discount. Most of the properties are familiar middle-range North American brands, such as Holiday Inn, Best Western, Days Inn, Red Roof, Super 8 Motel, Econo Lodge, Hampton

Inn, Quality Inn, La Quinta Inn, Ramada, Travelodge, Courtyard by Marriott, and Fairfield Inn. The properties are only obliged to honor the coupons for "walk ins" who arrive when there are extra rooms available:

www.roomsaver.com

One final word of caution when working with hotel brokers and discounters. There may be much less there than what initially meets the eye with advertising hype. In other words, before booking a room through one of the discounters, call the hotel directly (not the toll-free reservation number which will give you the central reservation system and probably the full rack rate) and ask about their current rates and any specials (Are you a student, teacher, over 60, a minister, member of AAA or some mileage club, or a business person going "commercial"?). You may discover the so-called discount broker's rate is actually higher than the front desk's rate. Again, the 65 percent discount claim is more advertising hype that the reality of these Internet operations. You won't know unless you check other options as well.

Hostels

Hostels are nearly synonymous with young backbackers and other budget travelers who rely a great deal on hostels to keep themselves within budget as well as in touch with friends and family back home and on the road through cybercafes located near their hostel. Indeed, you can save a great deal of money on travel when you only have to spend $5 to $15 a night on such accommodations. These are the places where many dedicated Lonely Planet guidebook followers sleep on the cheap as well as make contacts with other budget travelers, exchange travel tips, and basically travel in a highly networked community of like-minded travelers.

The good news for budget travelers is that the hostel business is very well organized on the Internet. Just visit a few of the following key websites and you will discover a well organized world of hostelling. The largest and most informative hostel website – boasting a huge database of hostels worldwide as well as chat groups, feature articles, travel tips, news, traveler tales, and related products and services – is the well-designed Hostels.com:

Hostels.com:	*www.hostels.com*
Backpacker:	*www.thebackpacker.net*
Hosteling International:	*www.iyhf.org*
American Youth Hostels:	*www.hiayh.org*
Hostels Europe:	*www.hostelseurope.com*
Budget Travel:	*www.budgettravel.com/hostels.htm*
Hostel Watch:	*www.hostelwatch.com*
Hostel Network:	*www.hostelnetwork.com*
4Hostels:	*www.4hostels.com*
Eurotrip:	*www.eurotrip.com*
YHA Australia:	*www.yha.org.au*
Backpackers Canada:	*www.backpackers.ca*
Backpack New Zealand:	*www.backpack.co.nz*
Stay4Free:	*www.stay4free.com*

Inns, B&Bs, and Homestays

Contrary to what many people may think, staying in inns and bed and breakfasts is not necessarily budget-style travel. Indeed, many inns and bed and breakfasts are definitely first-class, and with prices to match! Nonetheless, you'll find many budget inns and bed and breakfast accommodations throughout the world. They especially appeal to travelers who love to stay in quaint inns and homey B&Bs that have real character and where they have opportunities to meet interesting fellow travelers and swap road tales.

Like the hostel community of travelers, B&B and inn travelers also are relatively well organized on the Internet. If you're looking for inns and B&Bs, there's no better place to start than with the website Bed and Breakfast which includes a directory of more than 25,000 inns and B&Bs worldwide:

www.bedandbreakfast.com

While this site may meet all your B&B needs, you might want to explore several other useful bed and breakfast sites:

International Bed & Breakfast Pages:	*www.ibbp.com*
Internet Guide to Bed & Breakfast Inns:	*www.traveldata.com*

1 Bed & Breakfast Avenue:	*www.bed-and-breakfast-inns.com*
Bed & Breakfast List:	*www.bnblist.com*
Bed & Breakfast Online:	*www.bbonline.com*
North American Bed & Breakfast Directory:	*www.bbdirectory.com*
Bed & Breakfast Inns, America's Inn Directory:	*www.bedandbreakfast.nu*
Inn Site:	*www.innsite.com*
111 Travel Directory:	*www.triple1.com*
Bed and Breakfast Inns in North America:	*http://cimarron.net*
Professional Association of Innkeepers International:	*www.paii.org*

Many travelers enjoy participating in homestays, a form of accommodations where you actually live with a local family. The concept of homestays is very strong in the United Kingdom, Australia, and New Zealand. They are especially popular with young high school and college students who go abroad to study a foreign language and wish to also learn about the local culture and society by living with a local family. If you are interested in homestays, check out these sites:

British Homestays:	*www.homestays.co.uk*
	www.hpn.org.uk
Global Routes:	*www.globalroutes.org/high_school/homestay.htm*
American International Homestays:	*www.spectravel.com/homes*
North American Homestay:	*www.ici-canada.com/homestay*
Australia Homestay:	*www.homestay.com.au*
New Zealand Homestays:	*www.homestays.net.nz*
	www.homes.co.nz/Homestays
Russia Homestays:	*www.123russia.com*
Korean Homestay:	*www.koreanhomestay.com*
Cultural Homestay Intl:	*www.chinet.org*

Rentals and Exchanges

If you prefer accommodations in the form of vacation rentals and exchanges, go to these sites:

Vacation Homes:	www.vacationhomes.com
World Wide Travel	
Exchange:	www.wwte.com
Vacation Homes Unlimited:	www.vacation-homes.com
Vacation Spot:	www.vacationspot.com
Home Exchange:	www.homeexchange.com
Holi Swaps:	www.holi-swaps.com
Villa Rentals:	www.villa-rentals.com
HolidayBank:	www.holidaybank.co.up
ResortQuest:	www.resortquest.com
International Vacation	
Homes:	www.ivacation.com
Ocean Front Properties:	www.oceanfrontproperties.com
Stay4Free:	www.stay4free.com

Major Hotel and Resort Chains

While you can book most hotels and resorts online by using the various global booking systems we've identified thus far, you also may want to explore individual properties of the major hotel chains. In addition to researching the properties, you should check out their direct-booking prices. Some hotels will offer incentives to encourage you to book online with them rather than go to another site or travel agent that will receive a 10 to 15 percent commission for their services.

If top quality accommodations are important in your travels, be sure to visit these sites which represent some of the world's best properties:

Ritz-Carlton:	www.ritzcarlton.com
Four Seasons/Regent:	www.fourseasons.com
Amanresorts:	www.amanresorts.com
Mandarin-Oriental:	www.mandarin-oriental.com
Peninsula Group:	www.peninsula.com
Orient-Express:	www.orient-expresshotels.com
Shangri-La Hotels:	www.shangri-la.com
Rosewood Hotels & Resorts:	www.rosewoodhotels.com
General Hotel Management:	www.ghmhotels.com

Many of the world's top hotels and resorts – from big to boutique – belong to marketing groups that have websites for promoting the various properties:

Leading Hotels of the World:	*www.lhw.com*
Leading Small Hotels of the World:	*www.slh.com*
Preferred Hotels & Resorts:	*www.preferredhotels.com*
Relais & Chateaux:	*www.relaischateaux.com*
Design Hotels International:	*www.designhotels.com*
Boutique Lodging:	*www.boutiquelodging.com*
The Kimpton Group:	*www.kimptongroup.com*

Some of the top properties can be booked through a website that specializes in luxurious travel accommodations and tours (also see pages 89-92):

www.luxury4less.com

Other major hotel chains also have their own websites which allow you to explore their properties and make online reservations. The major hotel chains include:

Best Western:	*www.bestwestern.com*
Clarion:	*www.clarioninn.com*
Club Med:	*www.clubmed.com*
Comfort Inns and Suites:	*www.confortinn.com*
Courtyard by Marriott:	*www.courtyard.com*
Days Inn:	*www.daysinn.com*
Doubletree:	*www.doubletreehotels.com*
Embassy Suites:	*www.embassy-suites.com*
Fairfield Hotels:	*www.fairfieldinn.com*
Forte and Le Meridien:	*www.forte-hotels.com*
Hilton:	*www.hilton.con*
Holiday Inn:	*www.holiday-inn.com*
Hyatt:	*www.hyatt.com*
Inter-Continental:	*www.interconti.com*
Kempinski Hotels:	*www.kempinski.com*
La Quinta Hotels:	*www.laquinta.com*
Marriott:	*www.marriott.com*
Moevenpick Hotels:	*www.moevenpick-hotels.ch*
Nikko:	*www.nikkohotels.com*
Omni:	*www.omnihotels.com*

Radisson:	*www.radisson.com*
Ramada:	*www.ramada.com*
Sandals Resorts:	*www.sandals.com*
Sheraton:	*www.sheraton.com*
Sofitel Hotels:	*www.sofitel.com*
Sol Melia Resorts:	*www.meliahotels.com*
Swissotel:	*www.swissotel.com*
Travelodge:	*www.travelodge.com*
Trump Hotels & Casinos:	*www.trump.com*
Westin:	*www.westin.com*
Wyndham Hotels:	*www.wyndham.com*

If you want to explore some of the best three-, four-, and five-star properties around the world, we highly recommend visiting the accommodations section of the Fodor's travel site:

www.fodors.com

Relatively unbiased, the descriptions are based on the Fodor's highly respected travel guidebook series. Each hotel is summarized and the most highly recommended properties receive a red asterisk. You can usually depend on Fodor's getting their hotel recommendations, as well as their restaurant recommendations, close to the mark.

Expedia.com

Book a United F
30% of

home | flights | hotels | cars | packages | cruises | destinations & interests | maps

Search Expedia.com: [____] Go

My Trips

msn.com

Cruise Specials from $249
Expedia Cruises

National Airlines
Fare Sale
Ends September 16th

Alamo
Autumn deals on midsize cars and SUVs

CUSTOMER SUPPORT
- Privacy and security
- Credit Card Guarantee
- Agents on call 24 hrs.
- New to the site?

Welcome to Expedia.com! Already a member? Sign in

WHAT'S NEW

travels

Expedia Travels magazine: Get the first issue free
We'd like to invite you to soak in a free trial copy of the premiere issue of *Expedia Travels*, the pioneering publication brought to you by Expedia and Ziff-Davis.

Expedia goes wireless
Download flight information to your cell phone or handheld.

Join our Associates Program
Partner with Expedia.com to sell travel and earn a commission.

Adventure Travel: Go wild
We partnered with Away.com to bring you the best adventure vacations.

Beat air traffic jams: 10 survival tips
Sidestep the hassles of flight delays and enjoy your trip.

EXPRESS SEARCH

○ Flights   ○ Hotels   ○ Cars

TODAY'S DEALS
United promotion: 30% off
Northwest flights: 16% off
New travel magazine: free
More special deals

TRAVEL PROVIDERS
Lodging & Resorts
Family Vacations
Hawaii Vacations
Tee Times & Gear
Adventure Vacations
Vacation Packages
Cruises

EXPEDIA SERVICES
Associates Program
Mobile Services

SPECIALTY TRAVEL INDEX

- Destinations
- Activities
- Tour Operators
- Special Offers
- Subscribe Now!
- Travel Stories
- Advertising
- About Us

Home Contact Us

The #1 Source for Adventure and Special Interest Travel

Search our information from over 600 tour operators

Select below to view category listings:

Destination   Activity Index   Tour Operators

Editorial Features

Dancing with the Deities: A Brazilian Workshop

Sheila Mary Koch pursues the pulse of the ancients in an Afro-Brazilian dance workshop.

Roof of the World: Skiing France's Vallée Blanche

Hair-raising runs and surreal glacial vistas

Lorry Heverly finds regal repose in historic Portuguese palaces

---

WELCOME TO
americanexpress.com

My American Express | **Personal** | Small Business | Merchants | Corporations
For individual Card, financial, travel & shopping needs

CARDS

Apply for a Card
- Learn more and apply online – it's fast and secure
- Meet Blue from American Express

Manage your Card accounts Online
- Log in here
- Register to access your accounts online - Check and pay your bill, update your Card account information, and more.

Take advantage of great offers and rewards
- Go to the Offer Zone℠
- Learn about the *Membership Rewards*® program

Get more information about Cards
- Visit our Cards Center
- Got Blue? Click here

FINANCIAL SERVICES

Log in to Your Account
- Online Brokerage
- Online Banking
- Accounts with Advisors
- Retirement Services - 401 (k)

Invest, Bank and Borrow Online
- Online Brokerage – Qualify for FREE online trading.
- Online Banking – Receive great rates and superior service.
- Loans – Mortgages, education loans, credit lines, and more.

More Financial Products & Services
- Work with an Advisor
- Tools & Financial Planning
- Funds & Investments
- Insurance
- Retirement
- 401 (k) & Workplace Services
- Visit Our Financial Services Center – Learn more about reaching and enjoying your financial goals.

12

Middlemen and Their Key Suppliers

THE TRAVEL BUSINESS IS RUN BY THOUSANDS OF entrepreneurial middlemen and suppliers involved in sales and marketing of travel products and services. Most come in the form of travel agents, consolidators, and brokers who work with a variety of travel suppliers – airlines, hotels, cruise lines, car rental companies, and tour operators. Oriented toward sales performance, they derive their major income from commissions on actual sales, the middlemen are primarily in the business of booking airline tickets, hotel rooms, car rentals, cruises, and tour packages.

New Relationships and Challenges

The Internet has upset many of the traditional relationships between suppliers and middlemen. It has especially eroded the key element that bound them together – the 10-15 percent commission on each transaction. Suppliers – mainly airlines, hotels, and car rental companies – have discovered via new technology how easy and profitable it is to bypass the traditional middlemen and go online to sell their products and services directly to consumers. They also have been willing to work directly with a new group of travel middlemen – online booking agents and their affiliates that compete fiercely with traditional travel agents as well as amongst themselves. At least in the case of online travel, the Internet gold rush has centered on the activities of online booking agents who move billions of dollars in travel sales each month at the expense of traditional travel agents, many of whom have seen their businesses quickly erode because of new online competition for travel sales. Many travel agents have gone out of business or transformed their businesses into specialty travel agencies that primarily work with two relatively loyal travel suppliers – cruise lines and tour groups. The days of generating a large portion of travel agency income from issuing airline tickets and booking hotel rooms and car rentals has largely given way to the core business of promoting cruises and specialty tours. In so doing, savvy travel agents have learned to incorporate the Internet into their new specialty travel services.

At the same time, fierce competition is taking place between Internet travel businesses that primarily derive their income from booking airlines, hotels, and car rentals. Many Internet travel businesses have either consolidated (ITN with American Express, Preview Travel with Travelocity, and GetThere with Sabre) or closed their operations (Wal-Mart). And much of the newest competition is coming from travel suppliers who also are selling their products and services directly to the public. A case in point is the current Internet wars between Expedia and Travelocity/Priceline as well as the war that will take place between the soon-to-launch airline-owned Orbitz/Hotwire sites which may effectively eliminate, or significantly downsize, Expedia and Travelocity. The benefactor in these wars should be you, the travel consumer.

Travel Agents

Although they may not like this characterization, most travel agents are basically retail ticketing representatives and trip planners; some like to be called "professional travel consultants". They sell travel products produced by other companies, be it airline tickets, hotel rooms, cruises, and tours. Few offer a unique travel product, although a few travel agencies may organize specialty tours which then puts them more into the class of tour operators (see last section in this chapter). As such, they are vulnerable to the application of new technology to the ticketing and travel planning processes. Indeed, travel agents have become the poster boys for the negative impact of technology on traditional travel sales functions. Today there are 20 percent fewer bricks and mortar travel agents in North America than there were five years ago. Numerous travel agencies, many of which were always on the financial edge even in good times, have closed their doors or merged with larger agencies because of three factors: intense competition amongst agencies, the declining commission base forced by airlines, and the role of the Internet in eroding their customer base (over 30 percent of travelers now book their airline tickets online which represents a major lose in revenue for bricks and mortar travel agents). Even travel schools that used to primarily train travel agents have all gone out of business within the past two years. Not surprisingly, traditional travel agents are viewed as a dying breed.

But travel agents also are an entrepreneurial lot. While some are still in "Internet denial", others have adjusted to, indeed embraced, the new Internet travel era by becoming Internet savvy themselves and by shifting the focus of their businesses to cruises and specialty tours. Recognizing the need to become more customer service oriented, they have focused on developing a local client base of repeat travelers who turn to them for travel expertise that is not readily available on the Internet. They become knowledgeable about specific destinations and custom-design tours for both independent and group travelers. Linking their businesses to the Internet with their own home pages, many of these travel agent survivors have seen their businesses prosper. For them, the Internet

> *Travel agents have become the poster boys for the negative impact of technology on traditional travel sales functions.*

is an important part of their business rather than a competitor. While the Internet wars rage for booking airline tickets, hotels, and car rentals, this new breed of travel agent stays above the fray and continues to add value with specialty travel services – and new benefits for clients.

As we've said throughout this book, don't forget your travel agent; he or she may come in handy during various stages of your travel planning. If you work with one who really knows the travel business, you may find a happy medium for your Internet activities. Like many other travelers who use the Internet, they primarily use it to conduct travel research prior to contacting and using their travel agent. They gather destination information, compare airline and hotel prices, and join in discussion groups. But in the end, they may let their travel agent attend to all the details involved in booking flights, hotels, cars, cruises, and tours. Making all these arrangements yourself can be very time consuming. And in the end, you may not get as good a deal on the Internet as you may through a travel agent.

But how do you find a real live travel agent or specialist with whom you can speak over the phone or meet in person? Ironically, you initially find them on the Internet. Thousands of travel agents now have their own websites. If, for example, you are interested in traveling to Vietnam, Laos, Cambodia, or Myanmar, you may want to contact a travel agency, such as Global Spectrum (*www.vietnamspecialists.com*) that specializes in individual and group tours to these areas. If you are interested in traveling to India, just go to the New York City India Tourist Office site (*www.tourindia.com*) website for a listing of tour operators (under "Travel Info") focused on India. Alternatively, use various search engines to identify travel agents specializing in particular destinations.

One of the best sources for identifying specialty travel agents is the website operated by the American Society of Travel Agents (ASTA):

www.astanet.com

Click on to the "Traveler" section and then again on to "Find a Travel Agent" to locate all types of specialists in the travel industry. For example, you can use the search engine to find a travel agency specializing in bicycling in Europe by specifying these criteria from a list of specialties and destinations. Just click onto the search button and this program will search its database of over 26,000 members in 130 countries to find matches. Since this is a very reputable association of travel specialties, we highly recommend using this site for locating travel professionals. In Great Britain, the counterpart organization is the Association of British Travel Agents: *www.abtanet.com*.

Another useful website is the Institute of Certified Travel Counselors. This organization refers to itself as *"The certification organization that trains travel agents to become travel experts!"* It maintains an online directory of members that you can search by keyword:

www.icta.com

Just click on to the button to the left that says "Show Me the Certified Travel Agents in My Community".

If you are interested in contacting one of the top 1 percent of travel agents in North America, visit the exclusive Virtuoso site for personalized service from the "best of the best" in the business:

www.virtuoso.com

Alternatively, you may want to search for a travel agent by contacting some of the largest franchised travel agencies which have offices in many different cities and countries. Such travel agency brands as American Express, Carlson Wagonlit Travel, and Uniglobe represent three of the world's largest and most respected such agencies. Visit their websites to find the locations of their offices:

American Express Travel: *www.americanexpress.com*
Carlson Wagonlit Travel: *www.carlsontravel.com*
Uniglobe: *www.uniglobe.com*

These sites allow you to locate travel agencies by city, state, country, and/or specialty. These also are jam-packed with travel information, tips, and specials. Best of all, two of the sites (American Express and Uniglobe) have an extensive global network of offices.

Online Booking Sites and Resellers

Much of the commerce that takes place on the Internet focuses on booking airline tickets, hotel rooms, and car rentals and, to a much lesser extent, cruises, tours, and rail passes. In other words, many travel website sites are basically online travel agencies or resellers – the retail side of the travel business which does not produce any particularly unique travel products. As resellers, they are into selling travel products developed by other companies. Like their offline travel agent counterparts, these websites are in a fiercely competitive business which is vulnerable to the continuing application of new technology that may substantially alter the relation between producer, distributor, and consumer. Accordingly, the trend is to develop a direct link between producer and consumer and thereby eliminate the overhead and nuisance costs of these middlemen/distributors. Since the services of both online and offline travel agencies do not involve any heavy lifting of products – all transactions can be done electronically except for passing out glossy brochures and catalogs – the future viability of the new electronic middlemen in the travel business remains uncertain.

Before using any of the following booking websites, you may want to go to BizRate and ScoreCard to see how various travel agencies and their suppliers are rated by consumers:

BizRate: *www.bizrate.com*
ScoreCard: *www.scorecard.com*

These sites rate several online travel agents (Airlines on the Web, American Express, ByeByeNow, Carlsontravel, Expedia, Leisure Planet, Travel Hero, Travelocity, and Trip.com) as well as airlines, hotels, cruises, and car rental companies. However, keep in mind that the number of consumer evaluations of these sites may be very small and thus not representative of reality.

Most of the booking or reservation websites offer a comprehensive selection of choices for at least three of six major travel products – airlines, hotels, car rentals, cruise ships, vacation packages, and rail passes. The two largest sites – Travelocity and Expedia – as well as several other groups, also offer affiliate programs to other travel sites that enable them to provide what is known in the trade as "seamless" and "branded" systems. However, they feed into the same major reservation systems. For example, when you make an airline reservation through the popular Frommer's site (*www.frommers.com*), you're actually making this reservation through their affiliate link with Travelocity (*www.travelocity.com*) which "powers" their site. In other words, when you make an airline reservation through Frommer's, it goes directly into Travelocity's reservation system. The development of affiliate programs designed around these reservation systems has enabled many travel sites to offer comprehensive travel services along with their own unique content and thus dramatically increase the availability, and redundancy, of such travel services online.

One new development to look for in mid-2001 is what is known as "T5" in the industry. Five major airlines (American, Continental, Delta, Northwest, and United) have banded together to offer their own cooperative site called Orbitz (*www.orbitz.com*). The site has developed partnership relationships with other travel suppliers (Advantage and Hertz for car rentals and National Leisure Group for vacation and cruise packages) and content providers (Accuweather, Lonely Planet, Map-Quest, and Zagat). In addition, Orbitz will challenge Travelocity's affiliate relationship with reverse auction site Priceline.com by developing a similar affiliate relationship with a new reverse auction site (minus Priceline's onerous restrictions) called Hotwire (*www.hotwire.com*).

The implications of such a new mega-site player have been unsettling for many traditional travel agents, who already suffered the impact of decreasing commissions and competition from online travel suppliers. This new site could very well put many online travel suppliers out of business by undercutting their prices. Indeed, look for some fascinating online travel wars in 2001 as Orbitz takes on what have become the 800 pound gorillas of Internet travel planning – Travelocity and Expedia – neither of which are profitable Internet operations at present. We would expect further consolidation within the online travel community with the entry of this big new player. Orbitz signals what is a growing trend – further bypass, and thus eliminate, travel middlemen by dealing directly with customers through their own online travel sites.

The number of online booking agents is incredible. Here are some of the most popular sites. Most offer similar products and services, although the big two – Travelocity and Expedia – are increasingly diversifying their sites with more and more travel content, tips, news articles, message boards, and travel tools. Their goal is to become one-stop shops for all travel needs. The first five sites represent the mega booking sites with Orbitz and Hotwire scheduled to launch within the very near future. These five sites are the major players in the coming Internet travel war.

Mega Booking Sites

Expedia:	*www.expedia.com*
Travelocity:	*www.travelocity.com*
Priceline:	*www.priceline.com*
Orbitz:	*www.orbitz.com*
Hotwire:	*www.hotwire.com*

Other Booking Sites

1Travel:	*www.1travel.com*
Air4Less:	*www.air4less.com*
AirDeals:	*www.airdeals.com*
AirFare:	*www.airfare.com*
Airlines of the Web:	*www.flyaow.com*
Atevo:	*www.atevo.com*
American Express:	*www.americanexpress.com*
BestFares:	*www.bestfares.com*
Biztravel:	*www.biztravel.com*
ByeByeNow:	*www.byebyenow.com*
Carlson Travel:	*www.carlsontravel.com*

CheapTickets:	*www.cheaptickets.com*
Conde Nast Traveler:	*www.concierge.com*
Cruise Value:	*www.cruisevalue.com*
eBookers:	*www.ebookers.com*
EconomyTravel:	*www.economytravel.com*
ETN Links:	*www.etnlinks.com*
Etravnet:	*www.etravnet.com*
Faraway:	*www.faraway.com*
GetThere:	*www.getthere.com*
InformedTravel:	*www.informedtravel.com*
International Discount Travel:	*www.idttravel.com*
LeisurePlanet:	*www.leisureplanet.com*
Lowest Fare:	*www.lowestfare.com*
Moments Notice:	*www.moments-notice.com*
MrCheap:	*www.mrcheap.com*
MyTravelCo:	*www.mytravelco.com*
OneTravel:	*www.onetravel.com*
SkyAuction:	*www.skyauction.com*
SmarterLiving:	*www.smarterliving.com*
Superfare:	*www.superfare.com*
Ticketplanet:	*www.ticketplanet.com*
Travelbreak:	*www.travelbreak.com*
TravelersAdvantage:	*www.travelersadvantage.com*
TravelersNet:	*www.travelersnet.com*
TravelFile:	*www.travelfile.com*
TravelHero:	*www.travelhero.com*
TravelNow:	*www.travelnow.com*
TravelScape:	*www.travelscape.com*
TravelZoo:	*www.travelzoo.com*
Trip.com:	*www.trip.com*
Uniglobe:	*www.uniglobe.com*
USA Hotel Guide:	*www.usahotelguide.com*
Vacation.com:	*www.vacation.com*
Yahoo:	*http://travel.yahoo.com*

Last-Minute Deals

Several booking sites specialize in alerting travelers to late notice or last minute deals. For example, a seven-day cruise to the Caribbean that normally goes for $1195 per person may be discounted at the last minute for $595 per person. Offering excess inventories, these sites are of special interest to individuals who are flexible enough to take advantage of such deals:

Moments Notice:	*www.moments-notice.com*
Site 59:	*www.site59.com*
Bargain Holidays:	*www.bargainholidays.com*
BestFares:	*www.bestfares.com*
LastMinute:	*www.lastminute.com*
LastMinuteTravel:	*www.lastminutetravel.com*
Cruise Stand-bys:	*www.cruisestandbys.com*

Auctions and Reverse Auctions

A few sites operate online travel auctions. The major players include:

Travelfacts Auction:	*www.bid4travel.com*
Priceline.com:	*www.priceline.com*
HotWire:	*www.hotwire.com*

Travelfacts Auction, for example, functions similarly to eBay: individuals bid against travel products during set auction periods, with the highest bidders purchasing the products when the auction ends. Other sites, like Priceline.com, have pioneered the reverse auction – you state what price you are willing to pay for particular travel products. If, for example, the rack rate for a hotel room is $250 per night and you offer $150, Priceline.com checks its costs, calculates its profit margins, and then lets you know if it is acceptable to them (they want you to think the supplier is actually doing this calculating when, in fact, they control the pricing). The real downside of Priceline.com's system is its requirement that you give them a credit card number and automatically pay for the product if Priceline.com accepts your bid. In a recent example, someone bid $180 for a roundtrip ticket from Washington, DC to Chicago; Priceline.com accepted the bid, automatically charged the amount to the bidder's credit card, and issued the ticket. The only problem was the arrival and departure times: the plane departed late evening and returned early morning the next day. But the bidder had to automatically accept this terrible scheduling situation because he had agreed to Priceline.com's terms. The only way to make a change was to incur a $75 cancellation fee. Priceline.com is currently affiliated with Travelocity.

A new reverse auction site, Hotwire.com, in affiliation with Orbitz, will give Priceline.com a run for its money because it eliminates this automatic purchase requirement. Hotwire.com allows the bidder up to 30 minutes to either accept or reject the offer, which is enough time to rethink one's schedule and perhaps shop elsewhere. Needless to say, Hotwire.com's competition will probably result in changes in Priceline. com's current reverse auction rules. It should liven up the competition between the auction sites and discount brokers.

Consolidators and Around-the-World Deals

Consolidators offer some of the best travel deals. Like their room broker counterparts in the accommodations business, consolidators offer blocks of deep discounted air tickets to the public. Operating "bucket shops", and often running small dense box ads in the Sunday editions of major newspapers, consolidators usually beat the prices of travel agents and online resellers. For an excellent orientation into the world of consolidators, read Edward Hasbrouck's book, *The Practical Nomad* (Moon). The relevant chapter on consolidators, including many Q&As, is available online through Travel-Library.com:

www.travel-library.com/air-travel/consolidators

Many consolidators also offer excellent around-the-world fares which may be cheaper that point-to-point fares for many long-distance locations. The major online consolidators and around-the-world ticketing specialists include:

International Air Consolidators:	*www.intl-air-consolidators.com*
TicketPlanet:	*www.ticketplanet.com*
IDT Travel:	*www.idttravel.com*
Air Treks:	*www.airtreks.com*
Air Brokers:	*www.airbrokers.com*
Avia Travel:	*www.aviatravel.com*

Air Couriers

Air couriers offer another inexpensive airline ticketing option for many budget travelers who might otherwise take the train, bus, or freighter.

For a good overview of the "ins" and "outs" of flying as an air courier, visit this site:

http://budgettravel.about.com/travel/budgettravl/msubaircourier.htm

Many companies still use private couriers to transport valuable documents and products. If you work with an air courier, chances are you can acquire a deep discounted ticket for your leisure labor; occasionally you may be able to fly free. A roundtrip ticket from Los Angeles to Singapore, for example, which might retail for $1199, may be acquired through an air courier for $250. In other words, air couriers will subsidize the cost of your flight in exchange for your courier services. However, there are certain restrictions you must accept, including scheduling times, with these operations. The four major air courier organizations include:

International Association of Air Couriers:	*www.courier.org*
Air Courier:	*www.aircourier.org*
Cheap Trips:	*www.cheaptrips.com*
Air Hitch:	*www.airhitch.org*

The International Air Courier Association site includes lots of travel information, articles, tips, and a free handbook and newsletter for members (*Courier Handbook* and *Shoestring Traveler*) in addition to the courier specials, whereas Air Hitch is a basic no-frills courier information and sales site. Like many of the freighter sites identified in Chapter 10 (Travlips and Freighter World Cruises), all of the courier sites require membership in their programs in order to be eligible for the courier specials. Membership requires enrollment fees that run about $40 to $50 a year.

Tour Operators

Tour operators continue to do a booming business as more and more people decide to travel with organized groups. Finding a tour that's right for you is relatively easy if you use the Internet. Several websites function as gateway sites for identifying specialty tours involving everything from biking, rock climbing, and ballooning to culinary, golf, and spa tours. For online information and directories of various specialty tours, visit these sites which provide contact information to the major specialty tour groups:

Specialty Travel:	*www.specialtytravel.com*
InfoHub:	*www.infohub.com*
Shaw Guides:	*www.shawguides.com*
JourneyQuest:	*www.journeyquest.com*
Specialty World Travel:	*www.specialtyworldtravel.com*

For a complete alphabetical listing of specialty tour companies, go to Travel Smith's site (*www.travelsmith.com*) and click onto "The Best Travel Companies Directory."

You'll discover many major tour groups on the Internet, ranging from high-end Abercrombie and Kent and Travcoa to more modest and budget tour groups as Cosmos and Valtur. Many tour groups also specialize in African safaris. Some of the best tour groups, which also have a presence on the Internet, include:

Abercrombie & Kent:	*www.abercrombiekent.com*
Backroads:	*www.backroads.com*
Big Five Tours/Expeditions:	*www.bigfive.com*
Brendan Tours:	*www.brendantours.com*
Butterfield & Robinson:	*www.butterfieldandrobinson.com*
Collette Tours:	*www.collettetours.com*
Contiki:	*www.contiki.com*
Cosmos Tours:	*www.globusandcosmos.com*
Country Walkers:	*www.countrywalkers.com*
Cox & Kings:	*http://zenonet/cox-kings*
Distrav:	*www.distrav.com*
Geographic Expeditions:	*www.GeoEx.com*
Globus:	*www.globusandcosmos.com*
Insight Vacations:	*www.insighttours.com*
Intrav:	*www.INTRAV.com*
Ker & Downey Safaris:	*www.kerdowney.com*
Lindblad Expeditions:	*www.expeditions.com*
Micato Safaris:	*www.africansafari.org/micato*
Maupintour:	*www.maupintour.com*
Mountain Travel Sobek:	*www.mtsobek.com*
Odysseys Unlimited:	*www.odysseys-unlimited.com*
Off the Beaten Path:	*www.offbeatenpath.com*

Overseas Adventure Travel:	*www.oattravel.com*
Perillo Tours:	*www.perillotours.com*
Rascals in Paradise:	*www.rascalsinparadise.com*
Saga Holidays:	*www.sagaholidays.som*
Tauck World Discovery:	*www.tauck.com*
Trafalgar Tours:	*www.trafalgartours.com*
Travcoa:	*www.travcoa.com*
Valtur:	*www.valtur-usa.com*
VBT Bicycling Vacations:	*www.vbt.com*
Wilderness Travel:	*www.wildernesstravel.com*

Whether you're an independent traveler or one who enjoys specialty group travel, check out these many fine tour sites. If nothing else, they should stimulate lots of interesting travel ideas. You may even want to send them an email requesting their catalog or brochures. As much as we love the Internet for travel planning, there's still nothing like receiving the glossy travel catalogs and brochures in the mail from Abercrombie and Kent, Tauck World Discovery, Lindblad Expeditions, or Travcoa and then curling up in bed to dream about your next great travel adventure. The photos and itineraries are as fabulous as the trips many thousands of travelers take and praise each year with these outstanding companies. Like the incredible Crystal cruise line, these fine tour operators make travel dreams come true. Although some may be expensive, they do produce a top quality travel product that everyone, even the most ardent independent traveler, should some day have a chance to experience.

India

Dzień Dobry　　こんにちは　　Hola

Welcome to India

- India Online
- Travel Info
- Tourist Locales
- Regions & States
- State Tourism Sites
- Related Links
- Tourist Offices WW
- Tourism News
- Plan Your Trip

1132066

This site is supported by India Tourist Office, New York (Disclaimer)
Please send your comments and suggestions to WebMaster

also visit Government of India - Ministry of Tourism's site

---

digitalcity
Make It Your Town™

Welcome to Digital City

Choose a City in

Alabama	Missouri
Alaska	Montana
Arizona	Nebraska
Arkansas	Nevada
California	New Hampshire
Colorado	New Jersey
Connecticut	New Mexico
Delaware	New York
District of Columbia	North Carolina
Florida	North Dakota
Georgia	Ohio
Hawaii	Oklahoma
Idaho	Oregon
Illinois	Pennsylvania
Indiana	Rhode Island
Iowa	South Carolina
Kansas	South Dakota
Kentucky	Tennessee
Louisiana	Texas
Maine	Utah
Maryland	Vermont
Massachusetts	Virginia
Michigan	Washington
Minnesota	West Virginia
Mississippi	Wisconsin
	Wyoming

Local Entertainment, People, News, Sports and More!

Digital City Your complete guide to going out and getting stuff done in the nation's largest cities.

Your Town Local links, local tools and local people, from coast to coast.

Find a City

Type your zip code or the name of a city or town below:

[ ] Go

Ex. *Hollywood, CA* or *90210*

The Boston Globe's
boston.com

Boston.com home ▾
PULL DOWN FOR OTHER SECTIONS Go

CLICK HERE FOR
The Boston Globe
ONLINE

THURSDAY, SEPTEMBER 14, 2000

MAKE US YOUR HOMEPAGE
Here's how
Win $100

MARKETPLACE
Apartments
Auctions
CareerPath
Cars
Classifieds
Personals
Real Estate
Shopping

GARDENING

Fall-blooming anemones are little-known garden treasures of the season. ▸ Story
▸ Gardener's Week

SJC wants child support after death

Even if you die, your obligation to pay child support continues, Massachusetts' highest court ruled today.

SJC POLL
Should you have to pay child support after you die?
○ Yes | ○ No
Submit

Home Delivery
Special Offer

Market Watch

DOW　　11,100.40 (-81.8)

NASDAQ　3,947.66 (+53.77)

Wholesale prices drop in August
[Story]

Sports [Latest news]

13

Great Destinations

IN ONE RESPECT, TRAVEL IS LIKE THE REAL ESTATE business – it's all about location, location, location. Not surprisingly, most travelers are very destination-oriented. They are interested in going to specific places to indulge their travel fantasies. Accordingly, they want information about destinations that helps them make wise decisions on where next to best target their travel resources.

Business travelers are forced by the nature of their work to travel to places that may or may not be of compelling interest. They primarily travel to meet colleagues, see clients, or do deals. Mainly oriented toward acquiring good transportation, hotels, restaurants, meeting rooms, and business services, they may see or remember very little of their destination. If they are fortunate to end up in a great destination, they may extend their trip for a day or two to see and do things normally associated with activities of leisure travelers.

On the other hand, leisure travelers have travel dreams to fulfill. Indeed, many already have a priority list of "must visit" places – only time and resources seem to be limitations. Others are always looking for a very special trip, be it adventure, romantic, or just relaxing. They look at travel guidebooks, examine travel brochures, talk with travel agents and fellow travelers, and surf the Internet for information on great places to visit. Internet savvy travelers are always in search of URLs and websites – some with streaming video and audio – that might uncover another great place to visit.

But where do you go to discover those great destinations? Can the Internet yield as good quality information on destinations as a travel guidebook, travel brochures, travel agent, or fellow traveler? The answer is *"Yes, and then some."* You are about to be overwhelmed with destination information and services as you go online to discover regions, countries, provinces, states, cities, towns, villages, parks, mountains, rivers, and oceans. Focusing on geography, the sites identified in this chapter put both a face and name on destinations around the world. Here, you'll literally take a virtual tour of the globe as we unlock intriguing places that lie at the heart of travel.

Welcome to Street-Level Travel

In this chapter we focus on the most exciting dimension of travel planning – location, location, location! This is what travel is all about – the destination. We examine websites that take you to specific areas, cities, states, provinces, regions, and countries for planning your next trip or, hopefully, several trips over the next few years. These sites open a whole world of great destinations. This is where street-level travel takes place – the information from which you put together your detailed daily itinerary of places to visit and things to see and do. These sites constitute the real nuts and bolts of planning a trip by putting a unique face on your next destination – photos, names, addresses, telephone and fax numbers, and email addresses. They take you to the street-level of travel where you discover and plan for your hotels, restaurants, transportation, sightseeing, entertainment, and special events. These sites are of special interest to independent travelers who want to fill in the locational details of their travel itinerary.

Site Content and Syndicators

Many of the websites we've identified thus far include lots of destination information. Indeed, they frequently include a "Destination" section with a pull-down menu that takes you to city and/or country travel information. Much of the information is drawn from similar sources which come from affiliate relationships with the same group of destination "content providers", especially Lonely Planet, Frommer's, Fodor's, and Weissmann, which are in the business of syndicating their travel content to other websites. Just sample the destination information on such mega reservation sites as Expedia.com and Travelocity.com or the adventure travel site Away.com and you'll discover a high level of redundancy; they basically offer the same information that has its origins with the major travel guidebook publishers – Lonely Planet, Frommer's, Fodor's, Moon, and Rough. The latest mega-partnership arrangement for content is between AOL and Rough Guides; in September 2000 AOL partnered with Rough Guides for its travel content to more than 18,000 destinations. Many entrepreneurial sites, such as Away.com, go so far as to resyndicate the content they already get from several guidebook publishers. Some websites, such as AOL's Digital City create their own destination content which is often cannibalized from secondary sources ("creatively plagiarized" from travel guidebooks with Fodor's often being a favorite source for international destinations) rather than developed through independent research. The truth is that most travel websites are "content poor" when it comes to providing destination information; thus, many of these sites must lease content from a few content providers (Lonely Planet, for example, currently leases all 300+ of its guides to websites for $50,000 a year) or simply link to sites that already have easily accessible content. As a result, the destination content on these sites tends to reflect the particular travel style promoted by the guidebook series (budget, independent, business, upscale, history/culture, adventure, luxury). In fact, there is very little reliable original destination content on most websites. What's original is usually not reliable – lots of first-hand discussions of destination experiences by travelers, many of whom are young

> *Most websites are "content poor". Many lease content from a few content providers or simply link to sites that already have easily accessible "free" content. Destination content on these sites tends to reflect the particular travel style promoted by the guidebook.*

and inexperienced budget travelers, who frequent community forums and bulletin boards. When it comes to providing destination information, most travel websites are in the business of getting their content from other sources that are in the business of syndicating their content or trading it for linkages and services. Indeed, this is nothing new to us since we also are in the business of syndicating travel content through our own delivery site: *www.contentfortravel.com*. In so doing, we get a first-hand look at the nature of destination information that appears on many sites, including some of the largest and most popular travel sites.

Gateway Destination Sites

Before looking for information on a specific destination, you are well advised to visit a few of the gateway destination sites identified in this section. These sites offer a wealth of community-based information on specific destinations that should be of interest to travelers:

hotels	maps	sports
restaurants	news	recreation
entertainment	photos	art
shopping	auctions	medicine
sightseeing	autos	nightlife
weather	jobs	fitness
real estate	relocations	festivals

While the quality of the country or city-specific information on these sites is at times suspect, especially in the case of the fast changing restaurant business, nonetheless, these sites provide quick access to hundreds and thousands of cities, states, provinces, and countries. Many sites, such as Towd, Travel-Library, and Citysearch, have easy to use pull-down menus for countries and North American states and provinces. Others such as DigitalCity, Boulevards, and Travel50 include selected menus of destinations – mainly major cities and countries – from which to choose. Our favorite gateway destination sites include the following:

Tourism Offices
   Worldwide Directory: *www.towd.com*
USA City Link: *www.usacitylink.com*
City Search: *www.citysearch.com*
Travel-Library: *www.travel-library.com*
City Travel Guide: *www.citytravelguide.com*
Digital City: *www.digitalcity.com*
Boulevards: *www.boulevards.com*
Travel 50:   *www.travel50/com*
About.com: *www.about.com/travel/go . . .*
My Travel Guide: *www.mytravelguide.com*

By using such search engines as Google, iWon, GoTo, and AltaVista, you'll uncover many other gateway destination websites.

Community-Based Sites

All major cities and most other cities, towns, and counties in the United States have community websites either sponsored by local governments or by private organizations, such as the news media, working in cooperation with many organizations, including government. In fact, the United States is the most highly wired country in the world when it comes to community websites. Three of the top city websites in the United States focus on New York, Boston, and San Francisco. In many respects, these are model sites for other cities.

New York City:	*www.nytoday.com*
Boston:	*www.boston.com*
San Francisco:	*www.sfgate.com*

Some of the most interesting city and island sites outside the U.S. are found in the Asian city-state island of Singapore as well as in the island communities of Hong Kong and Bali:

Singapore:	*www.newasia-singapore.com*
Hong Kong:	*www.hkta.com*
	www.totallyhk.com
Bali (Indonesia):	*www.indo.com*

U.S. Destinations

While the United States is a big and challenging country for many travelers, the good news is that it's easily accessible on the Internet because most major destinations are wired to the Internet. Indeed, you can spend hours taking a virtual tour of the United States by clicking onto the many city, state, and county websites identified in this section. Start with these gateway sites for the United States:

USA City Link:	*www.usacitylink.com*
TOWD:	*www.towd.com*
DigitalCity:	*www.digitalcity.com*
About.com:	*www.about.com/travel/usparks*

Two excellent gateway sites based in Europe which are especially useful for anyone planning to visit the United States include:

USA Tourist:	*www.usatourist.com*
Travel-America:	*www.travel-america.co.uk*

U.S. citizens traveling within the U.S. also will find these sites very useful, especially the USA Tourist site with its many linkages to local websites.

For terrific content based on the bestselling guidebook series *The Insiders' Guide*, go to this site and click onto the destination map which will take you to over 60 cities and areas nationwide:

www.insiders.com

This site yields some of the best information on local accommodations, transportation, restaurants, nightlife, shopping, attractions, parks, recreation, day trips, neighborhoods, and real estate. Bookmark this one and return to it whenever you wish to survey one of the site's destinations.

For an excellent regional destination site that covers six states in New England, visit:

www.visitnewengland.com

You can find other gateway sites to U.S. regions, states, cities, and parks by using what has quickly become one of the fastest and most reliable search engines:

www.google.com

Some of the best sources for destination information are the various State tourism offices and visitor bureaus that often function as gateways to a State's major tourist destinations and related websites. As you review the following list of State and city websites, please note that we have indicated the official State tourism office or convention and visitors bureau in ***bold italics*** immediately to the right of the State name. Most other sites listed under each State focus on major cities, but some also include counties (*www.sonomacounty.com* in California) or major attractions such as recreation areas (*www.thecanyon.com* for the Grand Canyon or *www.ozarkmountainregion.com* for the Ozarks in Arkansas). The city sites represent a mixture of sponsors: city governments, convention and meeting bureaus, local news media (such as *www. latimes.com* and *www.washingtonpost.com*), community groups, commercial city websites (*www.cityseach...* or *www.allabout...*), or private businesses focused on advertising local services. Sample a few of these sites, as well as explore linkage and occasionally search by keywords through *www.google.com*, and you will uncover a fascinating world of travel in the United States.

➤ ALABAMA:	*www.touralabama.org*
	www.ain.state.al.us
Birmingham:	*www.birminghamnet.com*
➤ ALASKA:	*www.dced.state.ak.us/tourism*
	www.alaskanet.com/Tourism
	www.akrr.com
	www.state.ak.us
Anchorage:	*www.alaska.online.com/anchorage*
Fairbanks:	*http://fairbanks-alaska.com*
Inside Passage:	*www.alaskainfo.org*
Juneau:	*www.juneau.com*
➤ ARIZONA:	*www.arizonaguide.com*
	www.carizona.com
	www.arizonatourism.com
	www.accessarizona.com
Flagstaff:	*www.flagguide.com*
Phoenix:	*www.phoenix.linksee.com*
	www.allaboutphoenix.com
	http://phoenix.citysearch.com
	http://boulevards.com/cities/ phoenix.html
Tucson:	*www.ci.tucson.az.us*
	http://boulevards.com/cities tucson.html
	www.desert.net/tw/bot
➤ ARKANSAS:	*www.arkansas.com*
Fort Smith:	*www.fortsmith.org*
Hot Springs:	*www.hotsprings.com*
	www.hotsprings.org
Little Rock:	*www.littlerock.com*
North Little Rock:	*www.northlittlerock.org*
Ozarks:	*www.ozarkmountainregion.com*
➤ CALIFORNIA:	*http://gocalif.ca.gov*
	http://gocalifornia.about.com/travel
Anaheim:	*www.allaboutanaheim.com*

Berkeley:	*www.berkeleycvb.com*
Big Sur:	*www.bigsurcalifornia.org*
Los Angeles:	*www.losangeles.com*
	http://losangeles.citysearch.com
	www.lacvb.com
	www.latimes.com
Monterey:	*www.monterey.com*
Oakland:	*www.oakland.com*
Palm Springs:	*www.desert-resorts.com*
	www.allaboutpalmsprings.com
Palo Alto:	*http://boulevards.com/cities/*
	paloalto.html
Sacramento:	*http://sacramento.citysearch.com*
San Diego:	*www.allaboutsandiego.com*
	http://citysearchsignonsandiego.com
	http://boulevards.com/cities/
	sandiego.html
	www.sandiego.org
	www.legolandca.com
San Fernando:	*www.valleyofthestars.org*
San Francisco:	*www.sfgate.com*
	www.sfguide.com
	www.allaboutsanfrancisco.com
	www.sfvisitor.org
	www.sanfrancisco.com
	http://bayarea.citysearch.com
San Jose:	*http://sanjose.citysearch.com*
	www.sanjose.com
	www.sanjose.org
San Luis Obispo:	*http://boulevards.com/cities/*
	sanluisobispo.html
Santa Barbara:	*http://boulevards.com/cities*
	santabarbara.html
Santa Monica:	*www.santamonica.com*
Santa Cruz:	*http://boulevards.com/cities*
	santacruz.html
Sonoma County:	*www.sonomacounty.com*
	http://boulevards.com/cities
	sonoma.html

➤ COLORADO: *www.colorado.com*
www.coloradoadventure.net
Aspen: *www.aspen-colorado.com*
Colorado Springs: *www.colorado-springs.com*
Denver: *www.allabout-denver.com*
http://denver.citysearch.com
www.milehighcity.com
www.denver.org
www.denver.com
Vail: *www.visitvailvalley.com*
http://web.vail.net

➤ CONNECTICUT: ***www.tourism.state.ct.us***
www.visitconnecticut.com

➤ DELAWARE: ***www.visitdelaware.com***
www.delaware.com
http://visitors.delawareonline.com
Dover: *www.visitdover.com*
Wilmington: *www.wilmcvb.org*
Regions: *www.visitsoutherndelaware.com*
www.delmarweb.com

➤ DISTRICT OF
COLUMBIA: ***www.washington.org***
www.washingtondc.com
www.123washingtondc.com
www.seewashingtondc.net
www.citytravelguide.com/
washington-dc-usa.htm

➤ FLORIDA: ***www.flausa.com***
www.funandsun.com
www.infoguide.com
Daytona Beach: *www.daytonabeach.com*
Florida Keys: *http://floridakeys.com*
www.floridakeys.org
www.fla-keys.com
Kissimmee: *www.floridakiss.com*
Miami: *www.allabout-miami.com*
http://miami.citysearch.com
www.about.com/travel/gomiami
Orlando: *www.allabout-orlando.com*
http://orlando.citysearch.com
www.about.com/travel/goorlando

St. Petersburg:	www.stpetersburg.com
	www.stpete-clearwater.com
Tampa Bay:	http://tampabay.citysearch.com
➤ **GEORGIA:**	**www.georgia.org**
Atlanta:	www.allabout-atlanta.com
	http://atlanta.citysearch.com
	http://boulevards.com/cities/atlanta.html
Savannah:	www.insidesavannah.com
Regions:	www.gomm.com
➤ **HAWAII:**	**www.visit.hawaii.org**
	www.aloha-hawaii.com
	www.about.com/travel/gohawaii
Honolulu:	www.honolulu.com
Kauai:	www.kauaivisitorsbureau.org
➤ **IDAHO:**	**www.visitid.org**
Boise:	www.boise.org
Sun Valley:	http://sunvalley.com
➤ **ILLINOIS:**	**www.enjoyillinois.com**
Chicago:	www.allabout-chicago.com
	www.chicago.il.org
	http://chicago.citysearch.com
	http://boulevards.com/chicago
	http://centerstage.net/chicago/
	virtual-el
➤ **INDIANA:**	**www.enjoyindiana.com**
Indianapolis:	www.indianapolis.com
	www.indy.org
➤ **IOWA:**	**www.traveliowa.com**
	www.icvba.org
	www.jeonet.com/amanas
Des Moines:	www.desmonesia.com
Sioux City:	www.siouxlan.com/ccat
➤ **KANSAS:**	**www.kansascommerce.com**
Kansas City:	www.experiencekc.com
Lawrence:	www.visitlawrence.com
➤ **KENTUCKY:**	**www.kentuckytourism.com**
	www.tourky.com
Louisville:	www.louisville-visitors.com
➤ **LOUISIANA:**	**www.louisianatravel.com**
New Orleans:	www.allabout-neworleans.com

	www.neworleansonline.com
	www.bestofneworleans.com
	http://neworleans.citysearch.com
Regions:	*www.crt.state.la.us/crt/tourism.htm*
	www.cajunlife.com
➤ **MAINE:**	*www.visitmaine.com*
	www.visit-maine.com
	http://maineguide.com/travel
	www.chickadee.com/lobster
Portland:	*http://boulevards.com/cities/*
	portland-me.html
➤ **MARYLAND:**	***www.mdisfun.org***
	www.delmarweb.com
	www.travel50/com/delaware
	www.beach-net.com
	www.tilghmanisland.com
Annapolis:	*http://visit-annapolis.org*
Baltimore:	*http://baltimore.citysearch.com*
	http://boulevards.com/cities/
	baltimore.html
➤ **MASSACHUSETTS:**	***www.massvacation.com***
	www.visit-massachusetts.com
Berkshires:	*www.berkshires.org*
Boston:	*www.boston.com*
	www.bostonusa.com
	www.allaboutboston.com
	www.newbury.com/guide.htm
	http://boston.citysearch.com
	http://boulevards.com/cities/
	boston.html
Cape Cod:	*www.capecodchamber.org*
Martha's Vineyard:	*www.mvy.com*
Nantucket Island:	*www.allcapecod.com/nantucket*
Salem:	*www.salem.org*
➤ **MICHIGAN:**	***www.michigan.org***
Detroit:	*http://detroit.citysearch.com*
	www.detroit.com
	www.visitdetroit.com
	www.www.behere.com/runs
Mackinac Island:	*www.sheplerswww.com*
South Haven:	*www.bythebigbluewater.com*

Traverse City:	www.mytraverse.com
Region:	www.michiweb.com
➢ **MINNESOTA:**	**www.exploreminnesota.com**
	www.minneapolis.org
Minneapolis/	http://twincities.citysearch.com
St. Paul:	www.minneapolis.com
	www.downtownmpls.com
	www.saint-paul.com
➢ **MISSISSIPPI:**	**www.visitmississippi.org**
Gulf Coast:	www.gulfcoast.org/mgccvb
Vicksburg:	www.vicksburgcvb.org
➢ **MISSOURI:**	**www.missouritourism.com**
	www.mostateparks.com
	www.show-me-missouri.com
St. Louis:	www.allaboutstlouis.com
	www.stlouis.com
	http://stlouis.citysearch.com
	www.st-louis-cvc.com
➢ **MONTANA:**	**www.visitmt.com**
	www.travel50.com/montana
	www.wintermt.com
	http://gtlc.com
➢ **NEVADA:**	**www.travelnevada.com**
	www.2000nevada.com
Hoover Dam:	www.hooverdam.com
Las Vegas:	www.allabout-lasvegas.com
	http://lasvegas.citysearch.com
	www.lasvegas24hours.com
Reno:	www.playreno.com
➢ **NEW HAMPSHIRE:**	**www.visitnh.gov**
	www.visit-newhampshire.com
	www.whitemtn.org
➢ **NEW JERSEY:**	**www.state.nj.us/travel**
	www.go-newjersey.com
	www.virtualnjshore.com
Atlantic City:	www.allabout-atlanticcity.com
	www.altlanticcitynj.com
	www.acnights.com
➢ **NEW MEXICO:**	**www.newmexico.org**
	www.about.com/travel/gonewmexico

	www.nmculture.org
Albuquerque:	www.albuquerque.com
	www.abqcvb.org
Carlsbad Caverns:	www.nps.gov.cave
Santa Fe:	www.santafe.org
➤ **NEW YORK:**	**www.iloveny.com**
	www.canals.state.ny.us
Albany:	www.albany.org
Lake Placid:	www.lakeplacid.com
New York:	www.nytoday.com
	www.allabout-newyorkcity.com
	http://newyork.citysearch.com
	www.newyork.com
	www.nycvisit.com
	www.nyctourist.com
	www.boulevards.com/cities/ newyork.html
	www.about.com/travel/gonyc
	www.itp.tsoanyu.edu/~student/ elecpub/kain
	www.ci.nyc.y.us/html/dot/html/ transportation_maps/home.html
Western:	www.westernny.com
Upstate:	www.roundthebend.com
➤ **NORTH CAROLINA:**	**www.visitnc.com**
	www.travel50.com/north_carolina
	http://nc.org
	www.dot.state.nc.us/transit/ferry
Ashville:	www.gotoashville.com
Charlotte:	http://charlotte.citysearch.com
Durham:	www.durham-nc.com
Greensboro:	www.greensboronc.org
Outer Banks:	www.outerbanks.com
Raleigh:	www.raleighcvb.org
Raleigh/Durham:	http://triangle.citysearch.com
Winston-Salem:	www.wscvb.com
Smoky Mountains:	http://smokysearch.com
➤ **NORTH DAKOTA:**	**http://discovernd.com**
	http://discovernd.com/visiting/ travel.html

➤ **OHIO:**   *www.ohiotourism.com*
                                     www.ohiotravel.org
                                     www.travelohio.com
    Cincinnati: *http://cincinnati.citysearch.com*
                                     http://boulevards.com/cities/
                                         cincinnati.html
    Cleveland: *http://cleveland.citysearch.com*
                                     www.cleve-visitors-guide.com
    Columbus: *http://columbus.citysearch.com*
    Portland: *http://boulevards.com/portland-or*
➤ **OKLAHOMA:**   *www.travelok.com*
    Oklahoma City: *www.okccvb.org*
    Tulsa: *www.tulsaweb.com*
➤ **OREGON:**   *www.traveloregon.com*
                                     www.teleport.com/~coastal
    Portland: *http://portland.citysearch.com*
                                     www.travelportland.com
                                     www.pova.com/visitor/index.html
    Southern Oregon: *www.sova.org*
    Roseburg: *www.visitroseburg.com*
➤ **PENNSYLVANIA:**   *www.state.pa.us/visit*
                                     www.experiencepa.com
    Erie: *www.eriepa.com*
    Gettysburg: *www.gettysburgaddress.com*
    Lancaster Co.:   *www.padutchcountry.com*
                                     www.800padutch.com
    Philadelphia: *http://philadelphia.citysearch.com*
                                     www.philadelphia.com
                                     www.pcvb.org
    Pittsburgh: *http://pittsburgh.citysearch.com*
                                     http://boulevards.com/cities/
                                         pittsburgh.html
                                     www.pittsburgh-cvb.org
                                     www.pittsburghbnb.com
➤ **RHODE ISLAND:**   *www.visitrhodeisland.com*
                                     www.visitri.com
                                     www.coastalvillages.com
    Newport: *www.gonewport.com*
    Providence: *www.providencecvb.com*

➤ **SOUTH CAROLINA:** *www.travelsc.com*
www.sccsi.com/sc
    Charleston: *www.charlestoncvb.com*
www.tourcharleston.com
    Hilton Head: *http://hiltonheadisland.net*
www.hiltonheadisland.org
    Myrtle Beach: *www.myrtlebeachlive.com*
➤ **SOUTH DAKOTA:** *www.travelsd.com*
www.state.sd.us
    Rapid City: *www.rapidcitycvb.com*
    Sioux Falls: *www.travelsd.com*
➤ **TENNESSEE:** *www.tourism.state.tn.us*
www.tennweb.com/tnbkrds
    Chattanooga: *www.chattanooga.net*
    Knoxville: *www.knoxville.org*
    Memphis: *www.memphis.com*
    Nashville: *www.allabout-nashville.com*
http://nashville.citysearch.com
http://boulevards.com/cities/
nashville.html
www.nashvillecvb.com
    Smoky Mountains: *www.smokymountains.org*
www.rodsguide.com
➤ **TEXAS:** *www.traveltex.com*
    Amarillo: *www.amarillo-cvb.org*
    Austin: *http://austin.citysearch.com*
http://boulevards.com/austin
www.austin360.com/acvb
    Corpus Christi: *www.corpuschristi-tx-cvb.org*
    Dallas: *www.allabout-dallas.com*
www.guidelive.com
www.dallas.com
www.dallascvb.com
    East Texas: *www.easttexasguide.com*
    Fort Worth: *www.fortworth.com*
    Gulf Coast: *http://pw2.netcom.com/~wandaron/*
cotxroads.html
    Houston: *http://houston.citysearch.com*
www.houston.com
www.houston-guide.com
    San Antonio: *http://sanantonio.citysearch.com*

www.sanantonio.com
www.sanantoniocvb.com

➤ **UTAH:**   **www.utah.com**
   Moab: http://moab-utah.com
   St. Lake City: http://utah.citysearch.com
                 www.visitsaltlake.com

➤ **VERMONT:**   **www.1-800-vermont.com**
                 www.travel-vermont.com
                 www.visit-vermont.com
                 www.discover-vermont.com
                 www.ferries.com

➤ **VIRGINIA:**   **www.virginia.org**
   Coastal Cities: www.thevirginiawaterfront.com
   Gunston Hall: www.gunstonhall.org
   Mount Vernon: www.montvernon.org
   Newport News: www.newport-news.org
   Richmond: http://richmond.citysearch.com
                 www.richmondva.org
   Virginia Beach: www.allaboutvirginiabeach.com
   Williamsburg: www.williamsburg.com
                 www.history.org

➤ **WASHINGTON:**   **www.tourism.wa.gov**
                 www.travel-in-wa.com
                 www.waypt.com/opta
                 www.whalewatching.com
   San Juan Islands: www.sanjuanguide.com
   Seattle: www.allaboutseattle.com
                 http://seattle.citysearch.com
                 www.seattle.com
                 www.seeseattle.org
   Spokane: www.spokane.org
➤ **WEST VIRGINIA:**   **www.state.wv.us/tourism**
                 www.westvirginia.com
   Harper's Ferry: www.nps.gov/hafe
➤ **WISCONSIN:**   **www.travelwisconsin.com**
                 http://tourism.state.wi.us
   Madison: http://boulevards.com/cities/
                     madison.html
                 www.visitmadison.com
   Milwaukee: www.milwaukee.com

	www.milwaukee.org
Wisconsin Dells:	*www.dells.com*
➢ WYOMING:	*www.wyomingtourism.org*
	www.state.wy.us/state/tourism/
	tourism.html
	http://commerce.state.wy.us
Cheyenne:	*www.cheyenne.org*
Jackson Hole:	*www.jacksonholenet.com/mountaintcy*

Global Regions and Countries

While the United States is the world's most highly wired country, many other countries and cities, such as Canada, Australia, India, France, Germany, Italy, Hungry, Finland, Japan, South Korea, Taiwan, Singapore, and Hong Kong, have moved rapidly online. Even China, in its own way, is beginning to make significant moves into the online world. Visit the many websites in these countries and cities and you'll uncover a great deal of useful travel information.

At the same time, many countries, especially in Africa, the Middle East, Eastern Europe, Central Asia, and Latin America, are only slowly developing an Internet presence. Not surprising, poor countries tend to be poorly connected to the Internet; rich countries have a commanding presence; and a few countries, such as ostensibly poor India – with its huge high-tech population centered around major technology centers in Bangalore, Hyderabad, and Chennai – and the Philippines – with the world's largest per capita Internet specialists – are surprises. In cases where a country has few Internet sites, you may need to consult a travel guidebook on the country which may or may not be available online (see Chapter 8). In fact, several embassies still do not have their own websites. To check on embassies and their websites, go to *www.towd. com* or visit the following sites which we discussed in Chapter 7:

| **Embassy World:** | *www.embassyworld.com* |
| **Embpag:** | *www.embpage.org* |

You will find several gateway sites to countries and cities worldwide. Many of these function as directories and search engines for locating countries and cities. Some of our favor such sites include:

Best in the World:	www.thebestintheworld.com
Countries:	www.countries.com
Travel-Library:	www.travel-library.com
Travel Finders:	www.travelfinders.com

Since several guidebook series, which we discussed in Chapter 8, provide a great deal of syndicated content to many travel websites, you might want to visit these sites which also function as gateway destination sites:

Lonely Planet:	www.lonelyplanet.com
Frommer's:	www.frommers.com
Fodor's:	www.fodors.com
Moon:	www.moon.com
Columbus Publishing:	www.wtg-online.com

Several sites also function as regional centers which link several countries, cities, and other websites that promote the region. The following are good examples of these types of sites:

The Caribbean:	www.caribbean.com
South America:	http://gosouthamerica.about.com
	www.goodnet.com/~crowdpub/
	linksnew.htm
Europe:	http://goeurope.about.com
Africa:	http://goafrica.about.com
	www.allafrica.com
	www.newaftrica.com/tourism.htm
Middle East:	www.maghreb.net
	www.arabnet
	www.mideasttravelnet.com
Asia:	http://asiatour.com
	http://asiatravel.com
	www.worldroom.com
	www.asia-links.com
	www.goseasia.about.com
South Pacific Islands:	http://www.tcsp.com

We especially like WorldRoom (*www.worldroom.com*) which has begun to expand from Asia into Europe as it attempts to become one of the world's most important mega sites for business travelers. Its unique services and content go far beyond the typical destination site.

Most countries maintain a tourism office or bureau within their country, and many operate tourism offices in several countries around the world. In such cases, the offices usually have websites which include information about entry requirements, specific destinations, and linkages to other sites. Other countries may provide tourist information through their embassy or consulates. In these cases, you may need to check out their embassy website for such information. And some very small and poor countries, mainly found in Africa, do not maintain a tourism or diplomatic presence in many countries. In fact, you may not be able to get tourist information from their government offices. In these cases, you are well advised to consult travel guidebook series, such as Lonely Planet (*www.lonelyplanet.com*), which produce guides on such places.

> **ALGERIA:** *www.algeria-tourism.org*
> **AMERICAN SAMOA:** *www.samoanet.com/americansamoa*
> **ANGOLA:** *www.angola.org*
> **ANGUILLA:** *www.net.ai*
> **ANTIQUA &BARBUDA:** *www.antiqua-barbuda.org*
> **ARGENTINA:** *www.sectur.gov.ar*
> *www.wam.com.ar/tourism*
> *http://argentinae.com/english*
> **ARMENIA:** *www.armgate.com/travel*
> **ARUBA:** *www.aruba.com*
> **AUSTRALIA:** *www.australia.com*
> *www.aussie.net.au*

Canberra:	*http://canberra.citysearch.com.au*
	www.canberratourism.com.au
Melbourne:	*http://melbourne.citysearch.com.au*
New South Wales:	*www.tourism.nsw.gov.au*
Northern Territory:	*www.nttc.com.au*
	www.ntholidays.com
Queensland:	*www.queensland-holidays.com.au*
	www.destinationqueensland.com
	www.tq.com.au
Sydney:	*http://sydney.citysearch.com.au*
Tasmania:	*www.tourism.tas.gov.au*
Victoria:	*www.tourism.vic.gov.au*
Western Australia:	*www.wa.gov.au/gov/watc*

➤ **AUSTRIA:**   *www.austria-tourism.at*
                                www.anto.com
  Salzburg: *www.salzburginfo.at*
  Vienna: *http://info.wien.at/e*
➤ **AZERBAIJAN:**   none
  Embassy in U.S.:   none
  Guidebook info: *www.virgin.net/travel/guides/*
                                middle_east/azerbaijan/
                                travelinternational.htm

➤ **BAHAMAS:**   *www.bahamas.com*
➤ **BANGLADESH:**   *www.parjata.org*
➤ **BARBADOS:**   *www.barbados.org*
➤ **BELARUS:**   none
  U.N. Mission: *www.undp.org/missions/belarus*
➤ **BELGIUM:**   *www.belgium-tourism.com*
                                www.visitbelgium.com
                                www.hotels-belgium.com
  Bruges: *http://193.75.143.1/toervl*
  Brussels: *www.bruxelles.irisnet.en/homeen.htm*
➤ **BELIZE:**   *www.travelbelize.org*
                                www.belizenet.com
➤ **BENIN:**   none
  Embassy in U.S.:   none
  Travel Guide: *www.travelnotes.org/Africa/benin.htm*
➤ **BERMUDA:**   *www.bermudatourism.com*
➤ **BHUTAN:**   *www.kingdomofbhutan.com*
➤ **BOLIVIA:**   *www.infobolivia.net/english/*
                                tourmenu.html
➤ **BONAIRE:**   *www.infobonaire.com*
➤ **BOSNIA AND**
   HERZEGOVINA: none
  Embassy: none
  Travel guide: *www.travelnotes.org/Europe/*
                                osnia.htm
➤ **BOTSWANA:**   none
➤ **BRAZIL:**   *www.embratur.gov.br*
                                www.brazilinfo.com
                                www.bitourism.com
                                www.vivabrazil.com
  Brazilia: *www.civila.com/brasilia*

Rio:	*www.ipanema.com*
	www.rioconventionbureau.com.br
	www.riowithlove.com
➢ **BRITISH VIRGIN**	
ISLANDS:	***www.bviwelcome.com***
	www.britishvirginislands.com
➢ **BRUNEI:**	***www.brunei.gov.bn***
➢ **BULGARIA:**	*www.travel-bulgaria.com*
➢ **BURUNDI:**	none
➢ **CAMBODIA:**	***www.cambodia-web.net***
➢ **CANADA:**	***www.travelcanada.ca***
Alberta:	*www.travelalberta.com*
	www.discoveralberta.com
Banff-Lake Louise:	*www.banfflakelouise.com*
British Columbia:	*www.hellobc.com*
	http://bcadventure.com/adverture
Calgary:	*www.calgaryplus.ca*
	www.discovercalgary.com
Edmonton:	*www.edmontonplus.ca*
	www.discoveredmonton.com
Jasper:	*www.discoverjasper.com*
Manitoba:	*www.gov.mb.ca/itt/travel*
	www.travelmanitoba.com
Montreal:	*http://english.montrealplus.ca*
	www.tourisme-montreal.org
Newfoundland:	*www.gov.nf.ca/tourism*
Northwest Territories:	*www.northernfrontier.com*
	www.nwttravel.nt.ca
Nova Scotia:	*www.explore.gov.ns.ca*
	www.destination-ns.com
Ontario:	*www.tourism.gov.on.ca/English*
	www.tourottawa.org
Prince Edward Island:	*www.peiplay.com*
Quebec:	*www.quebecplus.ca*
	www.bonjour-quebec.com
	www.destinationquebec.com
Saskatchewan:	*www.sasktourism.com*
Toronto:	*www.toronto.com*
	www.boulevards.com/cities/toronto
	www.tourism-toronto.com
Vancouver:	*www.tourismvancouver.com*

	www.tourism-vancouver.org
Victoria:	*www.tourismvictoria.com*
Yukon Territory:	*www.touryukon.com*
➢ CAYMAN ISLANDS:	***www.caymanisland.ky***
➢ CENTRAL AFRICAN	
REPUBLIC:	none
➢ CHAD:	none
➢ CHANNEL ISLANDS:	*www.guernsey.net/~tourism*
	www.jersey.co.uk/jsyinfo
➢ CHILE:	***www.sernature.cl***
	www.chile-travel.com
	www.gochile.cl
	www.chiptravel.cl
	www.chileweb.net/valparaiso
➢ CHINA:	***www.cnta.com***
	www.chinats.com
	www.chinavista.com
	http://china.muzi.net
	www.chinaetravel.com
	www.chinatravelservice.com
	www.chinatour.com
	www.citsusa.com
	www.china-tours.com
	www.chinapages.com
Beijing:	*www.beijingnow.com*
	www.beijing.com
Hong Kong:	*www.hkta.org*
	www.totallyhk.com
Kunming:	*www.kunming-china.com*
Macau:	*www.macautourism.gov.mo*
Shanghai:	*www.shanghaiguide.com*
	www.shanghai.com
Shenzhen:	*www.shenzhenwindow.net*
➢ COLOMBIA:	*www.colomsat.net.co/viajescapinero*
Embassy in U.S.:	*www.colombiaemb.org*
	www.countries.com/travel_links
	www.thebestintheworld.com/
	colombia.htm
➢ COOK ISLANDS:	***www.cook-islands.com***
➢ COSTA RICA:	***www.tourism-costarica.com***

		www.cocori.com
➢	COTE D'IVOIRE:	none
➢	CROATIA:	***www.mint.hr***
		www.htz.hr
➢	CUBA:	***www.cubaweb.cu***
		www.cuba-casa.com
		www.gocuba.com
		www.cubaonline.org
		www.cuba-travel.com
	Havana:	*www.lahabana.com*
➢	CURACAO:	***www.curacao-tourism.com***
➢	CYPRUS:	***www.cyprustourism.org***
		www.kypros.org/Cyprus/tourism.html
		www.north-cyprus.com
➢	CZECH REPUBLIC:	***www.czechcenter.com***
		www.hotelstravel.com/czech.html
	Prague:	*www.a-zprague.cz*
		www.pragueiguide.com
		http://sunsite.mff.cuni.cz/prague
➢	DENMARK:	***www.visitdenmark.com***
	Copenhagen:	*www.oak.dk/Copenhagen/*
		Visiting_Copenhagen
		www.woco.dk
➢	DJIBOUTI:	none
➢	DOMINICA:	***www.dominica.dm/travel.htm***
➢	DOMINICAN REPUBLIC:	***www.dominicana.com.do***
		www.hispaniola.com
➢	DUBAI:	***www.dubaitourism.co.ae***
➢	ECUADOR:	*http://ecuadorexplorer.com*
		www.travelecuador.com/english
		www.viaecuador.com
	Quito:	*www.quito.org*
➢	EGYPT:	***www.touregypt.net***
		www.egypttourism.org
		www.egyptmonth.com
		www.egypt.com
		www.idsc.gov.ed
		www.arab.net/egypt
		http://ce.eng.usf.edu/pharos
	Cairo:	*http://goafrica.about.com/travel/*

	msubcairo.htm
	www.pharos.bu.edu/Egypt/Cairo
➤ EL SALVADOR:	none
Embassy in U.S.:	_www.elsalvadorguide.com/_
	consalvamia
➤ ESTONIA:	_www.visitestonia.com_
➤ ETHIOPIA:	_www.ethiopianembassy.org_
➤ FALKLAND ISLANDS:	_www.tourism.org.fk_
➤ FAROE ISLANDS:	_www.faroeislands.com_
	www.puffin.fo/travel
➤ FIJI:	_www.bulafiji.com_
North Americans:	_www.bulafiji-americas.com_
	www.fijiguide.com
➤ FINLAND:	_www.thekingsroad.com_
	www.finland-tourism.com
	www.stn.fi/english
Helsinki:	_www.hel.fi/mato_
➤ FRANCE:	_www.franceguide.com_
	www.francetourism.com
	www.fgtousa.org
18 Cities:	_www.officialcitysites.org/france.htm_
Cannes:	_www.cannes.com_
Nice:	_www.cityindex.com/nice/nice/html_
Paris:	_www.paris.org/parisfull.html_
	www.paris-touristoffice.com
➤ FRENCH GUIANA:	_www.guyanetourisme.com_
➤ GABON:	none
➤ GAMBIA:	_www.gambia.com_
➤ GEORGIA:	none
Embassy in U.S.:	_www.georgiaemb.org_
➤ GERMANY:	_www.germany-tourism.de_
	www.lodging-germany.com
Berlin:	_www.net4berlin.com/home.e.html_
Cologne:	_www.koeln.org/koelntourismus/_
	english
Frankfurt:	_www.frankfurt.de/index-e.html_
Munich:	_www.munich-tourist.de/english/_
	offers.htm
➤ GHANA:	_www.ghana-embassy.org_
	www.interknowledge.com/ghana

➢	GIBRALTAR:	*www.gibraltar.gov.gi*
➢	GREECE:	*www.gnto.gr*
	Athens:	*http://athensguide.com*
➢	GREENLAND:	*www.greenland-guide.gl*
➢	GRENADA:	*www.grenada.org*
➢	GUADELOUPE:	none
➢	GUAM:	*www.visitguam.org*
➢	GUATEMALA:	*www.inguat.net*
		www.guatemala.travel.com.gt
➢	GUERNSEY:	*www.guernseymap.com*
➢	GUYANA:	none
➢	HAITI:	*www.haititourisme.org*
➢	HONDURAS:	*www.honduras.com*
➢	HONG KONG:	*www.hkta.com*
		www.totallyhk.com
➢	HUNGARY:	*www.hungarytourism.hu*
		www.gotohungary.com
		www.globewalker.com
➢	ICELAND:	*www.icetourist.is*
		www.arctic.is
	Reykjavi:	*www.reykjavik.com*
➢	INDIA:	*www.tourisminindia.com*
		www.tourindia.com
		www.allindia.com/cities
		www.destinationindia.com
		www.indiabuzz.com
		www.indiacity.com
		www.indiainsight.com
		www.welcometoindia.com
		http://travel.indiamart.com
➢	INDONESIA:	*www.indonesia-tourism.com*
		www.indo.com
		www.tourismindonesia.com
	Bali:	*www.bali-paradise.com*
		www.travelbali.com
		www.balitravelforum.com
		www.balinetwork.com
	Jakarta:	*www.jakarta.go.id*
➢	IRAN:	*www.itto.org*
➢	IRELAND:	*www.ireland.travel.ie*

	www.irelandvacations.com
Dublin:	*www.visit.ie/dublin*
Northern Ireland:	*www.ni-tourism.com*
➤ **ISLE OF MAN:**	*www.isle-of-man.com*
➤ **ISRAEL:**	***www.infotour.co.il***
	www.goisrael.com
	www.inisrael.com
➤ **ITALY:**	***www.italiantourism.com***
	www.piuitalia2000.it
	www.enit.it
	www.itwg.com
Florence:	*www.arca.net/florence.htm*
Rome:	*www.romeguide.it*
➤ **JAMAICA:**	***www.jamaicatravel.com***
	www.jamaicatravel.com
➤ **JAPAN:**	***www.jnto.go.jp***
Kyoto:	*http://web.kyoto-inet.or.jp/org/hellokcb*
Osaka:	*www.tourism.city.osaka.jp/en*
Tokyo:	*www.boulevards.com/tokyo*
➤ **JERSEY:**	***www.jersey.com***
➤ **JORDAN:**	***www.seejordan.org***
	www.noor.gov.jo
➤ **KENYA:**	***www.kenyatourism.org***
	www.bwanazulia.com/kenya
➤ **KIRIBATI:**	none
➤ **KUWAIT:**	none
➤ **LAOS:**	***www.visit-laos.com***
➤ **LATVIA:**	***www.latviatravel.com***
➤ **LEBANON:**	***www.lebanon-tourism.gov.lb***
Embassy in U.S.:	*www.embofleb.org*
➤ **LESOTHO:**	none
Mission in U.S.:	*www.undp.org/missions/lesotho*
➤ **LIBERIA:**	none
➤ **LIECHTENSTEIN:**	***www.news.li/touri/index.htm***
	www.searchlink.li/tourist
➤ **LITHUANIA:**	***www.tourism.lt***
➤ **LUXEMBOURG:**	***www.etat.lu/tourism***
	www.www.ont.lu
	www.luxembourg.co.uk
➤ **MACAU:**	***www.macautourism.gov.mo***

➤ MADAGASCAR: none
➤ MALAWI: *www.malawi-tourism.com*
➤ MALAYSIA: *www.tourism.gov.my*
   Kuala Lumpur: *www.mnet.com.my/klonline*
   Sarawak: *www.sarawaktourism.com*
➤ MALDIVES: *www.visitmaldives.com*
➤ MALTA: *www.visitmalta.com*
                        www.www.tte.ch/Malta

➤ MARSHALL ISLANDS: none
➤ MARTINIQUE: *www.martinique.org*
➤ MAURITIUS: *www.mauritius.net*
➤ MEXICO: *www.mexicotravel.com*
                        www.mexconnect.com
   Acapulco: *www.acapulco-cvb.org*
                        www.acapulco-travel.web.co.mx/
                          ing.html
   Mayan Riviera: *www.mayan-riviera.com*
   Mexico City: *www.mexico-city-mexico.com*
                        www.mexicocity.com
   Oaxaca: *http://oaxaca.gob.mx/sedetur*
   Puerto Vallarta: *www.puertovallarta.net*
   San Miguel de Allende: *www.infosma.com*
➤ MICRONESIA: *www.visit-fsm.org*
                        www.destmic.com
➤ MONACO: *www.monaco-congres.com*
                        www.monaco.mc/usa
                        www.cityindex.com/mcarlo/
                          mcarlo.html

➤ MONGOLIA: *www.un.int/mongolia*
➤ MONTSERRAT: *www.visitmontserrat.com*
➤ MOROCCO: *www.tourism-in-morocco.com*
                        www.morocco.com

➤ MOZAMBIQUE: none
   Mission in U.S.:   *www.undp.org/missions/mozambique*
➤ MYANMAR: *www.myanmar.com*
➤ NAMIBIA: *www.tourism.com.na*
                        www.namibia-tourism.com

➤ NEPAL: *www.welcomenepal.com*
                        www.travel-nepal.com

➢ NETHERLANDS: *www.holland.com*
                         www.visitholland.com
                         www.hotelres.nl
                         www.noord-holland-tourist.nl
  Amsterdam: *www.cityindex.com/adam/adam.html*
➢ NEW CALEDONIA: *www.noumea.com*
➢ NEW ZEALAND: *www.tourisminfo.govt.nz*
                         www.nztb.govt.nz
                         www.purenz.com
  Mt. Cook: *www.mtcook.org.nz*
  Nelson: *www.nelson.net.nz*
  Wellington: *www.wellingtonnz.com*
➢ NICARAGUA: *www.intur.gob.ni*
                         www.nicaragua-online.com
➢ NIGER: none
➢ NIUE: *www.niueislandcom*
➢ NORTHERN IRELAND: *www.ni-tourism.com*
➢ NORWAY: *www.tourist.no*
                         www.norway.org
  Oslo: *www.hurra.no/html/virtual_*
                           sightseeing.html
  Trondheim: *www.trondheim.com/english/travel*
➢ OMAN: *www.tourismoman.com*
                         www.omanonline.com
➢ PAKISTAN: *www.tourism.gov.pk*
                         www.ptl.com.pk
  Karachi: *www.alephx.org/karachi*
➢ PALESTINE: *http://travel.to/palestine*
➢ PANAMA: *www.panamatours.com/ipat/*
                           ipat_home.htm
                         www.panamatours.com
                         www.pancanal.com
➢ PAPUA NEW GUINEA: *www.dg.com.pg/paradiselive*
                         www.niugini.com
➢ PARAGUAY: none
➢ PERU: *www.peruonline.net*
                         www.peru-explorer.com
➢ PHILIPPINES: *www.tourism.gov.ph*
                         www.sequel.net/RPinUS/Tourism

➢ POLAND:	*www.polandtour.org*
	http://poland.pl/tourism
Krakow:	*www.krakow.pl/WK/EN*
➢ PORTUGAL:	*www.portugalinsite.pt*
	www.portugal.org/tourism
Lisbon:	*www.eunet.pt/Lisboa/i/isboa.html*
Portugal:	*www.portugalvirtual.pt/_tourism*
➢ PUERTO RICO:	*www.prtourism.com*
	www.meetpuertorico.com
	www.welcometopuertorico.org
➢ ROMANIA:	*www.tourism.ro*
	www.rotravel.com
➢ RUSSIA:	*www.russia-travel.com*
Moscow:	*www.moscow-guide.ru*
St. Petersburg:	*www.guide.spb.ru*
	www.cityvision2000.com
➢ RAWANDA:	none
➢ SABA:	*www.turq.com/saba*
➢ SAMOA:	*www.samoa.co.nz*
➢ SAUDI ARABIA:	*www.arab.net/saudi/tour/saudi_*
	tour.html
➢ SARK:	*www.sarktourism.gov.gg*
➢ SCOTLAND:	*www.visitscotland.com*
Glasgow:	*www.seeglasgow.com*
➢ SENEGAL:	*www.earth2000.com/sengal*
	www.senegal-online.com
➢ SEYCHELLES:	*www.seychelles.uk.com*
	www.seecychelles-online.com.sc
	www.sey.net
➢ SINGAPORE	*www.newasia-singapore.com*
	www.sg.com
	www.makansutra.com
	www.catacha.com.sg
	www.cybray.com.sg
	www.sg.yahoo.com
	www.singaporeeverything.com
	www.travel.com.sg
➢ SLOVAKIA:	*www.www.sacr.sk*
	www.slovakia.org/tourism

➢ SOLOMON ISLANDS: *www.commerce.gov.sb*
➢ SOUTH AFRICA: *www.satour.org*
                          www.satour.co.za
                          www.southafrica.net.tourism
                          www.tourism.co.za
   Cape Town: *www.gocapetownco.za*
                          www.cape-town.net
   Durban: *www.durban.org.za/tourism*
➢ SOUTH KOREA: *www.visitkoreaor.kr*
                          www.knto.or.kr
   Seoul: *www.nmetro.com*
                          www.metro.seoul.kr/eng
➢ SPAIN: *www.tourspain.es*
                          www.okspain.org
                          www.red2000.com/span
   Andalucia: *www.andalucia/org/ing/*
                             homepage.html
   Barcelona: *www.barcelona-on-line.es/Angeles*
   Madrid: *www.madridman.com*
➢ SRI LANKA: *www.lanka.net/ctb*
➢ ST. BARTHELEMY: *www.st-barths.com*
➢ ST. EUSTATIUS: *www.turq.com/statis*
➢ ST. KITTS AND NEVIS: *www.stkitts-nevis*
➢ ST. LUCIA: *www.st-lucia.com*
➢ ST. MARTIN/   *www.st-maarten.com*
    ST. MAARTEN: *www.interknowledge.com/st-martin*
➢ ST. VINCENT AND
    THE GRENADINES: *http://vincy.com/svg*
➢ SURINAME: none
➢ SWAZILAND: none
➢ SWEDEN: *www.visit-sweden.com*
                          www.gosweden.org
   Göteborg: *www.stoinfo.se/england*
   Stockholm: *www.stockholm.com*
➢ SWITZERLAND: *www.myswitzerland.com*
                          www.switzerlandtourism.com
   Bern: *www.berntourismus.ch*
   Geneva: *www.geneve-tourisme.ch*
   Lucerne: *www.luzern.org/index_e.html*
   Zürich: *www.zuerich.ch*

➤ SYRIA:	*www.visit-syria.com*
➤ TAHITI:	***www.tahiti-tourisme.com***
	www.tahiti-explorer.com
➤ TAIWAN:	***www.tbroc.gov.tw***
	http://travel.cybertaiwan.com/taipei
➤ TANZANIA:	***www.tanzania-web.com***
	www.zanzibar.net
➤ THAILAND:	***www.tourismthailand.org***
	www.amazingthailand.th
	www/sanuk.com
	www.siam.net
	http://th.orientation.com/eg
Bangkok:	*www.bkkmet.com*
	www.bangkokpost.net
	www.nationmultimedia.com
Chiang Mai:	*www.chiangmai-chiangrai.com*
Phuket:	*www.phuketgazette.net*
➤ TONGA:	*http://vacations.tb.gov.to*
➤ TRINIDAD AND TOBAGO:	*www.visitnt.com*
➤ TUNISIA:	***www.tourismtunisia.com***
➤ TURKEY:	*www.travelturkey.com*
Istanbul:	*www.istanbulcityguide.com*
➤ TURKS AND CAICOS:	***www.turksandcaicostourism.com***
➤ UNITED KINGDOM:	***www.travelengland.org.uk***
	www.travelbritain.org
	www.visitbritain.com
Edinburgh:	*www.edinburgh.org*
London:	*www.londontown.com*
	www.boulevards.com/london
Scotland:	*www.holiday.scotland.net*
➤ U.S. VIRGIN ISLANDS:	***www.usvi.net***
	http://ecani.com/vi/sc/stcroix.htm
➤ UGANDA:	***http://ugandaweb.com***
	www.africa-insites.com/uganda
➤ UKRAINE:	***www.ukremb.com***
Kiev:	*www.unazone.net/Kiev.html*
➤ URUGUAY:	***www.turismo.gub.uy***
➤ VANUATU:	***www.vanuatutourism.com***
➤ VATICAN:	***www.vatican.va***

➤ VENEZUELA: *www.venetur.com.ve*
                          www.postalven.com
                          www.venezuelatuya.com
➤ VIETNAM: *www.vietnamtourism.com*
➤ YUGOSLAVIA: none
➤ ZAMBIA: *www.africa-insites.com/zambia/*
                             zntbhome.htm
➤ ZIMBABWE: *www.tourismzimbabwe.co.zw*
                          www.afrizim.com

Index

The Authors

RON AND CARYL KRANNICH, PH.Ds, ARE TWO OF Amerca's leading business, career, and travel writers who have authored more than 50 books. They operate Development Concepts Incorporated, a training, consulting, and publishing firm. A former Peace Corps Volunteer and Fulbright Scholar, Ron received his Ph.D. in Political Science from Northern Illinois University. Caryl received her Ph.D. in Speech Communication from Penn State University.

Ron and Caryl are both former university professors, high school teachers, management trainers, and consultants. As trainers and consultants, they have completed numerous projects on management, career development, local government, population planning, and rural development in the United States and abroad.

The Krannichs' career and business books focus on key job search skills, military and civilian career transitions, government and international careers, travel jobs, nonprofit organizations, and communication skills. Their body of work represents one of today's most comprehensive collections of career writing. Their books are widely available in bookstores, libraries, and career centers.

Ron's and Caryl's international and travel interests are based on their many years of living, working, and traveling abroad. These interests are well represented in their two popular international and travel career books – *International Jobs Directory* and *Jobs For People Who Love to Travel* – as well as through their innovative Impact Guides series (*"The Treasures and Pleasures of . . . Best of the Best"*) and two related travel websites: *www.ishoparoundtheworld.com* and *www.contentfortravel.com*. Authors of 14 travel guidebooks on various destinations in Asia, the South Pacific, Europe, the Middle East, North

Africa, and South America, the Krannichs are seasoned travel planners who regularly use the Internet for both business and leisure travel. When not found at their home and business in Virginia, they are probably somewhere in the world pursuing one of their favorite passions – researching and writing about quality arts, antiques, hotels, and restaurants. Their travel books have been featured in many newspapers, magazines, and newsletters as well as on radio and television.

If you have any comments for the authors – including recommended travel websites for the next edition of this book and for the weekly Internet travel tip section of *www.ishoparoundtheworld.com* (see form below) – please direct them to the authors:

Drs. Ron and Caryl Krannich
IMPACT PUBLICATIONS
9104 Manassas Drive, Suite N
Manassas Park, VA 20111-5211
Fax 703-335-9486
E-mail: *krannich@impactpublications.com*
www.ishoparoundtheworld.com
www.impactpublications.com
www.contentfortravel.com

RECOMMENDED SITES

I found these websites to be especially useful for travel planning. You may want to recommend them to your readers:

_____

_____

_____

_____

_____

_____

Travel Resources

THE FOLLOWING TRAVEL RESOURCES ARE AVAILABLE directly from Impact Publications. Complete the following form or list the titles, include postage (see formula at the end), enclose payment, indicate your mailing address, and send your order to:

IMPACT PUBLICATIONS
9104 Manassas Drive, Suite N
Manassas Park, VA 20111-5211
1-800-361-1055 (orders only)
Tel. 703-361-7300 or Fax 703-335-9486
Email address: *orders@impactpublications.com*
Quick & easy online ordering: *www.impactpublications.com*

Orders from individuals must be prepaid by check, moneyorder, Visa, Master-Card, or American Express. We accept telephone and fax orders. For a complete listing of hundreds of additional travel resources, including all major travel series (Frommer's, Fodor's, Lonely Planet, etc.), visit our online bookstores at *www.ishoparoundtheworld.com* and *www.impactpublications.com*.

Qty.	TITLES	Price	TOTAL
	Current Featured Title		
____	Travel Planning on the Internet	19.95	_____
	Other Internet Travel Planning Resources		
____	Buying Travel Services on the Internet	14.95	_____
____	Complete Idiot's Guide to Planning a Trip Online	16.99	_____
____	Michael Shapiro's Internet Travel Planner	18.95	_____
____	Sams Teach Yourself e-Travel Today	17.99	_____
____	Travel Planning Online For Dummies (with disk)	24.99	_____
	Featured Internet Primers (pages 17-18)		
____	Rough Guide to the Internet	9.95	_____
____	Teach Yourself the Internet	19.95	_____

The Impact Travel Guides

___	Treasures and Pleasures of Australia	17.95	_____
___	Treasures and Pleasures of the Caribbean	16.95	_____
___	Treasures and Pleasures of China	14.95	_____
___	Treasures and Pleasures of Egypt	16.95	_____
___	Treasures and Pleasures of Hong Kong	16.95	_____
___	Treasures and Pleasures of India	16.95	_____
___	Treasures and Pleasures of Indonesia	14.95	_____
___	Treasures and Pleasures of Israel & Jordan	16.95	_____
___	Treasures and Pleasures of Italy	14.95	_____
___	Treasures and Pleasures of Paris & the French Riviera	14.95	_____
___	Treasures and Pleasures of Rio & São Paulo	16.95	_____
___	Treasures and Pleasures of Singapore & Bali	16.95	_____
___	Treasures and Pleasures of Thailand	16.95	_____

International/Travel Jobs and Careers

___	International Jobs Directory	19.95	_____
___	Jobs For People Who Love to Travel	15.95	_____
___	Jobs in Paradise	15.00	_____

SUBTOTAL ------------------------------- _____

Virginia residents add 4½% sales tax   _____

POSTAGE/HANDLING ($5 for first
product and 8% of SUBTOTAL over $30) $5.00

8% of SUBTOTAL over $30 ----------------------- _____

TOTAL ENCLOSED --------------------- _____

❑ I enclose check/moneyorder for $ _____ made payable to
IMPACT PUBLICATIONS.
❑ Please charge $ _____ to my credit card:
     ❑ Visa   ❑ MasterCard   ❑ American Express   ❑ Discover

Card # _____

Expiration date: ____/____ Phone # _____/_____

Signature _____

SHIP TO: Please include your street mailing address.

www.ishoparoundtheworld.com